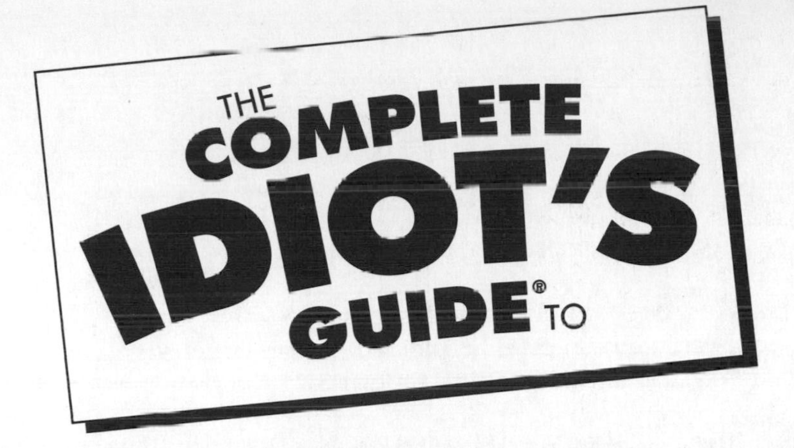

Getting Your MBA Online

by George Lorenzo

A member of Penguin Group (USA) Inc.

Dedicated to Gabe, Lisa, and Sal.

ALPHA BOOKS

Published by the Penguin Group

Penguin Group (USA) Inc., 375 Hudson Street, New York, New York 10014, U.S.A.

Penguin Group (Canada), 10 Alcorn Avenue, Toronto, Ontario, Canada M4V 3B2 (a division of Pearson Penguin Canada Inc.)

Penguin Books Ltd, 80 Strand, London WC2R 0RL, England

Penguin Ireland, 25 St Stephen's Green, Dublin 2, Ireland (a division of Penguin Books Ltd)

Penguin Group (Australia), 250 Camberwell Road, Camberwell, Victoria 3124, Australia (a division of Pearson Australia Group Pty Ltd)

Penguin Books India Pvt Ltd, 11 Community Centre, Panchsheel Park, New Delhi—110 017, India

Penguin Group (NZ), cnr Airborne and Rosedale Roads, Albany, Auckland 1310, New Zealand (a division of Pearson New Zealand Ltd)

Penguin Books (South Africa) (Pty) Ltd, 24 Sturdee Avenue, Rosebank, Johannesburg 2196, South Africa

Penguin Books Ltd, Registered Offices: 80 Strand, London WC2R 0RL, England

International Standard Book Number: 1-59257-349-5
Library of Congress Catalog Card Number: 2005925278

07 06 05 8 7 6 5 4 3 2 1

Interpretation of the printing code: The rightmost number of the first series of numbers is the year of the book's printing; the rightmost number of the second series of numbers is the number of the book's printing. For example, a printing code of 05-1 shows that the first printing occurred in 2005.

Printed in the United States of America

Publisher: *Marie Butler-Knight*
Product Manager: *Phil Kitchel*
Senior Managing Editor: *Jennifer Bowles*
Acquisitions Editor: *Tom Stevens*
Development Editor: *Nancy D. Lewis*
Production Editor: *Megan Douglass*
Copy Editor: *Keith Cline*
Cartoonist: *Richard King*
Cover/Book Designer: *Trina Wurst*
Indexer: *Heather McNeil*
Layout: *Rebecca Harmon*

Contents at a Glance

Contents

Appendixes

Foreword

According to a famous New Yorker cartoon, "On the Internet, nobody knows you're a dog." (Peter Steiner, cartoon in *The New Yorker*, July 5, 1993)

How true. In cyberspace it can be tough to differentiate the quality online MBA programs from the dogs. Have you tried yet? I just went to Google, typed "online MBA," and my search retrieved more than 7 million links. Start clicking away and you'll find that even the dogs (e.g., diploma mills) have high-quality web pages!

Is it even worth your effort to sort out all of this?

Viewed as an investment, I rate an MBA earned online a strong "buy" for a working adult. Distance learning has been around since the 1800s, but information and communication technologies have evolved to the point where the online learning experience is in many cases *as good as* the traditional classroom and in some cases *better than* what you'd experience going to class two nights a week. Two essential qualifiers: you have to be the right type of student, and you must choose a quality MBA.

How do you know if you have the right stuff, and which program has the right stuff for you? Consulting this book is like engaging the services of an experienced admissions counselor to assist you in both self-assessment and program evaluation. Most important, this counselor understands the issues of working adults, and has done extensive research on online MBA programs. Very few "live" counselors offer you that.

Interested in saving time and money? Use the author's advice to narrow the mind-boggling list of possibilities to a short list of quality programs. Then focus your attention and individual research on those. If you do it right, you may need to apply to only one program.

In the last third of the book, the author goes beyond the admissions counselor role and becomes your student advisor, giving you strategies for getting the best return on your online learning investment. Don't miss the chapter on financial aid and tax benefits—I haven't seen that material presented so completely and clearly anywhere.

The author peppers his advice with lots of insider tips from influential authorities: business school deans, program directors, and industry organization officials. These professionals are passionate about quality in management education. Speaking of insiders, the dozen or so profiles of current online MBA students are a great read.

What makes me such a distance-learning enthusiast? *Experience.* I've observed hundreds of working adults with impossible travel schedules or significant family obligations (many with both) buckle down and earn the MBA through our online program at Syracuse University. Each spring I watch our iMBA graduates walk across the stage to the thunderous applause of their proud spouses, children, parents, and significant others. I regularly hear of promotions and new positions that alumni attribute to the value of their MBA. They tell us they couldn't have done it any other way. I'm proud that we are able to provide this life-changing opportunity to our students and graduates.

If they can do it … can you? Yes. Go beyond the distance and get learning.

Paula C. O'Callaghan, J.D., M.B.A.
Director, iMBA Program
Whitman School of Management
Syracuse University

Paula C. O'Callaghan, J.D., M.B.A., is director of the Independent Study MBA Program (iMBA) at the Martin J. Whitman School of Management at Syracuse University (whitman.syr.edu/imba). Ms. O'Callaghan has been quoted in *Education Week*, *Harvard Management Update*, *InfoWorld*, the *Wall Street Journal*, and other regional and national publications. She has presented on topics of online MBA program administration at two national AACSB-International conferences, as well as being a member of the conference planning committee for the 2004 Distance Learning Conference of the AACSB-International. Ms. O'Callaghan is a member of the Professional Standards Committee of the Graduate Management Admission Council.

Introduction

In today's modern higher-education setting, you can earn an official, regionally accredited MBA from a respectable institution primarily over an Internet connection with the aid of sophisticated and relatively new educational technologies. And contrary to what you may have heard or believe, these online educational experiences are highly interactive for students and faculty. They are effectively communicating electronically and learning in ways that are equal to or greater than learning in a traditional face-to-face MBA program.

Some of these MBA programs are offered in a completely online teaching and learning environment, meaning you never have to set foot on campus to earn your degree. Other MBA programs have some face-to-face interaction, requiring relatively short "residencies" on campus and then doing the remaining 80 to 95 percent of your total course requirements in the online environment.

If you are a busy adult, working professional who can't fit a traditional part-time or full-time on-campus MBA program into your life, then a part-time online MBA program, with or without brief residency requirements, can absolutely be an educational pathway for you to seriously consider.

Just like any graduate-degree pursuit, earning an MBA online is no easy task. It's just as difficult as, and usually more difficult than, going the traditional route. And the degree you earn in the online learning environment will be no different from a degree earned on campus.

Start investigating the increasing number of online MBA program choices available to you. If you are not familiar with this new world of online higher education, you'll be surprised at what awaits you.

How This Book Is Organized

This book is divided into five parts:

Part 1, "Yes, You Can Earn a Legitimate MBA from Your Home," introduces the basic types of online MBA programs available as well as the terminology you will encounter while searching for the program that is right for you. I also go over how you can find reliable and possibly unreliable information online about MBA programs, and basically what's important to know during the early phases of your search process.

Part 2, "The Finer Details," goes deep into how online learning really works and how you need to take a close look at all the parameters, standards, and criteria that point to a program that fits in with your educational goals. This part of the book goes into things you should understand about faculty, students, institutional services, types of curriculums, the technology, and the way courses are taught before making a decision about which school to send your application to.

Part 3, "Getting Started," provides all those straightforward and important details about the admission process, how to possibly obtain financial aid, and the technical requirements for being an online learner. I'll take you through the essentials and more, with lots of advice on the best avenues to take when applying to and paying for your online MBA program, as well as what kind of hardware and software will suit your needs.

Part 4, "How to Be a Successful Online Learner," takes you through what's really necessary to work effectively in the online learning environment. You'll learn how to set up your home-based learning environment and how to develop and fine-tune your skills and work with your peers in order to succeed and get the most out of your education.

Part 5, "Your Career Evolution," deals with how you might take what you learn and apply it to a career change or enhancement, as well as what you need to know about the marketplace for online learners. I also provide some last-minute advice and a review of what you need to know about being an online MBA student and graduate. There's also an important chapter that features profiles of online MBA students from eight institutions.

Extras

You will notice that throughout the chapters there are some special elements along the way.

Online Term

Online higher education has its set of unique terms, defined here, that you'll run across during your decision-making process as well as during your actual education process.

Stat

This is not a large part of the book, but I do provide some interesting statistics about where online education is heading these days.

Guide on the Side

Advice from students, educators, and myself in relation to choosing a program, dealing with technology, applying and registering, succeeding as an online learner, and taking your education and career to the next level.

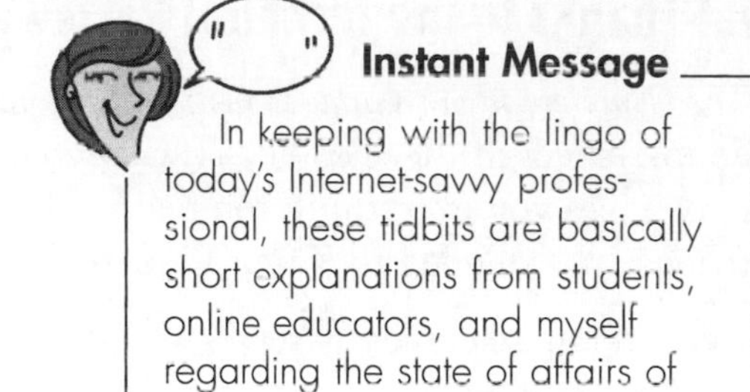

Instant Message

In keeping with the lingo of today's Internet-savvy professional, these tidbits are basically short explanations from students, online educators, and myself regarding the state of affairs of online MBA programs.

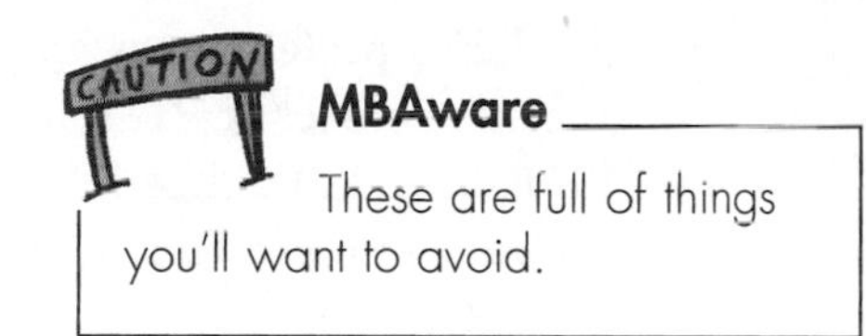

MBAware

These are full of things you'll want to avoid.

Acknowledgments

My sincere thanks go out to all the online educators and students who offered their invaluable insights. You'll see their names and quotes throughout. Talking to all these people was a wonderful experience. Thanks also go out to the more than 500 educators I have interviewed over the past three years as writer, editor, and publisher of Educational Pathways, a newsletter about online teaching and learning in higher education. All these interviews helped to form the backbone of this book.

A very special thank you to my wife who helped put together the two appendixes. Also as I pounded away at my computer keyboard during all hours of the day and night, I always welcomed those badly needed breaks when my children pulled me away. They are indeed the shining stars that keep me moving forward.

Also, a special thanks to Karen Vignare and Gordon Freedman, two friends and colleagues I can always count on for sound advice.

Finally, thanks to the people who are reading this book. I did everything I could to make it worth your effort. Having this book means you are embarking on a meaningful path to better yourself. If somehow this book contributed to you moving in a direction that turned out right, then I did my job and am grateful to have had the opportunity to help. Please don't hesitate to contact me if you have any further questions or concerns about getting your MBA online. I can be reached online, of course, at george@edpath.com.

Special Thanks to the Technical Reviewer

The Complete Idiot's Guide to Getting Your MBA Online was reviewed by an expert who double-checked the accuracy of what you'll learn here, to help us ensure that this book gives you everything you need to know about getting an online MBA. Special thanks are extended to Karen Vignare.

Karen Vignare currently serves as a Research Analyst and Instructional Designer for Online Learning at the Rochester Institute of Technology. In that position, she coordinates efforts to research all facets of online learning to improve online learning environments. She has published several pieces of research and instructor's manuals on distance and elearning. She is an adjunct professor teaching Customer Relationship Management and Marketing on Internet courses at RIT. Karen serves on several organizational boards—NUTN, Edpath, and Distance Education—and is a member of ASTD and the ADL-CoLab. Before coming to RIT, Karen was full-time faculty at SUNY Alfred State in the Marketing, Retail and Computer Technology. She also served as a Vice President and Political Economist for Wall Street financial firm. She has an MBA from the University of Rochester.

Trademarks

Part 1 Yes, You Can Earn a Legitimate MBA from Your Home

If you're like many hardworking professionals today, you may be investigating the possibility of going back to school to earn a Master of Business Administration (MBA) degree. What's stopping you? With flexible Internet-based degree programs growing in numbers across the country, you can work toward earning an MBA, without going to a college campus, at times that are the most convenient for you.

In this part of the book, you'll learn how to find these programs in order to get you started on a new online educational pathway. You'll be introduced to what types of online MBAs are available and what you need to do in order to begin the decision-making process that will take you toward earning your MBA sooner rather than later.

Chapter 1

A Higher-Education Revolution

In This Chapter

- How online learning is a growing phenomenon
- What's good and bad about online learning
- How online courses work
- The kind of student you'll need to be
- A starting point for finding the right online MBA

The growth of the Internet, along with a host of new education technologies, is bringing about revolutionary changes in the way modern colleges and universities offer their courses and degree programs. Today it is not uncommon to earn a legitimate, fully accredited degree from the comfort of your home desktop computer without setting foot on a campus.

This new method of learning in higher education is commonly referred to as *online learning*. Other terms frequently used to describe this modern higher-education landscape include distance learning, distributed learning, e-learning, computer-based learning, virtual learning, web-based learning, and open learning. All of these terms can fall under the umbrella term of *distance education*.

Online Term

Distance education means that teachers and students in a given course are not located in the same physical space.

Online learning is a type of distance education that entails students learning and interacting with their instructors, and with other students, over the Internet. It can include electronic communications, distributions and displays via e-mail, electronic discussion forums, chat rooms, streaming audio and video, electronic simulations, and other education technologies.

A Bit of History

Colleges and universities worldwide have been offering distance-education courses since the early 1800s, when it was commonly known as home study and was conducted by snail-mail correspondence. Today this traditional form of correspondence-based distance education has grown to become known as independent self-study, where students read and study course materials and textbooks on their own, without any interaction with other students, and manage their coursework under the guidance of an instructor or mentor whom the student communicates with by e-mail correspondence, telephone, mail, or a combination of all. This independent form of self-study is often referred to as open learning, which is based on the model used by the Open University of England, a world-renowned forerunner in distance education.

The vast majority of MBA programs offered in a distance education format in the United States and abroad are not provided in this independent-study, distance-education format. Instead, these programs are provided in a fully interactive online learning format where students and faculty communicate with each other through a wide variety of modern-day educational technologies, all discussed in detail throughout this book.

Online MBA programs offered by colleges and universities in the United States is what this book is all about, although I do briefly discuss online MBA programs available in Canada and England in Chapter 3. (Appendix B contains all the online MBA programs available in the United States, Canada, and England.)

The Move to Online

Online MBA programs are relatively new and have grown along with our adoption of the Internet. As noted in the definition of online learning, an online MBA program hosts courses where students and faculty interact with each other in a variety of ways over their Internet connections.

One of the earliest U.S. institutions to offer a *fully online MBA program* was Regis University, a private Jesuit institution located in Denver, Colorado, which launched its online MBA program in 1993. Today more than 2,200 online students from all over the world are enrolled in the Regis online MBA program.

Athabasca University in Alberta, Canada, is another early provider of a fully online MBA program, launched in 1994 and currently enrolling more than 1,100 online students.

The school with the largest number of online MBA students is the University of Phoenix, another early provider of online degree programs, with approximately 21,000 online learners.

Online Term

A **fully online MBA program** means that every course required for graduation can be completed through an Internet connection without ever setting foot on campus.

A good number of well-recognized public and private institutions also now offer online MBA programs, including Arizona State University, Drexel University, Florida State University, Indiana University, Syracuse University, University of Florida, University of Nebraska-Lincoln, and the University of Massachusetts-Amherst.

Overall, there are more than 100 online MBA programs of widely varied quality, content, and organizational structure located throughout the world. Besides reading this book, you can find a great deal of information about all these online MBA programs by visiting each school's website listed in Appendix B, as well as by visiting popular websites that aggregate plenty of information about graduate-level business education. In Chapters 2 and 5, I review the nature and content of these aggregator websites.

The majority of students enrolled in online MBA programs are busy working professionals, ranging in age from their late 20s to late 40s. Online learning has become an increasingly popular way for them to earn an MBA credential, primarily because online learning offers students flexibility. People who travel frequently for their jobs or have both work and personal responsibilities that limit their ability to physically attend classes are now going online. Additionally, employers are starting to see the benefits of this type of learning as web-based training and professional development programs increasingly move into the corporate mainstream.

The Regis University online MBA program website (see the figure that follows) provides details about its curriculum, how to apply, tuition costs, and how to contact representatives for more information.

Regis University's online MBA website.

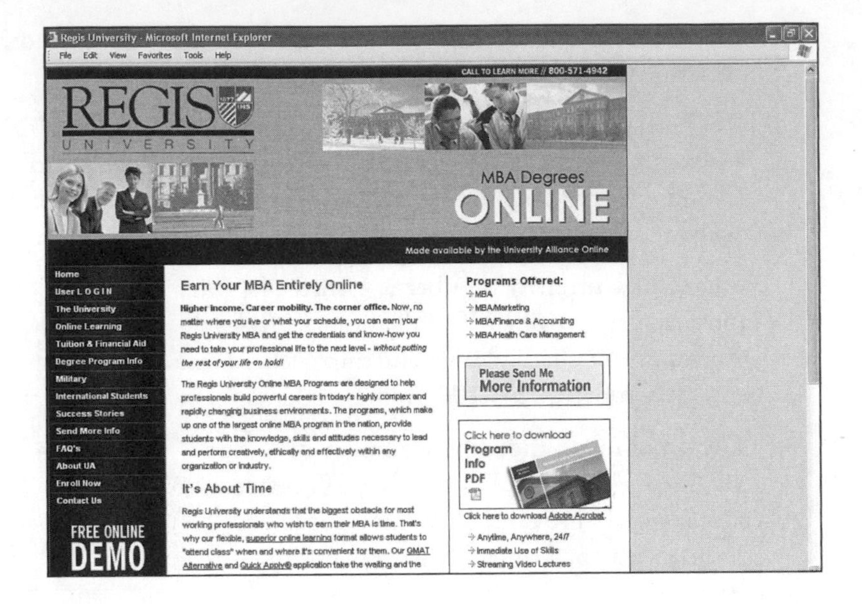

Pluses and Minuses

There are advantages and disadvantages to learning online. Students who require live, face-to-face, social interaction in an educational setting aren't going to particularly like or enjoy online learning. Typically, ideal online learners are students who enjoy communicating online; who tend to be self-directed, disciplined, highly organized; and who don't find it necessary to communicate with instructors or colleagues in person.

Online Learning Advantages

The primary advantage of online learning is that it offers the flexibility of managing your course responsibilities at times that are most convenient for you. Other pluses include the following:

- You don't have to drive to a campus and waste time in traffic or trying to find parking.
- You won't sit in an uncomfortable chair and space for an hour and a half or more at night, after a hard day's work, listening to a lecture that you may not be receptive to.

- You will listen to and view lectures (depending on the educational technology being used) and access course materials and assignments at your own pace (within the constraints of the class schedule) from any Internet-connected computer.
- If you are having difficulty understanding a concept or theory, you can always listen to and view online learning presentations and materials repeatedly until you do understand.
- You will have more time to better formulate significant ideas and concepts in online discussions, as opposed to spontaneously responding to live classroom discussions. Because all your classmates and faculty are doing the same thing online, these online discussions tend to be richer and more meaningful. Plus, students who tend to be shy in the live classroom are more likely to open up and add knowledge and insight to online discussions.

Online Learning Disadvantages

Of course, online learning has its drawbacks. I would not, for instance, recommend online learning for younger, nonworking professional students who have the time to commute to a campus for a full-time MBA program. Some of the minuses of online learning include:

- The often exciting and positive aspects of learning through face-to-face interaction between students and faculty do not exist. However, some schools have brief residency requirements where this type of interaction does take place (more details on this in Chapter 3).
- You won't visit the Student Union restaurant for a quick sandwich or people watch at the campus quad.
- You will experience frustrating computer software and Internet-access snafus on occasion.
- Your instructor or the institution itself may not be able to respond to your questions and concerns in a timely fashion.

Stat

In 2003, in the United States, 49 percent of public colleges and universities and 34 percent of all higher-education institutions offered fully online degree programs.

Source: The Sloan Consortium

- You may find it more difficult to do required work online with a project team or group, which is very common in online MBA programs. You may not get along with your cohorts, or you may find yourself doing a disproportionate amount of work.

Misinformed Perceptions About an Online Degree

Many people think that online degree programs somehow have less academic rigor and degree stature than traditional face-to-face programs. However, online degree programs are no different in rigor and stature than traditional face-to-face degree programs. Most diplomas given out after graduation do not stipulate whether a degree was earned online or on campus.

Taking courses online is in no way easier or less time-consuming than attending live, face-to-face classes. You still have to read the textbook and other course materials, take the obligatory tests, turn in homework assignments on time, write reports and research papers, participate in discussions, and possibly do a lot more work than you would in a traditional classroom environment, depending on the course you are enrolled in.

In addition, earning a degree online does not cost any less than earning a degree on campus.

Finally, you may hear people claim that online programs are not worth the effort because they lack some of the most important aspects of traditional face-to-face programs, such as the opportunities for networking and the importance of interaction with colleagues. To put it quite simply, these types of claims are not true. You'll see throughout this book direct quotes from educators and students about how online learning fosters excellent networking opportunities and meaningful peer-to-peer interactions. Chapter 17, in particular, covers how online learners interact with each other and network for success.

Instant Message

"Online education is growing; the technology is getting better; students are attuned to it; and it offers a whole lot of convenience and aspects that allow the extension of an educational experience to students who otherwise cannot attend a campus environment. We are very pleased to have adopted standards that we think are adaptable to the delivery of education at a distance."

—Jerry Trapnell, chief accreditation officer, Association to Advance Collegiate Schools of Business (AACSB)

Online MBA Programs Growing in Numbers

According to the United Bank of Switzerland (UBS) Investment Research, courses most frequently taken online are education (11 percent of all online students), computer science (9 percent), and business management (9 percent).

You may have seen some of the ads for online degree programs on television, or in direct mailers sent to your attention, or while surfing the web. These ads don't scratch the surface of what online learning is really all about. How institutions advertise and market their online MBA programs is discussed in Chapter 2.

Many of the most prominent and highly respected providers of online MBA programs don't advertise broadly, have stringent admission requirements, and are highly selective about whom they accept into their programs. Other programs generate relatively large promotional campaigns and have what can be considered less-stringent admission requirements and acceptance policies. Information about admission and acceptance policies is provided in Chapter 11.

As more institutions move to providing online MBA programs in an effort to better serve busy, working-adult professionals, the marketplace becomes busier and the level of noise and unreliable information increases. How to find good and dependable information about online MBA programs is discussed in Chapter 2.

CAUTION

MBAware

If you are surfing the web, keying in phrases such as "online MBAs," "distance learning," etc. through any of the popular search engines (Google, MSN, Yahoo!), carefully scrutinize your search results. Many Internet directories of online MBA programs that show up in search-engine results only list a very small portion of what's really available.

Is It Really Online or On-Campus?

Now, to make life confusing (nothing is simple these days), many so-called online MBA programs are not fully online. Some have short *residency requirements* that can vary in length from one weekend to one week or more each semester or quarter. Other programs may require only one brief orientation residency at the beginning of the first semester or quarter. There's more detailed information about residency requirements in Chapter 3.

Online Term

A **residency requirement** means that as part of the online MBA program you are enrolled in, you are required to pay a visit to the institution's main campus or an institution's satellite or off-campus office for a predetermined amount of face-to-face instruction.

Distance Education is Not Necessarily Online

Moreover, as you review what kind of online MBA program options are available, you may run into higher-education institutions that you might misinterpret as being online programs but, upon closer inspection, are not online programs. These are institutions that offer MBA programs in a distance-education format, which can often mean that courses are held off-campus in satellite offices, usually at more agreeable times of the day or week, such as weekends or evenings, and are thus geared for working professionals. For example, Clemson University offers a distance-education MBA program delivered by Internet, videotape, digital satellite broadcast, and/or videoconference broadcast, in traditional face-to-face, off-campus classrooms or on-site at various organizations. Virginia Tech offers a distance-education MBA program held at videoconferencing sites located throughout the state of Virginia.

Blended or Hybrid Programs

Other MBA programs that you will see referred to as "online" are really offered in what's called a *blended or hybrid learning* format. This means that completion of the program requires a substantial commitment to attending physical classes, but not as many physical classes as a traditional face-to-face *curriculum*. Many Executive MBA programs, for instance, are moving in this direction by having students switch every other weekend from live courses on campus to courses online to lessen the amount of time that time-crunched working professionals enrolled in these executive programs have to physically attend classes.

Online Term

Blended or hybrid learning is a form of education that replaces a portion of the traditional face-to-face classroom with an online learning format.

A good example of this kind of program is Pace University's Executive MBA program, which requires 9 residencies over a 2-year period—1 week-long orientation and 8 subsequent 3-day weekend residencies spaced about 11 weeks apart. The residencies are held at the Pace University campus in the Wall Street area of lower Manhattan, New York.

Another example of a hybrid online/on-campus MBA program can be found at Babson College, which offers a 27-month "Fast Track MBA" program in which students meet on the Babson campus once each month for three consecutive meetings beginning on Thursday evening through Saturday afternoon; the rest of the curriculum is conducted online.

Duke University's FUQUA School of Business Global Executive MBA program is frequently touted as being the premier online MBA program in the world, but it's definitely not fully online. This 19-month program requires five two-week face-to-face classroom sessions, two at the Duke campus in Durham, North Carolina, and one each in Europe, Asia, and South America.

Blended/hybrid MBA programs are not covered in this book, but MBA programs that do have relatively short residency requirements are covered. For more detailed information about the wide variety of fully and partially online MBA programs available today, see Chapter 3. Also note that Appendix B specifies whether any particular online MBA program has a residency requirement.

Graduate Degrees in Business-Related Fields

In addition to online MBA programs growing in numbers, online graduate degrees, without the MBA designation, in other business-related fields are increasing in number. At the Keller Graduate School of Management at DeVry University, for instance, online Master's degrees are offered in the following:

- accounting and financial management
- human resource management
- information systems management
- network and communications management
- project management
- public administration

At the University of Maryland University College (UMUC), which is the largest state-university provider of online degree programs, online Master of Science degrees are offered in the following:

- accounting and financial management
- accounting and information technology
- computer systems management
- e-commerce
- environmental management
- health-care administration
- information technology management

Appendix B also lists online business-related Master's degree programs.

How Long Will It Take?

The amount of time required to earn your MBA online can vary greatly. Online MBA programs are always slotted into the part-time graduate-level program category because they are geared toward busy professionals who don't have time to pursue a graduate degree on a full-time basis. This does not mean that you cannot carry a full load of graduate credits online and earn your MBA as quickly as possible. However, an academic advisor from any school that is noted for having a challenging curriculum will advise prospective students to take the part-time route.

Depending on the institution, program type, and your educational stamina and stick-to-itiveness, you are looking at anywhere from less than a year (for what could be considered a highly unique accelerated program that takes into consideration your educational background) to two or three years, or more, to complete an online MBA program.

The typical student in Syracuse University's iMBA program (which has 3 short residency requirements each year), takes 2 courses each term, each 15 weeks in length, for a total of 54 credits, and finishes the program within 3 years. American Intercontinental University promotes an accelerated online MBA program that can be completed in 10 months. Arizona State University's online MBA program (which has one 5-day residency requirement), can be completed in 24 months, with students taking 6 courses annually, each 6 weeks in length, for a total of 48 credits.

Chapters 3 and 8 provide more details about the variety of online curriculums offered. In addition, Chapter 3 reviews credit hours, length of courses, and academic schedules.

How Much Will It Cost?

What it costs to earn an MBA online also varies greatly. At the University of Nebraska-Lincoln (UNL), the 2004–2005 tuition rate for residents of the state of Nebraska is $190 per credit hour, or $9,120 for the 48 credit hours it would take to complete the program. Nonresidents at UNL pay $512 per credit hour, or $24,576. At the University of Colorado at Colorado Springs (UCCS), the 2004–2005 tuition rate for a 3-credit course in its online MBA program is $1,390—regardless of whether you are a resident of the state of Colorado—for a grand total of $18,070 for the 13 three-credit courses it would take to complete the program.

Both the UNL and UCCS programs do not have any residency requirements that would incur additional travel and room-and-board expenses. Both programs can also be considered bargains when you compare them to the tuition rates at some of the other institutions offering online MBAs. The 2004–2005 tuition rate per credit hour for the online MBA program provided by the Penn State University World Campus is $849 per credit hour for residents and nonresidents, or $40,752 for the 48 credit hours it would take to complete the program, not including expenses for 2 one-week residency requirements.

CAUTION

MBAware

When pricing out online MBA programs, make sure you are fully aware of the total cost of the program over and above tuition rates. You can find more detailed information about online MBA costs and how to possibly obtain financial aid in Chapter 12.

The University of Florida's 27-month online MBA program—if you can get accepted; it's one of the most selective online MBA programs in the country—runs about $37,000 for total program fees, which does not include expenses for seven weekend residency requirements.

In addition to residency-requirement expenses, other costs can come into play, such as technology fees, the cost of books and supplemental materials, and the necessary software and hardware you will need to purchase. For instance, when you factor in the additional costs for the Penn State World Campus program, the total increases to $46,000, which includes room and board for its required two one-week residencies.

How Classes Work

Lots of different media and software can come into play in any so-called online learning degree program, making them, speaking strictly from a technical point of view, not completely online. These include CD-ROM and DVD lectures with simulations, satellite and television broadcasts, videotaped programming, and printed textbooks. (Yes, you will still be required to read textbooks.) For the fully online side of things, however, you can expect to have a special account with your college that provides you with username and password access to the online library, to an e-mail account, and to what's called a *course management system* (CMS) that faculty and students use to organize their online coursework and the interactions that occur in them. See Chapter 9 for more information about course management systems.

Online Term

A **course management system** is software that provides most of the tools and interface to present an online course on both the student's and faculty member's computer. It is the shell that holds all of an online course's functions, including the course syllabus, discussion board, live chat room, reading materials, lectures, assignments, a grade book, electronic file exchange functions, and access to outside resources such as the campus library.

A Variety of Teaching and Learning Approaches

Of course, every institution uses a variety of education technologies in their own unique ways. For example, there are many different course management systems, some created and provided by commercial vendors, and others, known as home-grown systems, created and provided by the host institution. Each has unique features and functions that students and faculty are required to master.

Instructional approaches differ at each institution. Lectures, assignments, projects, and discussions may require a variety of student-to-student and student-to-faculty communications and collaborations, as well as a good number of independent-study, self-directed accomplishments. From a general point of view, the successful online student is active, creative, dependable, highly organized, and a skilled communicator with the written word. Chapters 9 and 10 and 15 through 18 contain detailed information about online class mechanics, as well as tips on how to use technology appropriately.

The Savvy Student

Basically, if you ultimately decide that earning an MBA online will be your educational pathway of choice, you'll need a certain skill set to get through the journey. Beyond having the obvious computer and Internet connection and the typical academic and software skills, you'll need to understand how to …

- download and install software.
- conduct research online.
- effectively communicate both *asynchronously*, primarily through discussion forums and e-mail, and *synchronously*, primarily through live chats and teleconferencing.
- attach, send, read, and archive electronic files.
- write clearly and intelligently, because almost everything you do in an online learning environment will involve typing on a keyboard to get your thoughts, concerns, and knowledge clearly understood by your instructors, fellow students, and the program administrators who support you.

Online Term

Asynchronous communication does not occur in real time. A discussion board, where students post topics and responses whenever they desire, is a form of asynchronous communication. **Synchronous** communication is live, occurring in real time. A live chat session is a form of synchronous communication.

In Parts 2, 3, and 4 of this book, you'll learn everything you need to understand to accomplish a smooth transition into online education and what it takes to ultimately earn your graduate degree.

Before You Take This Journey

Your search for the right online MBA program entails a close examination of a number of key ingredients. Here's a list of the types of questions you need to ask before making any kind of decision:

- What is the total cost of program, including all potential expenditures?
- What is the program length, including the typical start and end dates?
- What are the admission requirements?

- What kind of institution is it? Does it have a good reputation? Is it accredited?
- What types of students attend? What is the professional makeup?
- What kind of credentials do the faculty have? How long have they been teaching prior to online?
- What kind of online MBA curriculums are offered?
- How are online courses taught?
- What kind of online student support services does the institution have?

Guide on the Side

As a journalist, I can tell you that strong investigative skills and good telephone communication skills will get you a long way in your search for the right online MBA program. Don't rely only on information from websites and printed literature. Get on the phone and ask a lot of questions.

Many of the finer details of this list, and much more, are explained throughout this book.

Where Do You Want to Take Your Career?

Of course, embarking on any educational endeavor, especially at the graduate level, entails a thorough understanding of your goals and aspirations. If you are seeking a career with a major investment banking firm in New York City, then you might want to strongly consider an online MBA program from a nationally recognized school, such as the University of Florida, Arizona Sate University, Syracuse University, or Indiana University. However, if you are seeking career advancement at your current job as a marketing director or product manager at a manufacturing plant in your hometown, for example, you might want to consider enrolling in an online MBA program that is closer to home and not nearly as expensive as some of the aforementioned.

Instant Message

"I will take the top 10 to 15 percent of my students and stack them up against anybody else in this country. If you are looking for a job at a medium-sized business in any particular state you choose, then you don't need to go to Duke."

—Rick Niswander, East Carolina University dean of graduate business programs

The education you will get from a smaller school that has a local reputation as opposed to a national or international reputation may be just as rigorous as any program out there. So the odds are pretty good that the knowledge you will have gained from a school recognized in your local area will hold up quite well in most career-advancement pursuits (provided, of course, that you are not *really* an "idiot").

A Credential or Knowledge?

A big question for some people is do you need an MBA for the credential itself, which, in some cases can indeed get you that promotion, or do you want an MBA to help you move up the ladder of success through the knowledge you have gained and are ultimately capable of applying to your business life?

If you are a knowledge seeker, my advice to you is find an online MBA program that emphasizes learning over a lifetime, whereby you are taught business management foundational skills that can adapt to a business climate that is always fluctuating.

If you are looking "only" for the MBA designation to add to your resumé, enroll in the shortest, least-expensive, easiest-to-apply-to-and-get-accepted program you can find in the marketplace of available online MBA programs.

So, in short, choosing the right online MBA for you is relative to where you want to take your career, plus how much money and time you are willing to invest. The following chapters show you how to find the right school for you, how to get accepted, how to pay for it, and how to succeed during your educational experience and afterward.

Instant Message

"We do not just prepare students for how to do a particular thing. We incorporate the whole process that helps them with good decision-making skills. We produce decision makers who can think through new problems that they have not experienced in the program."

—Venkateshwar Reddy, interim dean, College of Business and Administration and the Graduate School of Business Administration, University of Colorado at Colorado Springs

The Least You Need to Know

- The number of online MBAs available today is growing rapidly.
- You need a certain set of computer and writing skills to be a successful online learner.
- There are both benefits and drawbacks to learning online.
- Earning a degree online carries the same academic weight and credentials as earning a degree on campus.
- Choosing an online MBA program means digging deep into your aspirations and doing extensive research on what's available.

Chapter 2

Finding Information Online

In This Chapter

- How to find information about online MBA programs
- A brief guide to higher-education web portals
- How programs are advertised online
- Filling out online request-for-more-information forms

Let the search begin!

Finding the online MBA program that fits in with your academic, career, and lifestyle plans requires a good deal of homework. The first layer of information that you can sift through is found on the web, which, at its worst, can be deceiving and sometimes inaccurate due to its heavy advertisement-laden nature.

At its best, and even at mediocre levels of accuracy, the information you'll find on the web will be a valuable jumping board for you to dig out more information about online MBA programs through e-mail and telephone inquiries, which I highly recommend, or through live campus visits with program administrators and faculty.

Suggestion: As you surf around the web looking at online MBA programs, organize the sites you find into folders labeled and categorized according to your personal preferences, such as location, tuition levels, admission levels, etc., inside the Favorites function of your web browser.

Searching Web Portals

You can begin web searching by combing through Appendix B and noting all the website addresses of the schools that might interest you. You can also visit ***higher-education web portals,*** which are one-cyberstop places that provide visitors with multiple online MBA listings, live links, and plenty of general information about getting an MBA that could prove helpful during this decision-making phase of your educational pathway.

Online Term

Higher-education web portals offer a comprehensive gateway to a wide variety of information related to higher education. They typically have links to other education-related websites, access to online communities with discussion forums and live chat rooms, specialized content about topics of interest, a search engine and directory function for finding degree programs, and a variety of online shopping services.

My four favorite higher-education web portals, in order of preference, for finding information about online MBA programs, are BusinessWeek Online, USNews.com, MBA.com, and DegreeInfo.com. Some of the websites, such as others owned by magazine publishers that I review in the sections that follow, are also described in more detail in Chapter 5, where I discuss higher-education ranking systems.

BusinessWeek Online

Located at www.businessweek.com/bschools, and from the publishers of the popular magazine, this website has a "B-Schools" section that is loaded with detailed information, mostly in relation to traditional on-campus MBA programs. However, much of this information, especially the career advice, admissions, and financial-aid strategies sections, can be applied to online programs.

BusinessWeek Online is also well known for its rankings of traditional on-campus MBA programs (see Chapter 5), and it does have a directory of unranked online MBA programs listed in a section of the website titled "Distance MBA Profiles." Click on any of the profiled institutions for information about when an online program was founded, how many students are enrolled, program length, tuition costs, application deadlines, a link to the school's website, and much more.

MBAware

You can register as a member of BusinessWeek Online, for free, and take part in its "B-Schools Forum," where online discussions cover lots of topics related to getting in and attending classes at business schools today. However, when seeking advice through any online forums, which can often be very good, avoid those messages claiming that online MBA programs are worthless. Such advice is not grounded in fact.

USNews.com

USNews.com is another site that ranks traditional, on-campus MBA programs. And like BusinessWeek Online, it provides a decent directory of online programs in its "E-Learning—Online Graduate Degrees" section (located at www.usnews.com/usnews/edu/elearning/directory/gradonline.htm). Online graduate-level business degree programs are listed under two categories: regionally and professionally accredited or regionally accredited only. See Chapter 3 for detailed information about accreditation.

USNews.com also provides information about admission requirements, tuition costs, number of students enrolled, when the program started, etc. It also has direct links to the websites of the online MBA programs listed in its database. Overall, USNews.com has some great content in its "E-Learning" section, including articles about how online learning works, a glossary of e-learning terms, and a forum on the topic of e-learning where you can start a discussion about online MBA programs.

MBA.com

This website comes from the owners of the Graduate Management Admissions Test (GMAT) and features plenty of helpful information about taking the GMAT, the overall application process, making an enrollment decision, assessing your business acumen and skills, career opportunities, the value of an MBA, and more.

For $50 you can get access to a self-assessment tool for MBAs called CareerLeader, which is currently used by more than 200 graduate business programs to help students design their career paths. The tool assesses skills, interests, and abilities in relation to the typical requirements of a successful business education and career.

DegreeInfo.com's Discussion Forums

DegreeInfo.com (www.degreeinfo.com/index.html) has respectable roots; it was once home to members of alt.education.distance, an early and very popular online forum that generated great discussions about distance education. As stated in the "About Us" section of this site, the founders (and regular contributors) of DegreeInfo.com are "dedicated to the dissemination of accurate information regarding quality distance-based higher education programs."

They add that "myth, rumor, ignorance, disinformation, and the unscrupulous business practices of a few people are often major obstacles to those who might benefit from a distance education. DegreeInfo.com's mission is to help remove these obstacles for as many people as possible." Part of this mission is accomplished through its fabulous discussion forums, where prospective and current students and distance educators from all over the world gather online to seek out advice and offer their opinions about online degree programs.

A good way to utilize DegreeInfo.com's discussion forums for information about any particular program is just to do a search through its thousands of posts on their discussion board (see the figure that follows). Input the name of the school you are investigating into the website's search function to see whether any discussions have been generated about that particular school. You can also post questions to the forums if you become a registered member, which entails filling out a relatively long, but painless, online form.

Guide on the Side

Go to www.degreeinfo.com and click on the "Discussion Board" link and then click on the "Search" link. Enter "online MBA programs" in the search box to view discussion threads that have many differing and interesting points of view about earning an MBA online. Or enter the name of any particular school you might be interested in to view discussions that have been generated about its quality.

Although my four favorite higher-education web portals are indeed loaded with useful information, the sections of these sites that feature directories to online MBA programs should be viewed with scrutiny, because they do not, in my humble opinion, offer a complete and fully accurate picture of the actual number of online MBA programs available today.

By the way, Appendix B contains the most thorough directory of online MBA programs you will find anywhere on the planet.

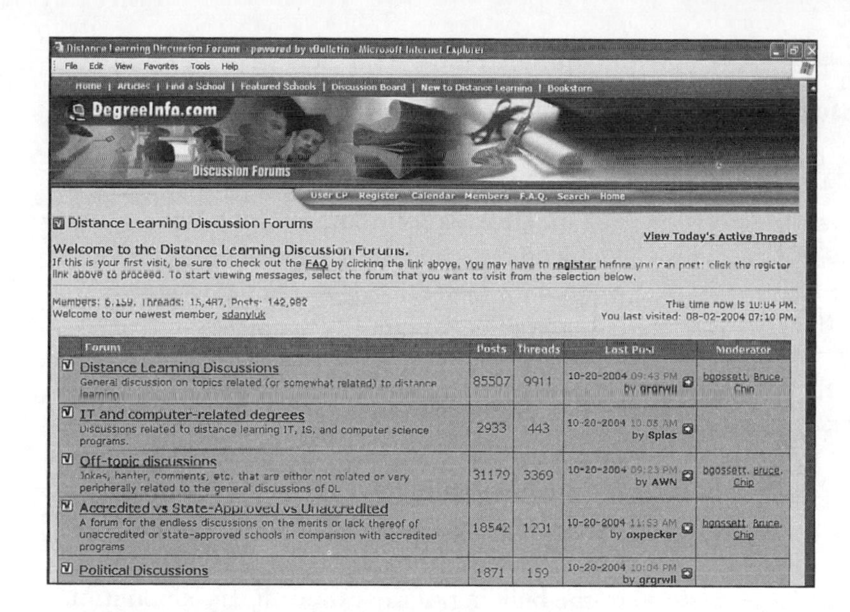

DegreeInfo.com's online discussion board is a great forum for getting opinions about online MBA programs.

Other Distinctive Websites

Following are other websites that have listings and a wide variety of information about earning a degree online. Some have their fair share of advertising, which can be annoying. However, beyond all the flashy advertising lies a good deal of useful information.

- **The *Financial Times*, the *Wall Street Journal*, and *Forbes***—In addition to the aforementioned BusinessWeek Online and USNews.com, you might want to browse through the education and career sections of the *Financial Times* at FT.com, the *Wall Street Journal* at WSJ.com, and *Forbes* at Forbes.com. See Chapter 5 for more information about how to utilize these websites.

- **Thomson Peterson's Distance Learning Channel**—Located at www.petersons.com/distancelearning, this site is hosted by Peterson's, a company long noted for its core products related to college search and selection, test preparation, and financial-aid services.

- **Worldwidelearn.com**—This site comes up in search engine results frequently because it has been around for a long time. It has a pretty decent section about online MBA programs.

- **eLearners.com**—Another good site with plenty of information about online MBA programs and online teaching and learning in general. The site also features an online assessment, called "eLearner Advisor," that helps students determine their readiness for an online degree program.

Instant Message

"I used Google to find online programs and compared the ones I found. I chose University of Maryland University College because it had no onsite requirement, was accredited, and my previous limited experience with them had been positive."

—Linda Couch, IBM Global Services business unit strategist and alumna of UMUC's online MBA program

- **mbajungle.com**—This site is geared toward traditional MBA students, but it has loads of advice about the admission process and career advancement.
- **distancelearn.about.com**—This is the About.com distance-learning channel, a good website for links to articles related to a wide range of topics about online education. Put "online MBA" in this site's search function to access a list of articles you may find interesting.
- **mbadepot.com**—This is a unique website founded by Jeff Blum, UT Austin MBA '98, that allows registered members to add links to MBA-related information and hence contribute to the building of the extraordinary amount of resources currently available (and growing) at mbadepot.com.

Numerous websites contain MBA-related information, many of which you may want to stay away from because they display and promote only a small list of online MBA programs that pay to advertise on their cyberpages. Also, as you are surfing around all these websites, you can experience a bit of information overload, so you may want to limit your page views to only one to three websites that pique your interest.

Virtual vs. Real

As in life, first impressions can fool you, and it's important to remember this adage when surfing around the web. Although I am a very strong advocate for finding valuable information online, I know from experience as a veteran web surfer since the early 1990s—when I had a Prodigy account and a very slow dial-up connection with a noisy modem—that slick, impressionable websites are all over the virtual world.

Any web designer worth his or her salt can make a website shine, and any talented promotional writer can generate content on a website that will make an online MBA program seem like a guaranteed ticket to a six-figure salary, promotion to the highest level of business management, and/or quick ladder to self-employed success.

My point is that what's presented virtually when compared to what's real can often be two different things. There are colleges and universities whose websites do not accurately represent their online MBA programs or purposely provide you with only a limited amount of information. As you surf around, you will be surprised at the different look and navigational feel of all these websites. An academically sound school might have a poor website simply because they're short on talented web-development staff. A school that could be considered less academically sound might have a truly wonderful, professional website because they have a top-notch web-development staff.

The Advertising and Marketing Game

Like many things in our profit-at-all-costs world, discovering the truth behind all the advertising can be difficult. The marketing methods utilized today over the web and through e-mail communications do not depict the real picture of online education.

For example, I get numerous unsolicited e-mails erroneously stating that I can earn a Master's degree or even a doctorate without taking any courses or studying. Or, as I mentioned earlier, a web search for "online MBAs" will frequently bring up results that are not, overall, an accurate representation of what's really available.

CAUTION

MBAware

As you are surfing the web for online MBAs, don't be surprised if you start getting all sorts of unsolicited e-mails from spammers who have captured your e-mail address through your web browser. Your best protection is to purchase anti-spam software that flags any incoming unsolicited e-mails you may receive. *PC Magazine* provides reviews on the variety of anti-spam software available, and is located online at www.pcmag.com/category2/0,1738,4795,00.asp.

On Filling Out Forms

The business model for many websites that promote online education, as well as the search engines that lead web surfers to them, revolves around a variety of marketing programs that institutions can buy into. One is called *pay-per-lead*. Another is called *pay-per-click*.

Here the name of the game is to get prospective students, such as yourself, to fill out and submit an online form that lets an institution know that you are seeking more information about its online degree program. Incidentally, the institutions pay for these completed forms to the tune of about $25 each.

Online Term

Pay-per-click (PPC) marketing is where an advertiser pays a predetermined amount of money to a web publisher or agency for every time a website visitor clicks on an advertisement or link that is listed on a hosting website. **Pay-per-lead** (PPL) marketing is where an advertiser pays a web publisher or agency to help generate information about as many prospective customers as possible through an online form that website visitors fill out and submit online. The information on the form generates a "lead" that the advertiser can follow up on.

The entire process typically begins and ends something like this:

1. You go to Google, Yahoo!, MSN, or any one of the many popular search-engine websites and enter something like "Where can I find an online MBA program" into the search box.
2. The search results come up, including "sponsored sites" listed prominently at the top and right side of the web page. You click on one of the sponsored links, which takes you to a higher-education web portal that lists about a dozen online MBA programs that have signed an advertising contract with the web portal.
3. These listings are flagged with "Request More Information" buttons that take you to an online form. You fill out the online form and a day later a school representative (with strong sales and public relations skills) contacts you by telephone and/or e-mail.

Depending on the institution you are interested in, and the person who gets assigned to contact you, this process will most certainly get you the detailed information and advice you need to apply—i.e., what forms you need to fill out, how to apply for financial aid, etc.—but it may not get you the finer information you need to make a decision (e.g., what the faculty and students in the program are really like and detailed information about course content).

Although filling out such online forms can be a quick-and-easy way to get information, you might want to skip this step and begin your search by visiting the actual websites of the institutions you are interested in and carefully reading through the information provided online. Then, if any particular program piques your interest, call the school's admissions office and ask to speak with an academic advisor.

Before you do this, however, I strongly suggest that you read Parts 1, 2, and 3 of this book, because, combined, these chapters have all the information you need to ultimately make an educated choice that is absolutely right for you, as well as what kind of questions you should ask when contacting schools.

The Least You Need to Know

- The web is a great resource for starting to get information about all the online MBA programs available to prospective students.
- Four great websites for finding information about online MBA programs are BusinessWeek Online, USNews.com, MBA.com, and DegreeInfo.com.
- What's presented online can sometimes be deceiving.
- Filling out an online form for more information about any given online MBA program may not be the best method for finding the information you need to know before making a decision.

Chapter 3

Program Types

In This Chapter

- Online graduate-level degree programs in the field of business
- Online MBA opportunities in Canada and England
- Enlisted and veteran military personnel online MBA programs
- Information about credits, course length, and schedules

Now that you have an idea of what to expect and what to look out for online as you navigate through the maze of websites related to MBA programs, it's time to discuss, in a little more detail, all the various types and categories of programs available to you in the online learning mode. You'll find, perhaps, that there are more options than you may have initially imagined.

Options, Options, Options

Before you take this plunge, you should understand what kind of online graduate-level business degree programs are out there. Some have relatively brief mandatory on-campus visits, and others do not. There are general MBA programs and specialized programs. There are customized programs, independent-study programs, dual-degree programs, consortium programs, corporate programs, online certificate programs, online programs available from schools outside the United States, and programs for military personnel. Moreover, credit-hour requirements and the length of courses and academic calendars differ from school to school.

Programs with Residential Requirements

As I have already mentioned, many online MBA programs require you to occasionally visit their campus once or multiple times over the duration of the degree coursework. For business people who travel frequently in their jobs, these types of programs may not fit in with their already busy travel schedules.

Residency requirements (defined in Chapter 1) and what they cover when you are physically on the campus differ from school to school. For many students, these residencies are welcome escapes from their daily grinds (although group-work and study intensive) and ideal for establishing friendships and networking opportunities with colleagues. Here are some examples of residency requirements at online MBA programs (from specific universities):

- Short-term residency requirement (for example, W.P. Carey MBA - Online Program at Arizona State University)
- Optional residency (for example, Regis University)
- Residency required (for example, Syracuse University)

The W.P. Carey MBA - Online Program at Arizona State University (ASU) residency requirement covers six days and five nights at the ASU campus in Tempe, Arizona, and includes an introduction to the W.P. Carey School of Business, faculty-led presentations, and team-building activities. M. Rungtusanatham, faculty director of the program, says the primary objectives of the mandatory residency are to have students get to know each other, the faculty, and the courses they will be taking, and to engage in educational activities similar to those asked of students who attend on-campus MBA programs at the W.P. Carey School of Business. Rungtusanatham says, "When they are here, we tell them this is not a vacation. Don't think about bringing your family. While you are here, forget about work. We are going to pretty much control you from 8 A.M. until 9 or 10 P.M."

The residency also exposes students to the education technology that will be used throughout the curriculum and the support staff that will help them throughout the duration of the program. Hands-on educational activities are included, such as having students play what's called "the beer game," which is a supply-chain simulation exercise. Students also engage in various group decision-making processes and creative team exercises and challenges, such as a team case competition, where students are given a business case, and, within a 12 hour period of time, are required to give a case analysis presentation that is judged by their peers. The team projects obviously help students become acquainted with each other as well as foster the development of networking channels.

Regis University offers optional "summer intensives." Held in mid-July, these five-day summer intensives, for those who choose to take them, give online students a chance to participate in a live accelerated course that includes additional seminars and presentations. Students have the option of staying in dorm rooms on the Regis campus in Denver, Colorado, or at local hotels, and are responsible for arranging their own transportation to Denver and their classes.

Guide on the Side

ASU has a very creative video stream with compelling music located at http://wpcarey.asu.edu/mba/online/curriculum_orientations.cfm. It shows, in vivid video, what their orientation week is all about.

Residencies at Syracuse University's (SU) iMBA program are not optional and are relatively frequent when compared to most online MBA programs that have residency requirements. The program runs on a trimester academic calendar with each trimester (January, May, and August) starting with a five-day residency on the SU campus that begins on a Saturday and concludes on a Thursday. Students attend two classes—usually one quantitative class and one qualitative class (see Chapter 8 for more on course structures)—taught by the same faculty who teach in the full-time, face-to-face MBA program at SU. The format of classes is similar to a traditional program, except with more intense class time and concentrated material.

Outside of class hours, students spend time reading, working on assignments, and getting to know classmates and faculty. SU also holds optional residencies in locations such as New York City; London, England; and Florence, Italy. However, all new students must begin with a residency in Syracuse, New York.

MBAware

Make sure you are fully aware of all the costs that are associated with residency requirements, such as hotel accommodations, airfare, rental car (if needed), and any textbooks that may be required for classes.

General and Specialized Programs

From a historical perspective, general MBA programs were created to help students who did not have strong business backgrounds to get up to speed in basic business theory and effective business practices. Today many pre-MBA students have accumulated this kind of basic knowledge through the business-related courses they took as undergraduates. Plus many prospective MBA students have gained practical business experience working a variety of jobs while they attended school or after they graduated. Others are entrepreneurs who have gained valuable business experience by starting up successful businesses themselves. This has brought about a change in MBA program offerings over the past few decades.

Although the general MBA program itself is still alive and well, there has been tremendous growth in specialized MBA programs that are geared toward students who already have the basic business preparation skills but need to acquire more expertise in a particular area of study.

At the University of Phoenix, for example, which is the largest provider of online MBA programs in the United States, students can enroll in a general MBA program, as well as take an MBA with concentrations in accounting, e-business, global management, health-care management, human resource management, marketing, or technology management. These types of programs are ideal for students who are seeking highly specialized skills.

Instant Message

"If you need general advanced business preparation and don't have a broad business background, you should enroll in a general MBA program because you will be surprised by what you don't know. You can't do an emphasis in a business subject area within the same number of credit hours without cutting corners off the general content, which can be critical in terms of the knowledge and expectations of a company hiring an MBA graduate."

—Regis University MBA Professor Ed Cooper

It's a good idea to determine whether the school has a solid academic reputation in any particular concentration area it might be offering online. For example, at Florida State University (FSU), students can enroll in an online MBA program with a specialization in hospitality administration or real estate finance and analysis. Not surprisingly, these are two areas of study FSU is well known for, especially because the state of Florida has a large tourism industry, in addition to a steady population growth.

Another good example of a specialty online MBA program can be found at the School of Management at the University of Texas at Dallas, which offers a Global Leadership Executive MBA (GLEMBA) that is one of the few AACSB (American Assembly of Collegiate Schools of Business) accredited Executive MBA programs that offers a full concentration in international business management. See Chapter 4 for more information about AACSB accreditation.

The GLEMBA program is not fully online, requiring six weekend residency requirements that it calls "retreats." The remainder of the program, however, is conducted entirely online.

Customized Programs

Can you customize an online MBA program so that you take only those classes you are interested in as opposed to the typical set schedule of core required courses that the institution says you must take to graduate? The answer is yes and no. A perfect example, and one of the very few examples, of where this kind of scenario might come into play is the Certified Public Accountant who wants to earn a general MBA. A CPA might find the typical financial accounting courses that are part and parcel of the core requirements of most general MBA programs to be a waste of precious time. In this case, the accounting course will more than likely be waived, allowing the CPA to replace it with an elective course.

Electives allow students to customize their online MBA course of study above meeting the required core courses of any curriculum. Although most online MBA programs offer a wide range of electives, other programs don't allow students to take any electives whatsoever and have a set schedule of classes that must be taken in a particular sequence. See Chapter 8 for more information about MBA curriculums and electives.

An Independent Self-Study Program

Independent self-study is another online MBA format, but one that is not widely available. Northcentral University in Prescott, Arizona, is one of the few schools in the country that offers an MBA program in this format. Here students do not take courses with other students. Each enrolled student is essentially a class of one. The base materials for independent self-study courses are typically a textbook, study guide, and final exam. At Northcentral University, students are assigned faculty mentors who support adult learners through one-on-one interactions. Contact between the learner and the faculty mentor can be achieved through telephone, fax, e-mail, snail mail, and, on occasion, person-to-person contact.

Online Term

Independent self-study is a teaching and learning format in which individuals enroll in a class of one (their self) and are typically guided by a faculty/mentor/coach whom they can communicate with for assistance with achieving their course objectives within a specified time frame.

Independent self-study students must complete clearly spelled-out course objectives within certain time frames. For example, at Northcentral University, students have 16 weeks to complete a course.

The Northcentral University MBA degree is a 36-credit/12-course program that offers specializations in applied computer science, criminal justice administration, electronic commerce, financial management, health-care administration, human resources management, international business, management, management of engineering and technology, management of information systems, and public administration.

Dual Degrees

Another highly unique curriculum in an online learning format is the MBA dual degree. The University of Maryland University College (UMUC), which is the largest public state university in the country to offer online degree programs, offers dual degrees that award an MBA in combination with a Master of International Management, Master of Science in E-Commerce, Master of Science in Health-Care Administration, Master of Science in Management, or a Master of Science in Technology Management.

Basically, a dual degree enables students to extend the breadth and depth of their studies based on the shared curriculums of two programs. Dual-degree students earn two degrees for substantially fewer credits than if each program were completed separately. For example, UMUC students who first complete all degree requirements for the MBA degree may then go on to earn a second degree by taking an additional 12 credits from one of the other available curriculums.

Consortium Programs

A number of state higher-education systems also offer online MBA programs by pooling together the resources of a group of schools within their state network. Systems that fit into this category include the University of Wisconsin Internet Business Consortium MBA Program, the University of Texas System TeleCampus, and the Georgia WebMBA Program. Following are brief descriptions of each.

The University of Wisconsin (UW) Internet Business Consortium MBA Program was built with the help of the University of Wisconsin Learning Innovations support group, which is the arm of the UW system that provides instructional design and development services to all 26 UW campuses. The MBA program courses were created by drawing on the combined expertise of business school faculty from the University of Wisconsin-Eau Claire, University of Wisconsin-Oshkosh, University of Wisconsin-La Crosse, and the University of Wisconsin-Parkside. UW-Eau Claire is responsible for reviewing graduate application files, so prospective students use a UW-Eau Claire graduate program admission application and send supporting documentation to UW-Eau Claire. Students who successfully complete the program receive their degrees from the University of Wisconsin-Eau Claire.

The University of Texas TeleCampus is the central support system for online education initiatives among the 14 universities and research facilities that comprise the University of Texas (UT) system. Eight participating institutions that offer traditional MBA programs (UT Arlington, UT Brownsville, UT Dallas, UT El Paso, UT Pan American, UT San Antonio, and UT Tyler) pooled their resources and expertise to create the UT TeleCampus fully online MBA program. Students must apply to and be accepted by one of the participating MBA programs, which becomes the home, degree-granting university. Criteria and deadlines for admission vary slightly from one university to another but are the same as the traditional residence programs. Students must take at least two courses from their home university. All courses taken from participating universities in the online MBA program can be transferred to the student's home university to fulfill degree requirements.

Five University System of Georgia institutions (Georgia College & State University, Georgia Southern University, Kennesaw State University, State University of West Georgia, and Valdosta State University) provide fully online courses that comprise the Georgia WebMBA program, which consists of 10 required courses. Each school of the five institutions admits students according to its own admission standards. Before starting their online courses, students must successfully complete a two-day orientation, held at the Kennesaw State University campus.

Instant Message

"One of the hardest parts about choosing a program is that a lot of what you need to know is not public. You won't know until you get there. I have great sympathy for the prospective student. It is difficult to transfer or move around once you are enrolled in a program, which makes their choice that much more critical."

—Paula O'Callaghan, director, Independent Study MBA Program (iMBA), Syracuse University

Corporate Programs

Some business schools have special customized online MBA programs that are provided to employees of specific companies. For example, Indiana University's Kelley Direct online MBA programs are divided into two categories: public and corporate. Its public online MBA is for anybody who can gain acceptance into the program, which is competitive. Its corporate programs are based on employers or affiliates that have made arrangements with the Indiana University Kelley School of Business to offer unique degree programs to their employees or contacts. Currently, Kelley Direct has corporate students enrolled through General Motors, John Deere, LOGTECH, Microsoft, and United Technologies.

Online Certificate Programs

For those who don't want to commit to a complete degree, there are *graduate-level certificate programs* in the field of business that are offered in an online learning format. Graduate-level certificates typically are for credit courses but can also be noncredit courses. The value of noncredit courses is they typically cost less, but these certificates are usually limited and cannot be applied to a degree. Graduate certificates can also be a help to students because sometimes a business will reimburse students for taking a certificate but not a degree.

For example, Capella University's School of Business offers concentrated 16-credit graduate-level programs of study, comprised of four 4-credit online courses, in the field of human resource management, information technology management, or business leadership. Certificate learners who want to pursue a Master's or doctoral degree at Capella University may apply all credit earned from completing a certificate toward a degree once admitted to the graduate program.

Online Term

A **graduate-level certificate** program is a non-degree-granting series of graduate courses. Upon successful completion, students are awarded a certificate. The number of courses in any certificate program varies by institution. Most award credit that can be applied toward earning a Master's degree.

Another institution that offers business-related graduate-level online certificate programs is Strayer University, which provides executive certificates in business administration, professional accounting, and computer information systems. The recipient of any executive graduate certificate, which consists of 6 courses totaling 27 credits (4.5 credits each), may apply all credits earned toward an MBA with the same emphasis.

Options North of the Border and Across the Atlantic

Students who might be interested in an online MBA program outside of the United States could find it difficult to obtain the information they need to ultimately enroll in such a program, but with the right amount of determination and a willingness to make long-distance overseas phone calls, it can be done relatively easily. However, to make life less complicated and as close to home as possible, due to some of the short residencies most of these foreign institutions require, I suggest looking at online MBA programs offered across the northern border in Canada and across the Atlantic Ocean in England.

There are some excellent online MBA programs offered by Canadian and British institutions that are noted for their strong emphasis on building global business management skills. These institutions typically have culturally diverse student bodies and faculty from numerous countries. Under the right circumstances, graduating from a Canadian or British program could turn you into a sought-after executive with a unique international perspective on business.

Guide on the Side

For a culturally diverse educational experience with a global business perspective, you might want to investigate some of the online MBA programs offered by institutions located in countries outside the United States. See the "Resources" section in Appendix B for online MBA program listings in Canada and England.

The sections that follow describe some of the foreign online options available to you.

Athabasca University

One foreign institution with an online MBA program that I have keen knowledge of through my work as a professional education writer is Athabasca University (AU), a Canadian "virtual university," which means that it does not have a physical campus and only offers distance-education programs (see the figure that follows). Its central office is located in the town of Athabasca, Alberta, located about 90 miles north of Edmonton. AU is currently a candidate for regional accreditation by the U.S. Commission on Higher Education of the Middle States Association of Colleges and Schools. If it wins accreditation, which is expected to occur sometime during the summer of 2005, it will be the first Canadian institution of any kind to be fully accredited in the United States. Regional accreditation is discussed further in Chapter 4.

AU's online Executive MBA program, which includes a one-week residency requirement, is noted as Canada's largest, and it has been included on the list of the world's top 75 Executive MBA programs by the *Financial Times* of London.

According to AU's director of external relations, Stephen Murgatroyd, AU's EMBA program has a strong focus on real-life business challenges, with students working on assignments that are directly related to their jobs, as opposed to theoretical or case-based problem solving. To be accepted into the program, students must have a Bachelor's degree and three years of managerial experience, or "an acceptable professional designation" with at least five years of managerial experience. Murgatroyd adds that students in the program, as well as the faculty, who are called "coaches," live in Europe, Asia, and all across North America.

In addition to a general EMBA, AU offers EMBAs with concentrations in information technology management, project management, and energy.

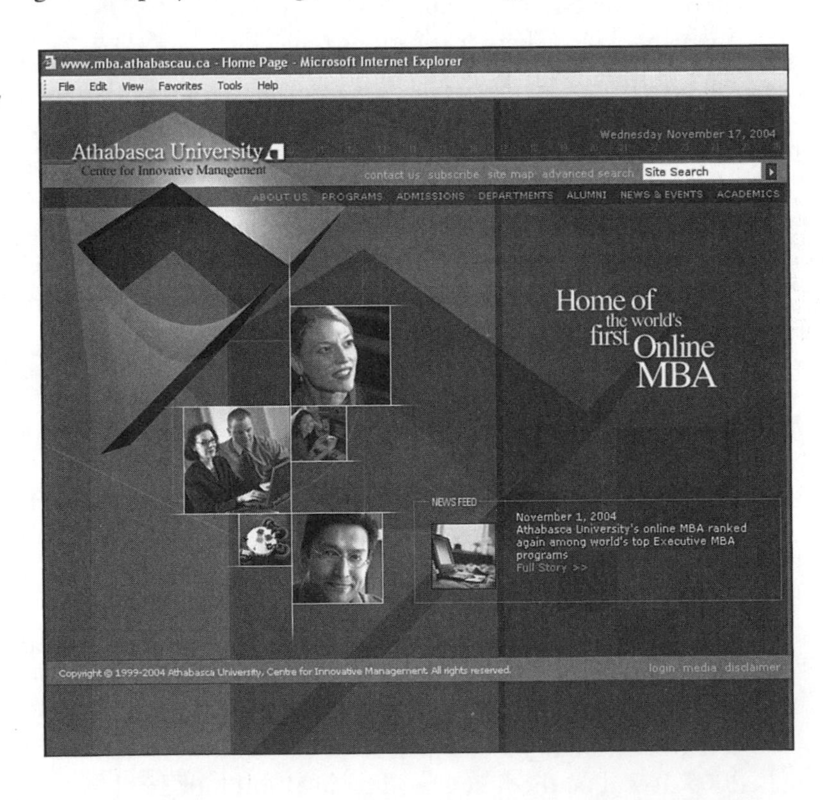

Athabasca University in Alberta, Canada, is currently a candidate for regional accreditation in the United States.

Henley Management College

Henley Management College's Distance Learning MBA and Diploma in Management is one of the oldest online MBA programs in the world. It has three week-long residencies—one each of the three years of the program at the Henley campus in Henley on Thames in Oxfordshire, England—that are complimented by a series of virtual workshops delivered as *webinars*, which are seminars conducted over the web.

Online Term

Webinars are live, synchronous seminars viewed through a web browser with audio communication through a teleconferencing connection or voice over Internet connection. They are typically recorded for viewing asynchronously.

Edinburgh Business School

The Edinburgh Business School MBA at Heriot-Watt University is another well-established early provider of an online MBA program featuring an independent self-study format that combines specially designed text-based instruction with online interactions and final examinations at the end of each course. More than 9,000 Heriot-Watt MBA students from 150 countries around the world are currently studying and taking examinations in more than 350 exam centers worldwide, including one in New York and another in Los Angeles. More than 6,500 students have graduated from the program since it started in 1990. Courses are written from a global perspective, and some of the courses have been written by faculty in the United States.

Several other well-known schools in the United Kingdom offering online MBAs include the Imperial College of London's Distance Learning MBA, the University of Manchester's Business School Worldwide, and the University of London Royal Holloway's Distance Learning MBA in International Management.

What Uncle Sam Offers

The U.S. military's history of providing educational assistance to soldiers and veterans through the GI Bill is well documented. Today that aid has been extended into the online world through a number of initiatives, such as the DANTES Distance Learning Program and eArmyU. These two initiatives, combined, have helped to educate tens of thousands of enlisted military personnel in the online learning format. Military veterans are also increasingly participating in online education programs through veteran assistance offices located on college and university campuses across the country.

DANTES

Defense Activity for Non-Traditional Education Support (DANTES) supports the education programs of the Department of Defense (DoD) and the U.S. military. DANTES has a distance-learning program that supports military personnel who want to earn their degrees but can't because their work schedules or duty locations do not permit physical class attendance. DANTES has an extensive online catalogue of regionally accredited online business-related graduate-degree programs that are approved for military personnel to enroll in. In general, subject to specified dollar limits and availability of funding, students in the DANTES program are reimbursed up to 100 percent of their tuition costs. Costs related to any possible residency requirements, as well as textbooks, are not reimbursed.

eArmyU

eArmyU is the U.S. Army's collaboration with 29 colleges and universities that offer online degree and certificate programs at the undergraduate and graduate levels (see the figure that follows). eArmyU launched in early 2001 with approximately 1,660 soldiers enrolled in online programs provided by 16 institutions during its first term. Today more than 50,000 U.S. Army soldiers are taking distance-education courses through eArmyU. To be eligible, soldiers must be regular active duty or active guard reserve enlisted, assigned to or in the area of geographic support of an eArmyU-designated installation. (At last count, there were a total of 16 eArmyU education centers, 14 in the United States, 1 in Korea, and 1 in Germany.) They must also meet a number of other prerequisites, including a specific service-remaining requirement (one to three years), and have approval from their unit commander.

Once enrolled, soldiers receive up to 100 percent funding for tuition, books, and course fees. They also receive a personal laptop, e-mail account, and Internet service provider (ISP) account. eArmyU also provides soldiers with 24-hour technical support and a host of academic advising services.

The majority of programs offered through eArmyU's 29 institutions are at the Associate's and Bachelor's level. Online MBA programs are also in the mix, with programs offered by Baker College, Nova Southeastern University, and the University of the Incarnate Word.

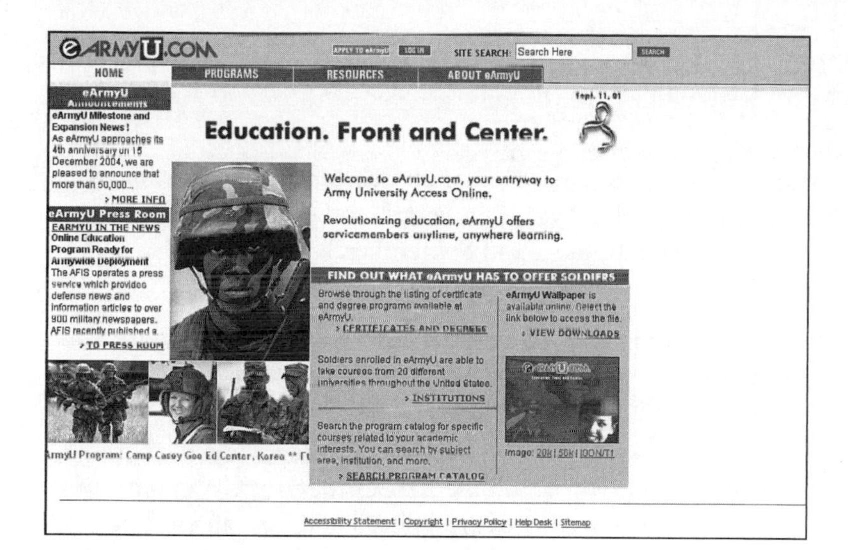

eArmyU.

Military.com

All enlisted military personnel, as well as all veterans, should be aware of Military.com. This is another excellent higher-education web portal. As noted in its "About Us" section, Military.com connects and informs the 30 million Americans with military affinity, including active duty, reservists, guard members, retirees, veterans, family members, defense workers, and those considering military careers. In particular, Military.com's "Education" section at www.military.com/Careers/Education is a wonderful source of information and links related to all of the education benefits and programs for active service members and veterans.

Credit Hours, Semesters, and Quarters

The number of credit hours required to complete an MBA, as well as the length of courses, semesters, and/or quarters, varies greatly from one institution to another, so much so that it can get very confusing at times.

Here are examples of the number of courses and credit hours required to earn an online MBA at four schools, as well as when these schools offer their courses:

- The University of Maryland University College program requires 43 credits: one 1-credit foundation course and seven 6-credit seminars, each of which is 14 weeks long with 3 weeks off between seminars. Courses are offered on a semester basis beginning in January, May, and September.

- The Capella University program consists of 48 credits or sixteen 3-credit courses that are 6 weeks long. Courses are offered every 6 weeks with a week break in between.
- The Drexel University program is comprised of 60 quarter credits distributed over twenty 3-credit courses, each 10 weeks in length and offered on a quarterly basis beginning in January, March, June, and September.
- The University of Baltimore program requires 48 credits or sixteen 3-credit courses, each 10 weeks in length and offered on a quarterly basis in January, May, June, and September.

So, in short, you can choose from a wide variety of credits required, course lengths, and academic calendars when searching for an online MBA program. Overall, it can be very difficult to decipher exactly when courses are offered and how an entire curriculum is actually sequenced for any given program, especially if you are only relying on information you see on websites. Your best bet for finding specific information about such important time-related and scheduling issues is to get on the phone and call the institution you are investigating and ask a lot of questions.

Before you make that call, however, note that this book covers a great deal more concerning what you will need to know to choose an online MBA program and ultimately succeed as an online learner, and, if all goes right, earn the status of an online alumni.

The Least You Need to Know

- A wide variety of online business-related graduate degree programs are available from institutions throughout the world.
- There are viable online MBA programs available from institutions in Canada and England that are noted for having culturally diverse students and faculty as well as a strong emphasis on global business strategies.
- The U.S. military has a number of programs that can help both enlisted and veteran personnel enroll in online MBA programs.
- You have a wide variety of credit requirements, course lengths, and academic calendars to choose from when searching for the online MBA program that is right for you.

Chapter 4

Accreditation and School Classification

In This Chapter

- Regional, national, and professional accreditation status
- AACSB, ACBSP, and IACBE accreditation
- Why or why not care about professional accreditation
- How to define an institution's Carnegie classification

There's a good deal more that you should consider when searching for and choosing an online MBA program.

In addition to knowing what the curriculum is like, which is covered in Chapter 8, and who the faculty and students are, which is covered in Chapter 6, you need to be aware of an institution's accreditation status. And that's what we are going to cover in this chapter.

To Be or Not to Be Accredited

There's a lot of literature available online about higher education *accreditation* standards. To cut right to the chase, I'll simply say that regional accreditation is the most important. You'll also want to understand what it means to be nationally accredited and professionally accredited.

Online Term

Accreditation is a process in which educational institutions are recognized as viable places to learn. Standards are established by various accrediting agencies that are composed of educational experts. If an institution meets the standards set by the agency, which is accomplished through a peer-review process, it is acknowledged with accreditation status.

Regional Accreditation

Regional accreditation means that an institution has been accredited by an agency that is recognized by the U.S. Department of Education and the Council for Higher Education Accreditation.

Credits earned at regionally accredited institutions can usually be transferred from one regionally accredited college or university to another. Transfer of credit is more common for undergraduate programs. Graduate programs typically limit transfer credit to 25 percent or less of the total credit needed to attain the degree.

Regionally accredited institutions, which are the majority in the United States, usually will not accept credits earned from non-regionally accredited institutions.

In short, make sure that the institution offering an online MBA program is accredited by one of the following six regional accreditation agencies:

- **MSA.** Middle States Association of Colleges and Schools Commission on Higher Education
- **NASC.** Northwest Association of Schools, Colleges and Universities Commission on Colleges and Universities
- **NCA.** North Central Association of Schools and Colleges, The Higher Learning Commission
- **NEASC.** New England Association of Schools and Colleges Commission on Institutions of Higher Education

- **SACS.** Southern Association of Colleges and Schools Commission on Colleges
- **WASC.** Western Association of Schools and Colleges Accrediting Commission for Senior Colleges and Universities

National Accreditation—DETC

Another notable accrediting agency is the Distance Education Training Council (DETC), which is recognized by the Department of Education and the Council for Higher Education Accreditation as a "nationally" accredited agency. DETC (www.detc.org) has been around since 1926 and was formerly known as the National Home Study Council. Most of the institutions and programs DETC accredits are related to specific trades or vocations, and many are print-based correspondence or home-study courses. DETC does, however, accredit a number of online MBA programs.

If you happen to enroll in an online degree program that is only DETC accredited, and you plan on transferring those credits to a regionally accredited institution at a later date, or pursuing a doctoral degree after you graduate, check with the regionally accredited institution's registrar before you proceed because those credits may not be transferable.

Professional Accreditation

In addition to regional and DETC accreditation, there are some professional accrediting bodies you may want to be aware of when it comes to online MBA programs:

- The Association to Advance Collegiate Schools of Business (AACSB) at www.aacsb.edu
- The Association of Collegiate Business Schools and Programs (ACBSP) at http://acbsp.org
- The International Assembly for Collegiate Business Education (IACBE) at www.iacbe.org

The AACSB is commonly known as the most prestigious accreditation any business school can achieve. ACBSP and IACBE are also regarded as viable accreditation bodies.

CAUTION

MBAware

Don't confuse "membership" with "accreditation status." An institution can be a member of AACSB, IACBE, and/or ACBSP and not be accredited by these professional accrediting bodies. The AACSB, IACBE, and ACBSP list both accredited and members-only institutions accordingly on their websites.

AACSB Accreditation

AACSB has been around since 1916. Institutions offering degrees in business administration or accounting may volunteer for AACSB accreditation review, which is conducted every five years. The review process includes an extensive self-evaluation and a peer review conducted by a team of about three business school deans from similar AACSB-accredited institutions.

In a nutshell, AACSB accreditation revolves around ensuring that a school adheres to standards that are consistent with its mission. Jerry Trapnell, AASCB chief accreditation officer, says, "We expect our schools to articulate the kind of student body they are trying to recruit, and then, of course, put together academic programs that are appropriate to serve that student body, consistent to the mission the school articulates."

Stat

According to statistics published in AACSB's 2004 Pocket Guide to Business Schools, 86.5 percent of full-time business faculty at AACSB-accredited schools in 2002 had doctoral degrees.

As noted in the preamble of an AACSB document titled "Eligibility Procedures and Accreditation Standards for Business Accreditation," it is important to note that "accreditation does not create quality learning experiences. Academic quality is created by the educational standards implemented by individual faculty members in interactions with students. A high-quality degree program is created when students interact with a cadre of faculty in a systematic program supported by an institution. Accreditation observes, recognizes, and sometimes motivates educational quality created within the institution."

An institution that is AACSB accredited means that all of the business programs offered by that institution, including any online degree programs, fall under the umbrella of AACSB accreditation status.

A list of AACSB accredited schools is provided in Appendix C. For updates, check the AACSB website (www.aacsb.edu) under the "Accredited Members" option on the "Accreditation" menu.

The average GMAT scores for part-time distance-education programs at 26 AACSB-accredited institutions in the United States, during the 2003-2004 academic year, were as follows:

- 75 percent had an average score of 588
- the median score was 549
- 25 percent had an average score of 532

ACBSP Accreditation

ACBSP was founded in 1988. The content of the ACBSP website reveals that this organization's mission "acknowledges the importance of scholarly research and inquiry and believes that such activities facilitate improved teaching. Institutions are strongly encouraged to pursue a reasonable mutually beneficial balance between teaching and research. And further, ACBSP encourages faculty involvement within the contemporary business world to enhance the quality of classroom instruction and to contribute to student learning."

A list of ACBSP accredited schools is provided on its website (http://acbsp.org) under the "Why Join ACBSP?" heading. As of October 2004, 145 four-year institutions were accredited by ACBSP.

IACBE Accreditation

I have to admit that the IACBE website does not look nearly as professional as the AACSB or ACBSP websites. Whether that means anything, I will leave up to you. The content on the IACBE website, however, reveals that this organization's mission is "to promote and support quality Business/Management Education worldwide through accreditation and outcomes assessment which involves: (1) the measurement of effectiveness, (2) the measurement of learning outcomes, and (3) the identification of changes and improvements that are needed as a result of the assessment activity." (Refer to Chapter 10 for more information about learning outcomes and how it relates to online MBA programs.)

A list of IACBE-accredited schools is provided on its website (www.iacbe.org) under the "IACBE Members" heading. The various accreditation statuses of all institutions offering online MBAs are included in the listing of schools in Appendix B.

The Great Debate About AACSB Accreditation

Most educators who work at AACSB-accredited business schools will tell you that one of the primary factors prospective students should consider when searching for an online MBA is whether a school is AACSB accredited. "AACSB accreditation is the good housekeeping seal of approval on your forehead," says Rick Niswander, dean of graduate business programs at East Carolina University, an AACSB-accredited school.

Educators who work at non-AACSB-accredited business schools will tell you that AACSB accreditation is not the be-all and end-all, so to speak. You'll also find students, employers, and recruiters who say that having AACSB accreditation is highly important as well as highly irrelevant. "Not being AACSB accredited has nothing to do with the quality of our program," says Online MBA Director Rosemary Hartigan from the University of Maryland University College, a *non-AACSB-accredited school.* "We probably have tighter assessment standards than any AACSB school."

Online Term

A **non-AACSB-accredited school** can either mean that they have not sought out AACSB accreditation or would most likely not achieve it if they did seek it out, perhaps because they don't meet AACSB's criteria for a variety of reasons.

So what's the bottom line? In my opinion, the answer is you, and how you can come to a decision, through your research, as to whether any particular online MBA program will ultimately fit in with your goals and aspirations. If you do enough investigating, you should be able to discover the school that is right for you, regardless of any outside accreditation body's stamp of endorsement.

Every school that is AACSB accredited typically displays this status on their program website. However, if you're not sure about a school's professional accreditation status, just ask an academic advisor.

Instant Message

"Many measures which are heavily marketed by institutions as hallmarks of quality—the quantity of research produced or even the number of terminally degreed faculty—are not necessarily related to the end product, which is student learning."

—Laura Palmer Noone, president of the University of Phoenix

"I look at the schools that are AACSB accredited and by and large they are schools that I consider to be peers, that are of high quality. Outside of the group (meaning those not AACSB accredited), we don't know."

—Paula O'Callaghan, director, iMBA Program, Syracuse University

Carnegie Classification

Another factor you may want to consider when doing your search is an institution's *Carnegie classification*, which is something that is often overlooked by prospective students. Although this is not a ranking or accreditation system, and may not be all that important in the grand scheme of things, an institution's Carnegie classification does tell you something about an institution's overall mission and function. There are a total of nine classifications. The following five, described in brief, can be related to your choice of an online MBA program:

- **Doctoral/Research Universities—Extensive.** Institutions that offer a wide range of undergraduate and graduate programs and at least 50 doctoral degrees per year across at least 15 disciplines.
- **Doctoral/Research Universities—Intensive.** Institutions that offer a wide range of undergraduate and graduate programs and at least 10 doctoral degrees per year across at least 3 disciplines, or at least 20 doctoral degrees per year overall.
- **Master's Colleges and Universities I.** Institutions that offer a wide range of undergraduate programs and at least 40 graduate degrees per year across at least 3 disciplines.
- **Master's Colleges and Universities II.** Institutions that offer a wide range of undergraduate programs and at least 20 graduate degrees per year.
- **Specialized Institutions.** Institutions that offer undergraduate, graduate, and doctoral degrees and typically award a majority of their degrees in a single field. For example, specialized schools of business and management, medical schools, and schools of law fall into this category, as well as other institutions that do not fit into any other Carnegie classification.

  Source: Carnegie Classifications of Institutions of Higher Education, available online at www.carnegiefoundation.org/Classification/CIHE2000/defNotes/Definitions.htm.

The latest classification was completed in 2000 and an updated version is slated for 2005. To see where your school of choice fits in with the mix, go to www.carnegiefoundation.org/Classification/CIHE2000/PartIfiles/partI.htm.

Online Term

As noted at www.carnegiefoundation.org, "The **Carnegie Classification** is a taxonomy of colleges and universities. It is *not* a ranking of institutions, nor do its categories imply quality differences. Each institution is assigned to one of several categories based on descriptive data about that institution. The categories are intended to be relatively homogeneous with respect to the institutions' functions as well as student and faculty characteristics."

What Do Carnegie Classifications Really Mean?

Although the Carnegie Foundation makes it clear that its classifications do not imply quality differences, it's perceived among some educators and lawmakers that they really are a strong indication of quality. In some states, for instance, budget allocations are determined by Carnegie classifications. In addition, some educators suggest that an institution's ability to recruit top-notch faculty, as well as top-notch graduate students, can be related to its Carnegie classification.

Also, some parents and private college-planning counselors use Carnegie classifications as a decision factor when choosing or suggesting which institutions high school seniors should apply to.

In general, Doctoral/Research Universities—Extensive institutions are perceived as the highest level any institution can achieve. However, as noted on the Carnegie Foundation website's "background" section, "the Classification is a great simplification of what colleges and universities do, and only one of countless ways that they might be grouped. It does not purport to identify the fundamental character of an institution, and many important facets of institutional activity and identity are not taken into account."

The Least You Need to Know

- The most important accreditation status you need to be aware of is whether an institution is regionally accredited.
- If a school you are interested in is not regionally accredited, find out whether any credits earned would be transferable to another regionally accredited institution should you decide to transfer or decide to purse a doctoral degree after you graduate.
- AACSB accreditation is the most prestigious of all professional accreditation standards, and you, personally, have to decide whether it has any meaningful bearing on what business school you choose to attend.
- Knowing an institution's Carnegie classification will give you an idea of its mission and overall structure.
- It's perceived among some educators and lawmakers that the Carnegie classifications are a strong indication of quality.

Chapter 5

The Rankings Game

In This Chapter

- How to interpret on-campus program rankings
- An unofficial ranking of four online MBA programs
- How to use ranking websites for finding information
- Advice for being an educated consumer

We've all heard about college rankings in the media. Schools in the upper echelon of the most popular rankings often boast about where they have been placed, and students use college rankings, perhaps more than they should, as part of their decision-making process before they start applying to schools. However, the first thing you need to know about rankings is that a reliable and valid ranking system for online MBA programs has not been invented.

All the rankings you see and hear about are for traditional on-campus programs, not for online programs. The second thing you need to know is that the popular ranking services have great websites that are packed with information about schools that you can use during your online decision-making process.

Using the Major Ranking Systems

When it comes to on-campus MBA programs, there are primarily four highly regarded and often touted ranking systems with great websites that, along with listing their rankings, provide huge amounts of information about graduate-level education:

- *Business Week* at www.usnews.com/usnews/rankguide/rghome.htm
- *Financial Times* at http://news.ft.com/management/businessed
- The *Wall Street Journal* at www.collegejournal.com/mbacenter
- *U.S. News and World Report* at www.usnews.com/usnews/rankguide/rghome.htm

CAUTION

MBAware

If you see a school proclaiming that its online MBA program is one of the top-ranked MBA programs by *U.S. News and World Report*, *Business Week*, or any of the other popular ranking systems, don't believe it. There is not any valid ranking system for online MBA programs in existence today.

Online MBA programs are very similar in content to their counterpart on-campus MBA programs. So, an on-campus MBA program with a counterpart online MBA program that has made it inside any of these four ranking systems could be unofficially considered a "top-ranked" program. I found four schools that fit within this unofficial ranking system for online MBA programs. They are, in alphabetic order—drum roll, please—Arizona State University, Indiana University, Syracuse University, and the University of Florida.

Here are the on-campus MBA program ranking stats for each:

- **Arizona State University.** Ranked 29th by *U.S. News and World Report*, "U.S. Next 20" (after Top 30) by *Business Week*, 60th by *Financial Times*
- **Indiana University.** Ranked 23rd by *U.S. News and World Report*, 18th by *Business Week*, 56th by *Financial Times*, 12th by the *Wall Street Journal*
- **Syracuse University.** Considered for ranking by *Business Week*
- **University of Florida.** Ranked 54th by *U.S. News and World Report*, considered for ranking by *Business Week*, 35th by the *Wall Street Journal*

All four of these programs are excellent choices, but they are by no means the only programs you should consider. Plus, any one of these four will cost you a good chunk of change.

The Princeton Review

Another well-known ranking is created by The Princeton Review, which publishes *Best 357 Colleges* and *Best 143 Business Schools*. Both have absolutely nothing to do with online programs, but these two books do provide numerous details that can give you a general sense about any of the schools listed. All of the best 357 colleges are also indexed, with links to more information, at www.princetonreview.com/college/research/rankings/rankingsBest357.asp. Schools offering online MBA programs that are part of the 357 include the following:

- Arizona State University
- Drexel University
- Florida State University
- Suffolk University
- Syracuse University
- University of Florida
- University of Massachusetts at Amherst
- University of Wyoming
- Worcester Polytechnic Institute

Forbes Magazine

Forbes Magazine, which is loaded with lists on a variety of things, including the best small and big companies, the world's richest people, and its famous Fortune 500, also has a best business schools list that it publishes online at www.forbes.com/2003/09/24/bschooland.html. Out of a list of 67 schools ranked by Forbes, 3 had online MBA programs: Indiana University came in 35th; Arizona State University was ranked 43rd; and University of Florida was ranked 50th.

Guide on the Side

A one-stop website where you can find links to all the higher education ranking systems—good, bad, and ugly—along with lots of great information about how rankings really work, including a "Caution and Controversy" section, is provided by the University of Illinois, Urbana-Champaign's Education and Social Science Library at www.library.uiuc.edu/edx/rankabout.htm.

The Economist Intelligence Unit

Another respectable ranking entity is the Economist Intelligence Unit (EIU), which is the London-based business information arm of The Economist Group, publisher of *The Economist*, *CFO* magazine, *Roll Call*, and other specialty business journals. EIU publishes its top 100 MBA programs worldwide at a website called "Which MBA," located at http://mba.eiu.com. Indiana University and University of Florida made the EIU list as well, ranking 54th and 89th respectively. The EIU website also provides news and information, in general, about pursuing an MBA.

The Center

The Center, which is based at the University of Florida, publishes another valid ranking system that is more academic in nature. The Center ranks entire colleges and universities. Its rankings are very much unlike the popular rankings previously mentioned, and they could be considered statistically significant due to the nature of the research and analysis it conducts. The Center publishes an in-depth annual report titled "Top American Research Universities." The report offers analysis and data useful for understanding American research university performance.

Universities are ranked according to a variety of measures, including research funding, endowment assets, annual giving, National Academy membership, prestigious faculty awards, doctorates awarded, postdoctoral appointees, and SAT scores of entering freshmen. You can download the report for free from http://thecenter.ufl.edu. Some of the schools listed in this report that have online MBA programs include, in alphabetic order, Arizona State University, Drexel University, Florida State University, Indiana University, Syracuse University, University of Massachusetts-Amherst, and University of Nebraska-Lincoln.

Nancy P. O'Brien, head of the Education and Social Science Library at the University of Illinois, Urbana-Champaign, says, "The Center (publisher of 'Top American Research Universities') is highly regarded for the work that it does. They use variables that are very research oriented. So there is a lot of significance to the factors that they use."

Questionable Rankers

Of course, the World Wide Web is by no means a perfect place, which is why you have sites such as one labeled "25 Best Distance Learning Universities." An immediate warning flag is that nowhere on this site did I see an explanation of the methodology that was used to arrive at their list of 25, not to mention who exactly created this list in the first place. Another website that left me wondering about the criteria actually used to reach their conclusions about leading MBA programs was a site called "Top 10" by Best Education. In short, numerous websites in cyberspace are similar to this in nature, and I would simply say these sites are not worth the time it takes to look at them.

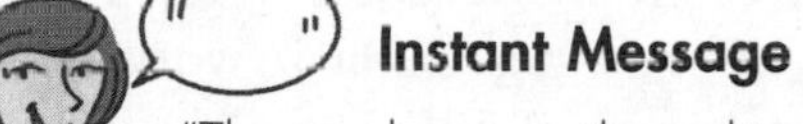

Instant Message

"Those who compile rankings will tell you they are valid, but to a great extent it depends on which factors are used to develop rankings, and I think that is where most of the controversy comes in."
—Nancy P. O'Brien, head, Education and Social Science Library, University of Illinois, Urbana-Champaign

Digging Out Information at the Rankings Websites

All of the big rankers have decent websites that can be utilized on a number of important fronts, including advice about MBA program admission strategies and financial-aid concerns that can be applied to online MBA programs. In my opinion, the best of all these sites in relation to providing information you can use is BusinessWeek Online. A lot of the good stuff, however, is only accessible through its "MBA Insider" web-based information service, which at the time of this writing was selling for $29.95. Nonetheless, there is a lot of free information and services you can use at the BusinessWeek Online website.

In Chapter 2, for instance, I mentioned its "Distance MBA Profiles" section. Another section you can use in relation to online MBA programs, even though it is geared primarily toward on-campus programs, is the "Part-Time MBA" section of the BusinessWeek Online website.

Online Comparison Tools

BusinessWeek Online (www.usnews.com/usnews/rankguide/rghome.htm) has a Part-Time MBA Comparator tool that you might find helpful. This tool enables you to compare up to four part-time on-campus MBA programs at a time. I used this tool to compare the part-time MBA programs (which would be very similar, if not exactly the same as, their online MBA programs) at the University of Massachusetts-Amherst, Florida State University, and the University of Nebraska-Lincoln—three similar public, nonprofit institutions that are Carnegie classified as Doctoral/Research Universities—Extensive. The results revealed such things as average GMAT scores, percentage of applicants accepted, average age of new entrants, percentage of international students, average postgraduate work experience of students, teaching methods used, and percentage of full-time and adjunct faculty members.

All the institutions offering online MBA programs are not listed in the Part-Time MBA Comparator tool, so it obviously cannot be applied across the board. However, it could prove useful for certain programs, such as the aforementioned example.

The USNews.com website has a similar online business school comparison tool, but you have to subscribe to its Premium Content Service ($14.95 at the time of this writing) to use it. For example, as a paid subscriber, I used it to compare three private, nonprofit institutions that offer online MBA programs: Drexel University, Syracuse University, and Worcester Polytechnic Institute. The service did not reveal as much information as the BusinessWeek Online tool, but it did provide a unique career prospects section that included average starting salary of its MBA graduates.

For an International Perspective

The *Financial Times* website (http://news.ft.com/management/businessed) looks like it has lots of great information, including a special section with articles that look insightful about online MBAs; however, you have to be a paid subscriber to view them, and to me it was cost prohibitive at $110 (at the time of this writing) annually. However, a good number of articles available for free are about getting a graduate-level education in business; and the *Financial Times*' editorial perspective is international in scope, which will perhaps give you an entirely different global view of MBA programs. See Chapter 3, where I briefly discuss international programs available in Canada and England.

WSJ's College Journal

The *Wall Street Journal*'s online MBA Center, which is a subsection of its College Journal website (www.collegejournal.com/mbacenter), is another excellent place to dig out general information about getting an MBA. In typical *Wall Street Journal* fashion, the articles on this website are very well written. The "Prepare for an MBA" section is my favorite part of the site because there are a couple of fun online assessments embedded in several of the articles that could help prospective students determine whether they really want to tackle a graduate degree in business. (See "Will Earning an MBA Help You Switch Fields?" and "Considering B-School for the Right Reasons?")

Another part of the website, "Advice for Business-School Applicants," had an interesting essay-question advice page that could prove helpful if you have to write an essay as part of the admissions process.

The other sections of the *Wall Street Journal*'s College Journal website could also prove very helpful because they cover admissions, financial aid, and career advancement. There is also an interesting selection of articles by some talented columnists, and information about salary expectations for a variety of jobs.

The Educated Consumer

As you can see, these ranking websites have some good online tools and information services available for free (and sometimes for a fee). You have to do a lot of navigating around—web page after web page after web page—which can be a bit cumbersome and slow-moving at times, especially if you are on a dial-up Internet connection. If you are a true "web-head," however, you might find it to be fun, interesting, and worth your while.

All this pre-choice homework I've been advising you to do—and there's a lot more throughout the rest of this book—is provided with the goal of making you the most educated consumer on the planet with regard to finding and choosing the right online MBA program. In addition, I obviously want you to succeed as an online learner when you start moving down this modern-day educational pathway. In my opinion, these ranking systems can help you in a relatively small way.

Instant Message

"You can't just go to one factor; you have to consider multiple issues, such as accreditation, reputation, quality of the program, quality of instruction, all of the issues that someone in the academic world would recognize."

—Nancy P. O'Brien, head, Education and Social Science Library, University of Illinois, Urbana-Champaign

More importantly, as with any major business transaction, you will be required to write a substantial number of checks to the institution that you choose to attend. That institution will be responsible for giving you the right tools and guidance to help you become a successful business manager or entrepreneur. If the school does not live up to your expectations, you can always drop out early, but then you will have wasted a lot of valuable time and effort (and money). Plus, whatever credits you may have earned may not be transferable to another program (see Chapter 11 for information about credit transferability). So my bottom-line advice is this: First educate yourself about how you can best educate yourself.

The Least You Need to Know

- A valid ranking system for online MBA programs has not been invented.
- You can use the information provided by most of the well-known ranking systems in a variety of ways to help you learn more about a program, even though these systems are based on traditional on-campus MBA programs.
- It's a bad idea to use ranking data as a primary decision-making standard.
- In the final analysis, you need to become an educated consumer, which will require that you do a lot more than just dig through information provided by the rankers.

Part 2

The Finer Details

Obviously there's a lot more to this educational pursuit you are embarking on than simply knowing what online MBA programs are available to choose from. You'll also want to put your investigative hat on and start asking questions, and this part of the book will help you know which questions to ask.

Who are the students? Who are the faculty? What kind of student services does the program provide? What's the curriculum like? What kind of course technology is utilized? What will I learn? Here's where you'll start to recognize all the details of an online MBA program that will help you make an informed decision.

Chapter 6

Faculty and Students

In This Chapter

- How to assess online faculty quality
- Learn about your fellow online students
- Questions to ask in relation to faculty and students
- What admission requirements reveal about online students

So suppose you have discovered which institutions and programs interest you the most and are satisfied that they are all appropriately accredited. What's next?

There are at least six major areas of concern that you need to investigate further:

- What kind of background do the faculty have who teach in the online MBA program?
- Where do the students typically come from?
- What kind of services does the institution provide to its online learners, and are there any value added aspects of the program?
- What's the program's reputation?
- What's the curriculum like?
- What do you need to know about the online courses?

This chapter covers faculty and students. Chapter 7 covers student services and value-adds. Chapters 8, 9, and 10 cover what you need to know about types of institutions, curriculums, and courses.

Who Are the Faculty?

In general, depending on the institution, the faculty teaching courses in an online MBA program are either full-time or part-time. The part-timers are typically referred to as non-*tenure*-track adjuncts, and they may teach for multiple online institutions on a part-time basis and only in the online mode. Full-time faculty members are typically on a tenure track, or already tenured, and they more than likely teach at only one institution on a full-time basis, and often in both traditional face-to-face classes and in online courses.

AACSB categorizes faculty as being either academically qualified, meaning he or she has earned at least a doctorate and is specialized in a particular field of study, or professionally qualified, meaning he or she has earned at least a Master's degree and is specialized in a particular field of study. AACSB qualifications require that at least 50 percent of faculty in the business schools it accredits be academically qualified. Additionally, AACSB-accredited business schools are required to demonstrate that their faculty are current in their fields and capable of delivering the education they profess to teach in their courses.

According to Jerry Trapnell, AACSB's chief accreditation officer, "Faculty must maintain their currency by their research, consulting, and/or appropriate professional development activities. Just because you have a doctorate does not mean you are current in your field." So basically, any AACSB-accredited program is expected to have qualified faculty who are up to date with today's business practices. Otherwise, the program could lose its professional accreditation status.

Online Term

Tenure is a system whereby faculty can obtain lifetime job security by passing a long-term evaluation period in which they must demonstrate academic achievement, typically through publishing research and contributing substantially to a body of knowledge. An **adjunct** faculty member is a part-time teaching employee. In online MBA programs, an adjunct will typically hold a full-time teaching position at another institution, or they may hold a full-time management-level position with a corporation. Some adjuncts teach part-time for multiple institutions.

Professional Academics and Professional Business People

When it comes to discussions about MBA faculty, there are basically two primary points of view. There are the programs that use a good number of part-time *adjuncts*, such as the University of Phoenix, and some of the other so-called "for-profits." These institutions are proud of the fact that their faculty are primarily business practitioners. This means that they are professionals who are currently working in the business world and enjoy sharing their real-world business acumen with students in their online courses.

Then there are the programs that use primarily full-time faculty, such as Arizona State University, Florida State University, and the many other traditional, not-for-profit institutions. They are proud of the fact that their faculty are contributing to the overall knowledge base in their areas of specialization through their academic research (they have to publish their research to reach tenure) and possibly have consulting contracts with major corporations.

Perhaps the ideal faculty member is one who is both a successful academic researcher and theorist and a knowledgeable real-world practitioner.

Stat

To be a faculty member for the University of Phoenix Online, one must have a Master's or doctoral degree in the field in which they teach. They must also be employed full-time in their profession. Approximately 75 percent of the University of Phoenix Online's faculty have Master's degrees, and 25 percent have doctoral-level degrees.

Digging Up Information About Faculty

However, the question really is how do you find information about what kind of faculty teach in any online MBA program you are considering? In many cases, you will be hard pressed to find decent faculty bios on any online MBA website. So what's the next best thing? Call or e-mail the program director, introduce yourself, and say you are very interested in enrolling in their online MBA program and that you would like to have more information about the faculty who teach online. Here's a short list of questions you can ask:

- If the school has a full-time MBA program, do the same faculty teach in the online program?
- What percentage of faculty are part-time adjuncts? What percentage are full-time faculty? How many have doctorates?

- Can you provide a list of faculty and links to their resumés or bios that may be on your institution's website? Or can you e-mail the *curriculum vitas* of your online faculty members?
- Are there any faculty in your program who are conducting specialized research and are thus contributing knowledge to the field? If yes, can you point me to whatever they have gotten published?
- Can you provide information about where some of your faculty are employed (if practitioners)?

If you have the names of faculty teaching in an online MBA program and you can't find information about them on the program's web pages, try going to the main home page of the institution and entering their names into the home page's search box. Sometimes this will take you to links of faculty members' personal websites that show their curriculum vitas, mug shots, and more.

Pedagogy

Pedagogy is a word that is frequently brought up when talking about faculty. It basically refers to the science and art of teaching. For example, one form of effective pedagogy in an online MBA program could be a teacher's utilization of competency-based assessments, whereby students are tested on their ability to make certain business-related decisions. Another form of pedagogy would be the case-study method of teaching and learning, where students review documented simulations of real business problems and challenges and then discuss and present relevant business-solution strategies. See Chapter 10 for more information on competency-based learning and case studies.

Online Term

A **curriculum vita** is similar to a resumé in that it lists a person's employment history and education. In higher education, it is usually a much longer document that also includes a faculty member's full publishing history, professional memberships, special recognition and awards, and other biographical information.

Pedagogy is a term that is used to describe how teaching and learning occurs in a course. It is often referred to as the art and science of teaching and learning, or the study of the manner and function of educational concepts and theories and how knowledge and learning are applied and accomplished.

The ironic thing about pedagogy is that most higher-education faculty members are not taught pedagogical concepts and theories, except those who were education majors. Most professors are basically "thrown to the wolves" and learn how to teach through trial and error. Some professors become very good at teaching and others do not.

When it comes to online teaching, the same truths apply. Many faculty are not adequately taught how to teach an online course, which, obviously, entails a different set of skills than teaching face to face. That is why it is very important that any business school providing an online MBA has a strong online teacher support system in place that trains teachers how to effectively teach online.

Training Teachers How to Teach Online

So one more question you might want to ask is what kind of infrastructure is in place for supporting faculty who teach online. Some business schools are still trying to find their way with regard to providing adequate support for online faculty. However, most business schools that teach in the online environment have sophisticated and efficient teaching, learning, and technology centers that provide the necessary support and expertise for helping faculty build and teach online courses. For example, Florida State University, which launched its first online MBA program in the fall of 2004, has an Office of Distributed and Distance Learning that supports FSU's College of Business by providing faculty with online class design support and a continuously updated series of live workshops for faculty to learn how to effectively use such educational technologies as online discussion forums, PowerPoint lectures, and electronic testing and grading functions. See Chapter 9 for a much more detailed discussion about how educational technologies are utilized in online teaching and learning. Also look at Chapter 10 for information about how faculty use a variety of teaching and learning styles in online MBA programs.

Unfortunately, there's really no surefire way to discover whether an online MBA program is doing a good job of training its faculty how to teach online. The only thing you can do is ask the program administrators and try to make an educated guess based on the response you get. Short answers such as "we provide a five-week training period for all our faculty before they teach online," might tell you something negative. A more thorough

Guide on the Side

To get a sense for the numerous considerations that higher-education faculty need to be aware of with regard to teaching in an online environment, see the University of Washington's online faculty support website at http://catalyst.washington.edu/partner/distance.html.

answer that explains how an institution teaches online-related pedagogies and how it helps faculty incorporate effective learning technologies into its overall curriculum might tell you something positive. In the end, however, you are really not going to know how good the faculty are until you actually sit through an online course and interact with them.

"There will always be a range of professors," says Paula O'Callaghan, director, iMBA Program, Syracuse University. "The core in the middle will be very good and very responsive. There will be some professors who have high expectations, and you will struggle to meet them, and there will be a few who might not meet your expectations. You can't expect that it will be all that different from what you experienced as an undergraduate."

Who Are the Students?

The next part of your homework entails finding out what kind of students enroll in the programs you are investigating. This investigative assignment is just as important, if not more important, than all the other steps I have thus far suggested you take when searching for the right online MBA program.

In Chapter 19, you'll find some very interesting profiles of online MBA students. One thing they all have in common is that they are busy, working adult professionals in their late 20s to late 40s, and most have Type A personalities. These are the kind of students you will be interacting with throughout your educational experience and very possibly after you graduate if you form some meaningful bonds with fellow students, which is actually not uncommon in the online environment. The other part of the student equation is the networking angle, which is discussed in Chapter 17. The students you meet online can indeed become an important part of your business network during and after the program, just like they would in any traditional face-to-face MBA program.

What's great about online learning is that it brings out the voices of those people who might normally sit in the back of a face-to-face class and say nothing. People who are shy in a physical social environment are known to open up and contribute valuable information and readily share their work experiences in an online course. Plus, it is hard to hide in an online course. There's basically no back of the class. Online MBA students are almost always partially graded on their ability to post significant comments to online discussions, and they are frequently put into teams that work on projects together as part of their course requirements and grades.

Especially if you enroll in what's called a *lock-step cohort* program (see Chapter 8), you'll want to find out as much information as possible about fellow students.

So in short, because you'll be interacting with these people for the duration of your MBA education, you'll want to get a sense of who they are before you enroll, which, by the way, is not the easiest task in the world. Because of privacy rules and regulations that institutions must honor with regard to providing information about any students, you won't be able to get any detailed information about a particular cohort before you enroll. However, an academic advisor should be able to give you a generic sense of what kind of students you will be working and studying with, including what kind of occupations they hold, without naming names.

Online Term

A **lock-step cohort** online MBA program is one in which a group of students are enrolled in a program and all take the same predefined courses together and in the same sequence as strictly outlined by the school.

Digging Out Student Data

Of course, you can always start by looking at information about students that might be available on a program's website. Syracuse University's iMBA program, for instance, features student profiles at http://whitman.syr.edu/prospective/imba/connections/alumni. Arizona State University has a web page that profiles the entire student body of its most recent online enrollees, including the companies they represent, their average age (33), years of working experience (9), average GMAT scores (605), their undergraduate majors and schools they attended, and more at http://wpcarey.asu.edu/mba/online/onlineprf.cfm. However, most online MBA programs do not supply this kind of relevant information about students on their websites. Why, you may ask? Because they simply haven't got their act together when it comes to developing websites with relevant information. Nonetheless, I must add that having a website that's lacking the appropriate amount of informational content does not necessarily mean that an institution has lower-quality faculty and/or students. If you ask a program administrator for information about students, they will give you whatever they can dig up for you, regardless of whether it happens to be posted on their website.

Instant Message

"I greatly enjoyed the discussion threads, as there were always one or two that were provocative."

—UMUC online MBA graduate Linda Couch

"Sometimes I found my classmates to be tiresome, but then I reminded myself that everyone is different and with a little effort I could find something interesting in every one of them; and, I could grow and expand my own awareness if I just tried to meet everyone halfway."

—Regis University online MBA graduate Katherine Porter

"Just like a regular face-to-face group, the more you work with people, the more you come to know what they are really good at and what they are not so good at, and you divvy up responsibility accordingly."

—Dawn McAvoy, online MBA student, East Carolina University

Tips for Learning About Students

There are at least four more things you can do to enlighten yourself about the makeup of any online MBA program's student body:

- **Look at admission requirements.** The criteria students must meet to be accepted into an online MBA program can, indeed, tell you something about your future online colleagues. At the University of Florida, for instance, admission is highly selective and based on students demonstrating high performance in academic ability (average of a 3.3 GPA and a score of 655 on the GMAT), professional experience (at least two years of full-time post-baccalaureate work experience and two letters of reference from current or former supervisors), and personal character (proof of concept of which is provided through written essays and an invitation-only personal interview). At the University of Phoenix, admission requirements include a minimum average GPA of 2.5 and at least three years of significant work experience. GMAT test scores, essays, and reference letters are not required for admission to the University of Phoenix online MBA program.

  Overall you'll hear differing points of view regarding admission requirements and selectivity processes and how these all relate to what a student body comes to represent in any particular online MBA program. Stiff academic requirements do indicate that students in the program are typically conscientious, hardworking, and dependable classmates who contribute vast energy and knowledge to the online learning environment. Students in other programs, who are not good test takers and wouldn't come close to meeting stringent admission requirements because they have been out of school for many years, typically have more than enough practical, real-life working experience and knowledge to contribute sound and useful information to any online course. Regardless, in most online learning environments, the slackers and noncontributors will more than likely drop out in due time.

- **Try to find out where the students live and work**. Most online MBA programs show that the majority of their students live and work in areas relatively close to the physical campus. However, there is also the reverse of this trend, with students living as far away as another country that is across an ocean. Take a look at Syracuse University's iMBA alumni profiles, for instance, and you'll see an entrepreneur from Russia, an executive from a suburb of Syracuse, a pilot from Chicago, a product manager from northern California, and a marketing specialist from Japan.
- **Ask about student surveys**. Most online MBA programs regularly conduct student surveys in which students are asked a series of questions about their work habits, online learning skills, professional working skills, satisfaction levels, and the overall efficiency of their online learning experiences. Often the results of such surveys are aggregated into internal reports not for public consumption. However, you can ask an academic advisor to give you a sense of such survey results that could help paint a picture of students' typical working and learning behaviors.
- **Ask whether you can communicate with some students and/or alumni.** When talking to advisors and other administrators of the programs you are investigating, just come right out and ask them whether they have any students or alumni who are willing to share their phone numbers and e-mail addresses with prospective students such as yourself. You may be surprised that they do, in fact, have such contacts. Plus, most online programs have alumni services just the same as they do for on-campus students. So you can always contact a school's alumni department and ask if they can connect you with any online graduates. The problem with this, of course, is that the institution's contact list is always full of very positive ambassadors. However, if you can form a short and friendly relationship with such contacts, you can get them to open up more about any of the negative aspects of their online learning experiences. My advice in these kinds of situations is to be friendly, thankful, very polite and humble, and ask a lot of questions until you feel you have gotten the right answers and lots of good information.

So with a little homework on your part and a willingness to ask a lot of questions, you should be able to dig up some relevant information about the students you will be interacting with on a regular basis and getting to know quite well during your graduate school experience. Nonetheless, you really won't get to know your colleagues until you actually start learning and working with them. As you go along through trial and error you'll pick and choose interactions with those students with whom you communicate most effectively.

Ask Questions and Listen Carefully

According to AACSB accreditation standards, online learning programs raise questions about the opportunities students actually have for the right kinds of interaction among each other, as well as the interactions they have with faculty, and "the school will have the burden of demonstrating that it provides significant interaction opportunities." Because online courses do have the unique feature of being able to capture electronically all the student-to-student and student-to-faculty interchanges that have occurred over time, the administrators of such programs should be able to give you a pretty good historic sense of what their online student body is really like, as well as how well their faculty have been doing in this relatively new form of teaching and learning. Again, you'll have to listen carefully and try to make an educated guess based on the responses you get.

The Least You Need to Know

- You need to dig up as much information as possible about the faculty and students in the online programs you are investigating.
- There are many criteria you can use and questions you can ask online MBA program administrators related to faculty and students, but you may not find out what a program is really like until you actually take a class and interact with faculty and students on a regular basis.
- Although some online MBA administrators will tell you otherwise, admission requirements may not necessarily be a sound indicator of what the actual student body is really like at any institution.
- Communicating with online students and alumni can be an excellent way of digging out more information about any program, provided that you are a smart and friendly communicator and know how to ask a lot of polite questions.
- In many cases, you'll have to make an educated guess about a program's overall faculty and student makeup based on the responses you get to the questions you ask.

Chapter 7

Student Services and Value

In This Chapter

- The most important student services
- Student services made available to online learners
- Questions you can explore regarding an institution's value

Every institution has a set of on-campus customer services it offers to its students through various offices and departments, ranging from the financial aid and registrar's offices to dormitory residencies and a campus infirmary. This chapter covers those services important to online learners, such as enrollment and registration services, academic advising, the library and bookstore, technical support, and much more.

Online Student Services

Student services is a term used by higher-education institutions that covers a lot of ground. It relates to all those offices and services one would expect to find on any real campus, such as admissions and financial aid, the registrar, the library, health services, athletics, student clubs and organizations, alumni services, job and career services, academic advising, tutoring services, food and beverage services, residential services, and even recreational and entertainment services that an on-campus student would typically find at the student union. Many, but not all, of these services can be and are provided to online students. In particular, today it is not unusual for students to go through the admissions, financial aid, and registration processes almost entirely online.

Capella University is a good example of an institution that has developed a sophisticated online admissions process that allows prospective students to apply and track the application process with relative ease, all online (see the figure that follows). In addition to being able to complete all the necessary admissions forms online, prospective students can enter into live discussions with enrollment counselors in an online chat or through a toll-free phone service as they are filling out their online applications. Prospective students can also send their questions about the application and admissions processes via e-mail.

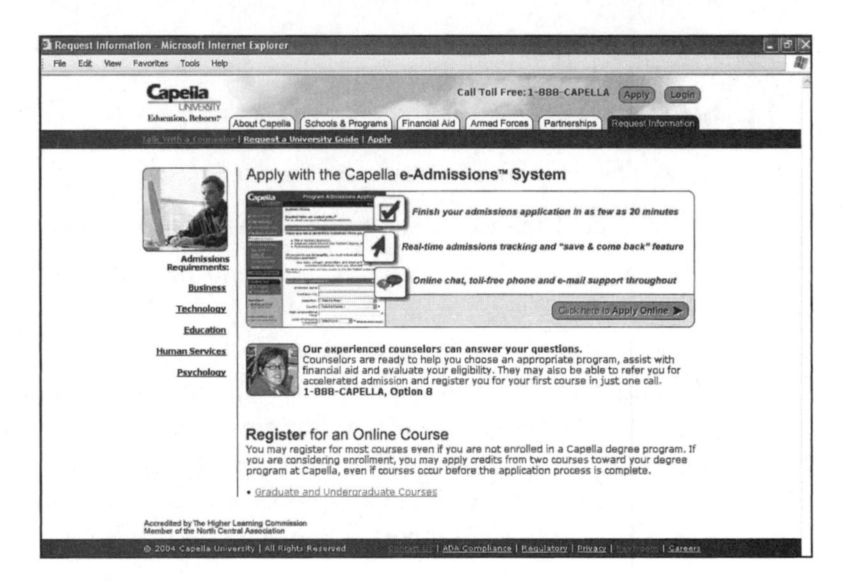

Capella University's e-Admissions system website.

Regardless of how an institution provides services to its online learners, you are entitled to the same student services as an on-campus student.

If you were to walk onto the campus of the school you are attending online, you will, indeed, be able to go to the campus library and use its services just like any other student; you will be able to visit any of the aforementioned student services-related offices and take advantage of any or all of the services they offer their student body. After all, you are a card-carrying, tuition-paying student, too.

In fact, if you happen to be interested in an online MBA program that has a physical campus located close to where you live, you could get the best of both worlds by visiting the campus whenever you desire to take advantage of the student services provided by the institution. You could, for example, arrange to meet with your faculty, attend school-sponsored social events, use the campus library, and attend graduation ceremonies at commencement time without having to travel a long distance.

You'll need to judge how thorough, organized, and efficient a business school handles the services it offers to its online student population. Just like in business, some schools have a long list of excellent customer services and others don't.

Guide on the Side

Online students do get all the institutional student services they need to enroll and succeed as online learners. However, if you enroll in an online program that has a physical campus located close to your home, you'll be able to easily visit the campus to take advantage of all those student services that are available to on-campus students in the face-to-face environment.

Are Student Services Up to Par?

The Western Cooperative for Educational Telecommunications (WCET), a organization that is an advocate for effective policies and practices in support of distance education, has done extensive research on the topic of student services for online learners. WCET, whose membership includes colleges and universities from across the U.S., and some foreign countries, that offer online degree programs, claims that many institutions are still struggling with providing the same level of services for their online students as they do for their on-campus students. WCET's research has resulted in a set of guidelines to help institutions provide student services in an online environment—a tall task that requires a working collaboration between a school's information technology infrastructure and all its many student services-oriented departments working in concert with the business school offering the online MBA program.

Instant Message

"The library service was wonderful, but the advising and administrative services were obviously not developed with international students in mind. I became very frustrated when basic issues (enrollment, credit card payments, answering phone messages) could not be resolved via e-mail or online."

—Anonymous online MBA student

WCET explains that all student services can have some online presence, even if only at the level of simply providing the right amount of information online. What this means is that as an online student you should expect a certain amount of important student services to be provided smoothly over an Internet connection. Additionally, WCET notes that there should always be a way to easily connect with a live person who can answer any questions or concerns you may have via telephone, fax, or other synchronous methods, such as live chat and instant messaging. Or, if seeking answers via e-mail, you should get a response within 24 hours.

Enrollment Services

Depending on the institution, prior to actually going through the official application and admission process you'll communicate with the first level of the school's advisement staff, who are admissions and financial-aid counselors. These are the people who will help you with understanding all the forms you will need to fill out and basically how to effectively deal with all the bureaucratic red tape you'll need to go through to apply and possibly get financial assistance. They will also be able to explain academic requirements, any prerequisite courses you may need to take to get up to the appropriate academic speed, estimated timelines to ultimately graduate, and how much hard work and determination will be required of you, in general, to complete coursework.

> **Online Term**
>
> An **academic advisor** is a professional staff member of an institution (usually a professor) who has been assigned to assist a certain number of students with the course selection process and other decision-making processes concerning one's academic and professional objectives.

Although these counselors do indeed provide an invaluable service, for many people the information they provide is really secondary to finding detailed information about a school's academic structure. This is where professional *academic advisors* come into the picture.

Academic Advising

Academic advising is one of the most important student services you can take advantage of prior to actually going through the application and admissions process, as well as during your stint as an online student. After you are accepted into your program of choice, you will be assigned an official, professional academic advisor, who is usually a professor or may be a dean or assistant dean. Your academic counselor will be your friend and mentor throughout your MBA experience.

However, if you are really concerned about the academic side of your MBA endeavor, you'll want to get in touch with an academic advisor before you go through the typically cumbersome application, admissions, and financial-aid processes. Many online MBA program websites list contact information for academic counselors whom you can talk to by telephone or communicate with via e-mail. Other programs don't make academic counselors so readily available to prospective students who are in the early phase of the decision-making process, but instead have them talk primarily with their admissions and financial-aid staff, who are in many cases trained professional salespeople.

Because some of the most informative advice you can get would typically come from a professional academic advisor, you should simply tell the school you are investigating that you would prefer to speak with a full professor, dean, or program director.

Instant Message

"Advising services have been great via a peer counselor and the program administrator, who were quick to answer all of my concerns and questions."

—Errol Robateau, fall 2004 online MBA graduate, University of Colorado at Colorado Springs

"You need to get past the screening forces and see if they will let you talk with *real* faculty members."

– Regis University MBA Professor Ed Cooper

Registration Services and Student IDs

When you become a bona-fide accepted student in an online MBA program, you will be able to register and pay for your classes online, and much more. You'll be assigned a student ID username and password that gives you access, through a web-based learner's portal environment, to a host of online services that are typical of almost every institution, such as library services, the online bookstore, online career services, technical support services, and a wide variety of online study aids and resources. Chapter 9 discusses how this first phase of the basic online student infrastructure operates.

Library Services

I talk more extensively about what students really need to understand about library services and conducting research online in Chapter 18. For now, however, as you are searching for the right online MBA program, be aware of what kind of online library and research services will be made available to you from the schools you are investigating. First of all, the library and research service portion of your online courses should have an easily accessible and relevant collection of online materials related to what MBA students read and study, including business-oriented scholarly journals and other modern business research databases and resources.

At the University of Colorado at Colorado Springs, for instance, all online students get a subscription to the online version of *Business Week*. Also many online MBA programs use a company called Xanedu that provides customizable access to an impressive collection of digitized case studies from the Harvard Business School, the American Graduate School of International Management, the Stanford Graduate School of Business, and many other highly respected publishers of case studies. See Chapter 10 for information about Xanedu and about how the case-study approach to teaching and learning is used in online MBA programs.

In addition, you'll want to know whether the online library subscribes to a good supply of business research databases, of which there are many, such as Bloomberg, Business Source Elite, Gartner Group Reports, Hoover's Online, and others.

Guide on the Side

If the school library does not have an extensive electronic database of online business-related resources, ask whether they have made interlibrary loan arrangements with other university libraries.

Finally, in relation to online library services, you'll want to know whether the school has a special distance-learning library staff that works specifically with online students and whether the library provides any online information literacy/research skills training to its students.

Distance-learning librarians could turn into some of your most valuable allies. They are typically charged with teaching and guiding online students how to conduct effective research, and more, through the many online resources available through a library system's information labyrinth. For instance, distance-learning librarians, in addition to showing online students how to use its electronic reserves, will also readily provide information about the proper way to write research papers, how to avoid plagiarism, and how to honor and abide by the latest copyright laws.

The Online Bookstore

In addition to obtaining research materials from the online campus library service, you will be dealing with an online campus bookstore service. Many institutions partner with an online bookstore solution provider, such as MBS Direct, which carries a large inventory of textbooks and other course reading material in both printed and digital form. These bookstore solution providers handle customer service and online ordering and delivery—both physical and via online modalities—of course material to online students. Other institutions have their own sophisticated bookstore services and do not rely on an outside provider for such services.

At Indiana University's Kelly Direct Online MBA program, for instance, students receive an e-mail approximately one month before the start of the quarter containing their textbook order forms. Students use these forms to order the textbooks, course packs, and/or software necessary for the courses they are taking. All textbook orders are shipped from the campus bookstore to the address the student indicates on the textbook order form.

Technical Support

How a school provides online technical support is another important element that you should consider. A school's technical support services become particularly important during the beginning phases of when you actually start and begin learning how online education really works. Specifically, it is important that a school provides live technical support at all hours of the evening, when most students are accessing their online courses and working on assignments.

Things inevitably go wrong when working with a variety of web-based software. You may not have your software configured properly. Your username and password logon might not work, or you may have trouble posting to a discussion forum. These are only a small sample of some of the technical problems you may encounter. When disaster strikes, you'll want to immediately talk with an expert who can rectify your problem, especially because you are time-crunched enough as it is and can't afford to fall behind.

That's why some schools provide 24/7 technical support services to their online students, often through a third-party provider. One such provider is a company called Embanet out of Toronto, Canada, which provides round-the-clock technical support and help desk services for the University of Texas System TeleCampus students and a number of other providers of online MBA programs. The UT TeleCampus is a good example of an institution that has all its bases covered in the area of technical support (see the figure that follows).

In addition to providing 24/7 support, the UT TeleCampus has a thorough technical support website that covers everything online students need to know about running the right software, maintaining their Internet connections, and generally moving smoothly through their online courses at all times.

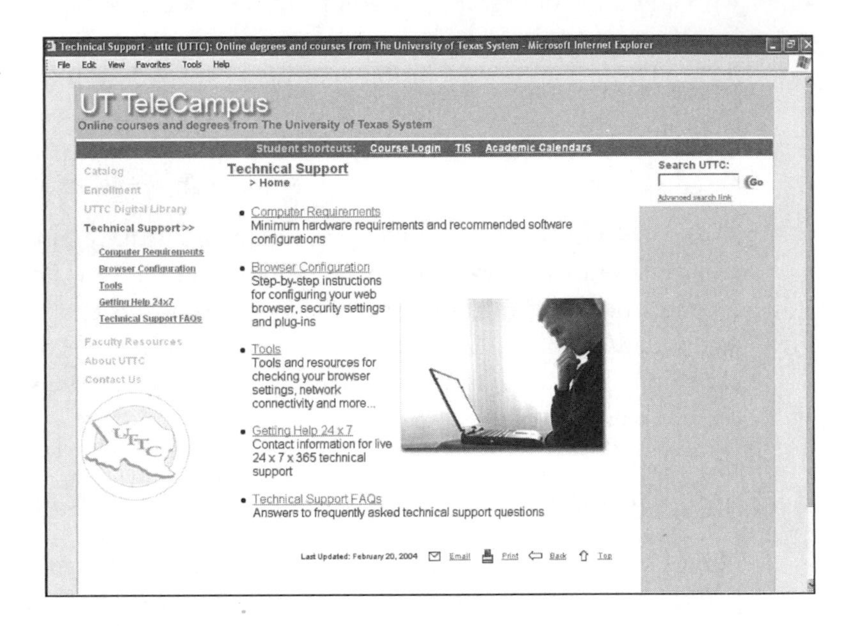

Technical support services website for the University of Texas System TeleCampus.

Instant Message

"Accrediting organizations require adequate and appropriate support for the students served by the institutions in a distance-learning environment. This includes a major emphasis on technical support."

—Council for Higher Education Accreditation, from the publication "Accreditation and Assuring Quality in Distance Learning"

Additional Academic Aid

In addition to utilizing the services of their academic advisors, students at many schools can take advantage of additional services of an academic nature, such as special online writing courses that are separate from the program curriculum, various mentoring and tutoring services, and information literacy tutoring services that may be provided by the campus library.

The University of Phoenix, for example, has a Center for Writing Excellence resource for all its online students that includes an automated and proprietary "WritePoint" paper review service that provides feedback on grammar and formatting, completed in minutes, on the papers that students upload to the service (see the figure that follows).

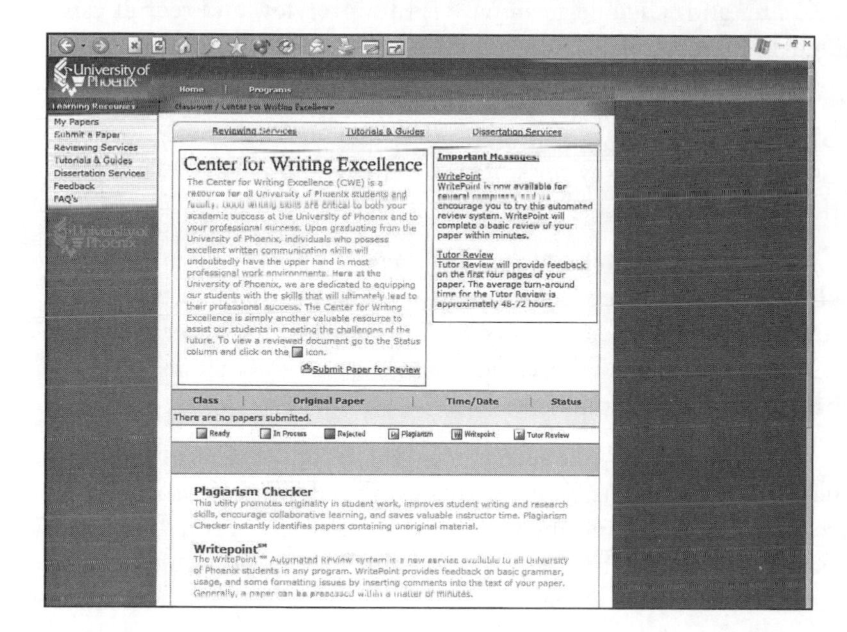

The University of Phoenix's WritePoint proprietary online service automatically checks a student's uploaded paper for grammar and formatting errors.

At Capella University, students can take advantage of a professional coaching service to get advice related to applying what they have learned in their courses to their current job responsibilities (described in greater detail in Chapter 10).

The University of Maryland University College (UMUC) has a live "Chat with a Librarian" service available to students on a 24-hour basis. The UMUC library also provides a full slate of online interactive tutorials for its online students on such subjects as how to use the web for research; how to cite sources in research papers; and how to search for company, financial, and industry information in its library databases.

Career Services

Career services is one area of online MBA programs where students generally lose out. Most traditional on-campus MBA programs have a very full slate of employer recruitment and career-advancement services that physically put their students in front of the businesses that may be seeking to employ them, and vice versa. For example, at the University of Buffalo (UB), which has a highly ranked traditional MBA program, students can take advantage of a number of creative career services offered by the UB School of Management's Career Resource Center. Most of these services require a face-to-face meeting, such as on-campus recruiting events where employers contact the Career Resource Center and schedule a campus visit to interview and recruit candidates for employment at a later date.

UB also hosts employer information sessions where employers visit the UB campus and provide valuable information about their prospective permanent and summer positions. Such information sessions are a great way for students to meet and network with professionals from a variety of companies.

As an online student, you will not be able to take advantage of opportunities such as those provided by UB's Career Resource Center, unless, of course, you can travel to the face-to-face recruitment events when they occur. All is not lost, however. Some online programs have very sophisticated career-development services that are provided to students who can't come to campus.

Capella University, a virtual university without a campus, has an online Career Center that is part of its Advising and Academic Support division. In addition to providing a full array of job-search and career-advancement information services through the Career Center's website, there's an "Ask a Career Counselor" e-mail service. Through this service, online students can e-mail career counselors assigned to the School of Business their questions regarding resumés, cover letters, marketing an online degree, salary negotiation, and career-advancement strategies. Capella promises to respond to any career-related questions within four business days.

Finally, many of the career services offered both online and on-campus are not that vital of a concern to the majority of online MBA students, who are typically mid-career professional already fully employed. If you are a student who is seeking that first substantial job in the world of business management after you earn your MBA, however, you'll want to ask the schools you are investigating to determine what kind of career services they provide.

Guide on the Side

Here's the bottom line regarding career services for prospective online MBA students: Ask the schools you are interested in what kind of career services they offer to their online student population, and whether you can come on campus, when feasible, to attend any student recruitment-oriented events and/or live information sessions.

Chapter 18 covers the MBA job marketplace, including advice about how to handle possible negative perceptions about online learning that you may encounter with prospective employers. Chapter 18 also includes some great information about strategies you can use for finding career advancement online.

Alumni Services

Alumni services is another area where online students typically do not participate nearly as much as on-campus students, but this does not mean that you cannot become an active alumni. Many online programs are encouraging their students to take a more active role in alumni organizations and are updating their websites to better promote the many services and business networking benefits provided by such organizations to both online and on-campus students.

The Kelly Direct Online MBA program at Indiana University recently built a website, called the Kelly Direct Network (KDN), that is geared toward helping its online business graduate students obtain guidance and professional services for a post-MBA job search. The site also has a KDN message board where fellow alums can seek out advice from each other as well as do some business networking. There's also a nifty service that allows Kelly Direct Online students to buy, sell, and trade books, electronic items, and just about anything else within reason, all online through the Kelley Direct Network.

Instant Message

"I am still involved with the alumni group, which welcomed me with open arms even before I graduated. Based on my experience, students would find it easy to use all the services Regis offers. You never feel like you're an outsider, or in some other category just because you're part of Regis's online programs."

—Regis University online MBA graduate Katherine Porter

What's the Real Value-Add?

Again, just like in business, every institution should have some value-added goods and services that make it stand out among its competitors. In other words, what parts, or sum of all parts, give added worth to a program beyond the fundamentals? In that spirit, here are three broad questions you might explore as you continue your search for the online MBA program that is right for you:

- Does the institution have a good track record for graduating successful business professionals?

- Does the school's student support system seem packaged and presented in a way that makes it easy for you to find information and easily access and take advantage of all the student services the school provides?
- What kind of tangible results related to career advancement and overall practical business acumen and skills will you derive from earning an MBA from this particular institution?

Instant Message

"Students should ask themselves if the degree from that school is going to have value, and to some extent that is difficult to determine, even once you have done all the research. If I am going to work in South Carolina, employers are going to understand the value of an MBA degree from East Carolina University more than they are going to understand one from Idaho State."

—Rick Niswander, dean of graduate business programs, East Carolina University

The following chapters examine more ways you can fine-tune your decision-making process. They also discuss in greater detail the inner workings of online learning and teaching and how it is a viable way to get your MBA. As you can already tell, there is indeed a lot to consider. Don't let that discourage you, though. After all, this is a decision that will affect the rest of your life, not to mention cost you a great deal of money and time in the short term.

The Least You Need to Know

- The same student services that are available to on-campus students are available to online students and should be equal in quality and efficiency standards.
- In particular, you should ask school administrators whether you can take advantage of academic advising services before you enroll.
- Make sure you have a clear understanding of what kind of enrollment, library, career, alumni, and technical support services are available to online students.
- Try to determine what makes a school stand out over and above the fundamental services it provides and what kind of added value its degree will give you in your career.

Chapter 8

Every School and Curriculum Is Unique

In This Chapter

- Differences in for-profit and nonprofit institutions
- Virtual universities defined
- A broad review of curriculum types
- A note about quantitative and qualitative courses
- Elements of a well-designed program

Although an institution's accreditation, ranking, student body, faculty members, and the number of student services and value-added services it may or may not provide are all important decision-making criteria, it also pays to understand what type of institution you're investigating (in addition to its Carnegie classification and accreditation status, as noted in Chapter 4) as well as what kind of curriculum its business school is offering to online MBA students.

This chapter covers institution types and classifications as well as what you need to understand about how academic online MBA curriculums are organized and what kind of courses you can expect to find in most programs.

Traditional vs. For-Profit Institutions

Broadly speaking, colleges and universities can be divided into two camps: *nonprofit* and *for-profit*. The majority of colleges and universities today are either public or private nonprofit entities. In relatively recent years, however, the rise of for-profit colleges and universities, which are also called proprietary institutions, has altered the landscape of higher education like never before, especially in relation to online higher education.

Online Term

A **nonprofit** higher-education institution operates under the notion of serving the public good, with all earnings being utilized only for the institution's improvement. A **for-profit** higher-education institution operates under the notion of accruing earnings that can be utilized for the institution's improvement but also for the benefit of the shareholders and/or individuals who own the corporation that runs it.

The University of Phoenix, owned by the Apollo Group, Inc., is the largest for-profit institution in North America. Established in 1976, the entire University of Phoenix system comprises 151 on-campus facilities in 30 states within the United States, Puerto Rico, and Canada, and it enrolls more than 200,000 students. In 1989, the University of Phoenix started to offer online programs and today serves more than 100,000 online students. Its online MBA programs serve about 21,000 students (and growing), which is a significantly larger online MBA student body than its closest private nonprofit counterpart in the United States, Regis University, which enrolls about 2,200 online MBA students.

For federal aid eligibility, the U.S. Department of Education strictly defines a higher-education institution as being "a public or other nonprofit institution." What this ultimately means is that although many for-profit institutions can qualify to offer their students federal student loans and grants, they cannot qualify to receive federal institutional-improvement monies.

If you want to know whether an institution operates as a for-profit or nonprofit entity, go to the National Center for Education Statistics IPEDS College Opportunities On-Line service at http://nces.ed.gov/ipeds/cool/. Enter an institution's name in the IPEDS Search field to view a description of the institution, including whether it has an agreement with the U.S. Department of Education for eligible students to receive federal financial aid.

Business Approach or Traditional Approach?

So what does all this have to do with getting your MBA online? Public nonprofit institutions that offer online MBA programs, such as Florida State University and the University of Maryland University College, to name only two, are required by law to operate for the public good, meaning that they are not driven primarily by the prospect of pleasing "company" shareholders.

The for-profit institutions, like corporate America, run on the basis of applying business efficiencies that ultimately please their shareholders. Part of those efficiencies are related to how an institution such as the University of Phoenix advertises and markets itself—and this is where the whole notion of nonprofit versus for-profit gets controversial.

The argument goes something like this: Nonprofit institutions take a traditional academic-oriented approach to what they offer students and do not allocate large sums of money to advertise and market their online programs to the prospective student marketplace, although this is starting to change in order for them to remain competitive in the marketplace as for-profits invest heavily in advertising campaigns. Nonprofits believe students recognize an institution's academic strengths through an understanding of the institution's history of providing education to the public. They believe that large amounts of slick and costly advertising only exaggerate the truth about an institution's academic viability, and that too much competitive advertising makes it difficult for prospective students to make wise choices about their higher-education alternatives.

On the other side, for-profit institutions take more of a business approach in their relationship with students. They want students to understand that they are proud of their educational products and services and are more than willing to invest in sophisticated advertising and marketing initiatives to let prospective students know that they provide academically sound programs that are highly beneficial to helping students reach their career goals (which is why you see so many advertisements from these institutions all over the web).

In my opinion, each camp has a valid point of view. At the end of the day, you need to review the numerous considerations that are described throughout this book and choose the online MBA program that's right for you.

Instant Message

"We believe passionately and strongly in our product and the good it will do for our students and their organizations and communities. Providing access requires that you let people know who you are."

—Craig Swenson, provost and senior vice president for academic affairs, University of Phoenix

"Just like you have fast-food chains to serve different people, you have restaurants that serve certain people. The same notion applies to online MBA programs. The question is where do you want to eat?"

—Venkateshwar Reddy, interim dean, College of Business and Administration and the Graduate School of Business Administration, University of Colorado at Colorado Springs

Virtual Universities

Another type of higher-education institution that you should know about is the *virtual university*. Two that immediately come to mind are Jones International University (JIU) and Capella University. These are universities that offer only distance-education programs and courses and do not have a physical campus. Both Jones and Capella, by the way, are also for-profit institutions that offer online MBA programs.

Online Term

Virtual universities are higher-education institutions that do not have a traditional physical campus but instead operate out of a central office that is the management hub of its distance-education-only degree programs and courses.

Jones International University holds the unique distinction of being the first virtual university to achieve regional accreditation (which it achieved in 1999). It is owned by Glenn R. Jones, who is also JIU's chancellor. JIU's main office is located in Englewood, Colorado. Capella University is a rapidly growing virtual university, formerly known as the Graduate School of America, and is privately held by the Capella Education Company (based in Minneapolis).

What's the Curriculum?

Regardless of the type of institution offering an online MBA program, you also need to know as much as possible about the overall academic curriculum being provided.

In short, you want to understand what courses you have to take, as well as what they are all about. I know this sounds rather obvious, but there is more to this than you may think.

For one, make sure that the courses you are about to take are relevant to today's business world as well as steeped in the traditional time-honored business skills that every good business manager needs to know.

Rosemary Hartigan, director of the University of Maryland University College (UMUC) Online MBA program, explains that all courses within the UMUC program are constantly being updated. "Our students demand it," she says, adding that "certainly there are also management classics out there written in 1980 or even earlier that still have a lot of validity today. But when students see an article that is old, they will question it."

Regis MBA Professor Ed Cooper adds that just because a program might use case studies that are not current does not mean that a curriculum is out of date. "Some of the best lessons are historical lessons," he says. "The base issues and situational business context may be just as relevant today and provide lessons from the past."

You'll find course descriptions on school websites, but most really don't tell you much, which is why, as I mention throughout this book, you have to speak with school administrators and professors to glean information about the actual content of courses. See Chapter 10 on course objectives and learning outcomes for more information about teaching and learning styles used in online MBA programs.

Core Required Courses

MBA courses, in general, are geared toward helping the student develop strong managerial skills that can aid in the overall decision-making processes that enable a business to succeed. All online MBA programs have core required courses, also frequently referred to as foundation courses, that cover certain aspects of business that all MBA graduates must understand. Examples are marketing, accounting, finance, economics, statistics, organizational structure and theory, technology management, business strategy, business ethics, international strategic management, entrepreneurship, and business law.

Core required courses are very similar across the landscape of online MBA offerings, it's just that they all have different course titles and descriptions. For instance, a core required marketing course might be titled marketing and brand management, marketing strategy and planning, or marketing management. All cover everything a business manager needs to know about evaluating and managing a marketing department or marketing plan. For accounting courses, you'll see such titles as accounting foundations, managerial accounting, and introduction to accounting. All cover what every business manager needs to know about accounting.

Regardless of what core required courses are called, you have to take them, unless you may have taken an equivalent course somewhere else that the school will consider as transfer credit. Every school has different policies with regard to the possibility of granting course waivers and transferring credit.

Quantitative and Qualitative Courses

Many MBA professors and administrators refer to courses as being either quantitative or qualitative. Quantitative courses have a lot of math and/or statistical analysis and basically deal with numbers and factual information. Qualitative courses are more about decision-making and management issues that may or may not require a related numeric element.

The quantitative courses, in particular, require that you have a certain amount of math skills, such as how to work with spreadsheets, and a good understanding of basic business math, from algebra through calculus, as well as knowledge of statistics, accounting, and finance.

Qualitative courses, which are typically conceptual by nature, are generally viewed as being easier and more fun to take than quantitative courses. Examples of qualitative courses are marketing, business communications, entrepreneurship, and human resources management.

See Chapter 16 for a review of the skills you need to succeed as an online learner.

Instant Message

"Some courses are more numerical, factual, and quantitative in nature, but even these courses will be geared toward what you are going to do with the numbers. How are you going to use those numbers in the decisions you need to make? Other courses may not have as many numbers to deal with and may involve more complex situations, such as how do you motivate an employee?"

—M. Rungtusanatham, faculty director of the W.P. Carey MBA - Online Program at ASU

Electives

Depending on the overall curriculum, you may or may not have the option of taking electives. Some business schools outline the entire course of study for you (see the lock-step cohort model that follows), explaining exactly what courses you have to take, or the school may offer a relatively limited number of elective courses within various categories. Other schools allow you to choose from a long list of elective courses after you have completed a set of core required courses.

Often the set of electives you decide to take can become a concentration, if you complete, on average, 12 to 18 credits in a particular subject area, such as finance, technology management, international business, supply-chain management, or human resources management.

Overall, the choice of electives varies greatly from school to school. As you review complete curriculums, you need to consider the required courses as well as possible electives to choose the best fit for your career goals.

Cohort-Based

If you prefer to have all of your coursework very clearly spelled out for you in advance, with no room for electives, the lock-step cohort online MBA program format was made for you. A lock-step cohort online MBA program is one in which a group of students are enrolled in a program and all take the same predefined courses together and in the same sequence as strictly outlined by the school.

Some institutions that offer online MBA programs, such as the University of Florida, Drexel University, Arizona State University (ASU), and UMUC, have lock-step cohort programs. Depending on the school, an average-size cohort would contain about 30 students, and that may be broken down into smaller cohorts of 5 to 6 students who work on team projects together. The smaller cohorts will change through the entire length of the program, but the larger group of 30 may remain the same up through graduation day.

The beauty of a lock-step cohort program is that it facilitates strong relationships with fellow students, and these relationships could develop into meaningful business networking opportunities throughout your business career. Additionally, the strictness of a predefined program in which you take specific courses at specific intervals of times, along with the support systems that develop among students who are all doing the same thing, are strong motivators to complete your course of study on time, which is particularly important in the online learning modality. According to

M. Rungtusanatham, faculty director of the W.P. Carey MBA - Online Program at ASU, "We know from experience and from research that when you have individuals learning remotely, there is negative pressure for them to continue unless they can feel as if they belong to something and that there are others in the same situation, under the same learning agenda, whom they can rely on from both a teamwork and interaction perspective."

The negative side of a lock-step cohort is that you are locked in, meaning that for approximately two years you are encouraged to enroll in each term, regardless of what may be on your future agenda. In most cases, however, schools are flexible about this and will allow students to drop out of a cohort and then drop in later and enter a new cohort where they left off. Also most schools will allow students at least five years to complete a two-year lock-step program. However, depending on your circumstances, dropping out and coming back in might not be the best option, especially if you happen to be in a really tight group of very experienced and knowledgeable professionals that is working very well together.

Corporate Input and Modernity

Many MBA programs have built sound relationships with corporations that result in changes to the courses being offered to students. In an effort to stay modern, schools seek out the advice of business managers about what kinds of courses they should develop. At schools such as Capella University and the University of Phoenix, for example, professors in their online MBA programs are mostly practicing professionals who frequently contribute their insights to the overall makeup and design of the school's curriculum and course content. At ASU and at Indiana University, their histories of offering customized MBA programs to major international corporations has helped to form online curriculums that have remained up to date on some of the latest business practices and strategies.

For example, "Companies have told us that they need people who have project management skills," says Rungtusanatham. "So we have a course titled Project Management and another titled Management of Technology and Innovation, which represent an attempt for us to help managers understand that change is something that has to be planned for and executed properly." Rungtusanatham further explains that through one-on-one conversations with executives and former students from companies such as Deere & Company, United Technologies, Lucent, and Chevron that have participated in customized corporate programs offered by the W.P. Carey School of Business, as well as through direct and indirect feedback he obtains from working professionals enrolled in the courses he teaches, the W.P. Carey School has been able to create an academic-development environment that is continuously changing and improving.

As a prospective online MBA student, you need to take a look at whether the school you are considering has any corporate influences affecting its course content and overall curriculum-development processes. One important and relatively basic question you can ask is this: "Please tell me how your school is keeping up with modern business practices."

For instance, business ethics courses are popular today due primarily to all the corporate scandals that have occurred in recent years. Thus, since the spring 2004 term, the University of Maryland University College (UMUC) has integrated business ethics components into all courses in its online MBA program. "We are religious about keeping our course materials up to date," says Rosemary Hartigan, UMUC's online MBA director. "Students are very skeptical of material that is not up to date, and they will call us on it."

Instant Message

"We do as much as we can to listen to our students and listen to our alumni to keep abreast of the market to understand which courses would be of most value to them."

—Alex Sevilla, director of Executive and Professional MBA programs, University of Florida

The University of Florida's Internet MBA program provides another example of a relatively modern course in e-commerce. When the University of Florida first started its MBA Internet program (five years ago), this was not an available (or perhaps envisioned) course offering.

Integration Is Key

Another approach you can take when investigating a curriculum is to examine how a complete course of study as a whole learning experience will encapsulate everything you need to know to succeed in the world of business. This is where the term *integration* comes into play. At UMUC, the integration of business ethics components into its overall curriculum is only one part of the online MBA program's complete curriculum integration process, says UMUC's Hartigan. Themes are integrated throughout the online MBA program, making courses more like "combinations of subjects. There is not just a marketing course, or a business law course, or a business ethics course. Instead, we integrate these subjects, and others like quantitative methods, throughout the curriculum."

Aspects of a Well-Designed Program

According to Bartholomew Jae, former vice president of products for Acadient, a Boston-based company that designs graduate-level business courses for higher education, students should look for the following elements in an online MBA curriculum:

- **Standards based.** Is the curriculum built according to regional and/or professional accreditation standards?
- **Highly structured.** Do the students know exactly where they are in the program, how they are doing, and what they need to do next? Do they understand the purpose of each assignment in a course and how to get help when they need it, as well as how they will be graded?
- **Learning outcomes-oriented.** Every module, course, lesson, or assignment within the overall curriculum should tie back to a desired learning outcome (see Chapter 10).
- **Balanced workload.** Are courses designed so that you have a reasonable period of time to complete self-paced assignments, as well as team-based assignments, along with enough time to actively participate in discussions related to such assignments?
- **Highly interactive.** Students should be engaged through a variety of methods, including exercises, graphics, and assignments that keep them in contact with their fellow students and the faculty teaching the courses.
- **Transparent technology.** Students should encounter minimal distraction from the usability and reliability of the technology being used.
- **High-quality content.** The depth of the content within courses should be educationally rigorous, accurate, and clear.
- **Flexible instructor influence.** There should be built-in flexibility for instructors to change assignments on the fly to reflect current events and changes in regulation or practice.
- **Individualized.** Faculty need to cater to various adult learning types and styles to ensure that ample opportunities are available for students to reflect upon their understanding of the material being taught and apply them to real-life scenarios.
- **Highly relevant.** Courses should have abundant examples that help students understand how the knowledge and skills they are learning will be applied to actual work situations.

The Details Beneath the Surface

As this chapter informs you, there's a lot of detail beneath the surface of an institution itself and the way it organizes its online MBA at the program level. In the next chapter, the details trickle down to the course level and the types of educational technologies you'll typically see in an online course. In Chapter 10 there are more details, including information on a variety of teaching and learning techniques and strategies that online MBA programs use to ensure that you are actually learning something of value.

The Least You Need to Know

- There is a difference between how nonprofit and for-profit institutions operate.
- Online MBA curriculums come in different shapes and sizes with their own unique way of providing core required courses and electives. You need to pick the one that fits in best with your career goals.
- It is important to look at how a complete course of study may or may not cover everything you need to understand and practice to succeed.
- Some programs are offered in a lock-step cohort format, which has lots of benefits, provided that you don't mind the rigidity of such a program.
- The elements of a well-designed online MBA program deal with course and curriculum structure, learning outcomes, relevancy, quality, and everything in between.

Chapter 9

The Technology of Online Courses

In This Chapter

- Educational technologies used in online MBA programs
- How online courses are created
- Information about online course material
- What online lectures are actually like
- Information about innovative online communication tools

There's some pretty slick technology that is utilized for online courses. When online teaching and learning first came on the scene in the late 1980s, it comprised mostly text-based lectures and e-mail correspondence. Today that has changed considerably as online learners are now able to take advantage of all kinds of sophisticated educational technologies that enable them to interact with each other in ways that are highly conducive to learning.

In Part 4, I specify how you can utilize educational technologies effectively and ultimately succeed in today's revolutionary high-tech online learning environments. For now, however, the focus is on explaining what's available to online learners more from a technology point of view so that you understand what you may or may not see in your online courses.

Educational Technologies

There are numerous examples of how *educational technologies* are used in online MBA programs (and, in fact, in all higher-education disciplines). All sorts of electronic and web-based teaching and learning tools form the interfaces and functions of online courses, and it takes a talented group of professionals to make online teaching and learning operate smoothly and effectively.

Some institutions are better at implementing effective uses of educational technologies, and are better equipped, than others. A lot depends on what kind of staff, as well as what kind of investment in software and technology-support infrastructure, the institution allocates toward the technology side of these programs. For instance, some programs may have easy access to and the staff to support video productions, for creating web-based video streaming lectures, and/or *simulation*-creation software and services, for creating slick electronic representations of real-world business challenges that students can interact with. Other programs may not have the means to create multimedia course elements and rely more on text-based lectures and discussion forums for teaching and learning.

Online Term

Educational technologies comprise the set of software tools and electronic and/or web-based functions, features, and tools of a course of study or program used by both students and faculty. Educational technologies can include CD-ROMs and DVDs, all educational-related software, video- and audiotapes, Internet-based communications, telecommunications, and streaming multimedia. **Simulations** are electronic replicas of business challenges users interact with online and make decisions about. The simulations then assess the user's behavior and choices and provide feedback.

What follows are some of the educational technology elements you may or may not see in your program of choice. Getting a basic understanding of these elements could form the basis of technology-oriented questions you can ask before applying to any program.

How Online Courses Are Created

Many institutions have *teaching, learning, and technology centers*, sometimes referred to as TLTs, with a staff of instructional designers, webmasters, writers, content experts, graphic designers, software and multimedia experts, and other information technologists who help build online courses.

Faculty are the main drivers behind what goes into the online courses they teach. They are the content or subject-matter experts who typically start out the course-development process by sharing the course outlines and learning objectives of their courses with the TLT staff. The TLT staffers and faculty members work as a team to hopefully create an effective online teaching and learning environment that students can easily access and work through from their home or business-office computer workstations or laptops.

Online Term

A **teaching, learning, and technology center** (TLT) is composed of a group of information technology and education professionals who build and maintain the electronic and web-based infrastructure and functionalities used inside online courses.

Instructional designers can be considered the second most important drivers behind the development of an online course. These professionals help with the organizational structure and methods used for presenting online courses. They will introduce faculty to online teaching strategies, course content resources, student activities, testing methods, and what kind of technologies may best fit their desired teaching goals. They might advise a faculty member, for instance, to replace a long text-based lecture, or a cumbersome list of links to academic resources, with a well-designed PowerPoint presentation with audio components.

Regardless of the kind of educational technologies being used in any online course, these technologies are not as important as the interactions you will have with faculty and students, nor the actual learning you will accomplish by completing all the required reading and assignments.

Your Course Management System

In simple terms, the course management system (CMS), which may sometimes be referred to as a learning management system (LMS), is the electronic shell or graphical interface that holds all the elements of your online courses. The CMS also provides most of the underlying operational software that controls such things as file management, grading, online testing, asynchronous and synchronous discussions, and more.

There are basically two interfaces in any CMS: the one used by faculty and instructional designers to build out an online course, and the one used by the student to take an online course. Overall you need not concern yourself with the technical aspects of a CMS. The school will give you an orientation on how everything works and what you need to know to utilize all the functions and features of the CMS.

Most institutions will lease a CMS from a vendor. The three largest CMS providers to higher education are Blackboard, WebCT, and eCollege. For example, Arizona State University uses Blackboard, Drexel University uses WebCT, and the University of Colorado at Colorado Springs uses eCollege. There are other smaller providers such as CyberlearningLab's Angel CMS, which is used by the Pennsylvania State World Campus; Desire2Learn, used by the University of Wisconsin system; and IntraLearn, used by the University of Massachusetts Amherst. Other institutions may have built their own CMS, which is referred to as a home-grown system, such as the one used at the University of Maryland University College, called WebTycho; and the CMS used at the University of Florida, called iNet; and the CMS used by the University of Phoenix, called eResource. All these CMS products pretty much have similar features and functions.

Guide on the Side

If you are interested in knowing more about CMS products, go to the Western Cooperative for Educational Technologies edutools website at www.edutools.info, where there are web-based tools for analyzing information about course management systems.

You will access a CMS, which is hosted on servers either at the campus you are enrolled in or on remote servers owned by the CMS provider, through a username and password authentication process. Once you're in, the fun begins.

It All Starts with a Welcome Message and a Syllabus

Just like in a traditional classroom environment, your instructor will provide you with a welcome message and a syllabus that outlines all the elements of your online course. Like almost everything else in the course, the syllabus resides in your CMS. The syllabus starts with an introductory message from the instructor, including contact information and office hours he or she may hold via live chat, e-mail, or telephone.

All textbooks and any online supplemental course materials, such as online lectures and other readings, required for the course will be duly noted, along with the course objectives, a description of how you will be graded, and a course outline that lists what is required of you on a weekly basis.

Most weekly course requirements include a good deal of reading, listening, and/or viewing of a variety of course materials and resources, depending on the educational technologies being used; a list of discussion topics related to the readings, with deadlines for when you need to post your comments and respond to other students' comments on the discussion board; a number of exercises, online quizzes, and exams; and possibly some precise days and times when you need to participate in an online web conference, or live chat, or in a teleconference, to interact in real time with your fellow students and the teacher.

Your weekly coursework will typically be broken up into modules, which is basically a way of dividing up the entire course into smaller pieces that are more easily digestible. These modules will be related and integrated with each other to form the structure of an entire course (see the figure that follows).

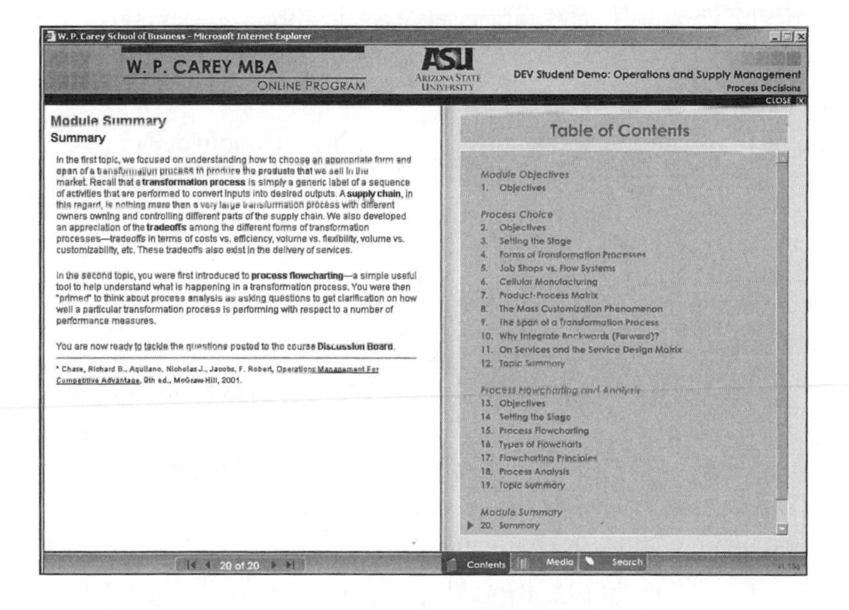

A module inside an Arizona State University online MBA course in operations and supply management.

Textbooks and Other Reading Materials

Depending on the school, the textbooks and other supplemental course materials you will need as you move through your coursework may come in many different shapes and sizes. Textbooks, which you will be able to purchase online through the campus bookstore, may be supplied as digitized electronic books over the web or in the more typical hardcover printed form, which will be shipped to you. Even if a textbook is available only in print, many of today's textbooks have accompanying websites and/or supplemental reading and viewing material supplied on CD-ROMs.

There is a relatively new movement by the textbook publishing industry that is pushing more textbooks into the digitized format because they are less expensive to produce and thereby less costly for students to purchase, as well as easier to distribute and to update.

The University of Phoenix has spearheaded what could be a sign of the future of digitized textbooks, also called eBooks, in online MBA programs through a new service it offers to its students called eLibrary.

eLibrary is a customized publishing service whereby instructors can pick and choose segments of a variety of electronic textbooks to include as reading material in a course, instead of having students purchase one or two primary textbooks that may have some superfluous information or may not cover absolutely everything an instructor wants to cover in a particular course. The eLibrary service also allows students to search through numerous electronic textbooks to obtain segmented information by their topic of choice.

Supplemental reading materials can include research papers, business journal and magazine articles, digital library resources, business-related websites, and lots of case studies in digitized form. Much more information about how electronic case studies are used in online MBA programs is provided in Chapter 10.

Lectures in an Online Course

Obviously, all courses, be they online or on-campus, have lectures. One of the most innovative and modern methods of providing faculty lectures to online students can be found at the University of Florida's Internet MBA program, where faculty burn their lectures onto DVDs. These DVDs might also include Microsoft PowerPoint presentations, supplemental video clips, and animated simulations.

According to Alex Sevilla, University of Florida MBA program director, "The DVDs we use are much more of a show than a talking head where you put a disk into your computer and hear a faculty member drone on about a particular topic. It is very much meant to simulate a real lecture environment, where faculty talk on a particular topic, show their PowerPoint slides, and highlight certain content and resources that interact with their lecture."

PowerPoint is pretty much the software of choice used by businesses for viewing presentations online, in a live meeting, or via external media such as DVDs and CD-ROMs. In the online learning world, it's not any different. Many faculty compose their lectures with PowerPoint slides and add audio and animation to them. Depending on the program's technology infrastructure, you may be able to access PowerPoint lectures with audio through your CMS over the web. Other programs will ship you CD-ROMs or DVDs that hold the PowerPoint lectures.

Still others may have lectures video streamed and provided online through such software plug-ins as RealPlayer, Macromedia Flash, or Windows Media Player. (Refer to Chapter 13 for information about technical requirements, including video streaming plug-ins.) Other schools may not use any of these educational technologies and have lectures put on videotape that are shipped to you. Still others may have text-based lectures provided in Microsoft Word or as PDF-formatted documents, or simply posted on a web page. The beauty of all of these methods—although anything that is purely text-based these days is pretty boring—is that the lecture is recorded and can be viewed again and again. So, if you're not getting the subject matter under discussion, you can always go back repeatedly until you do.

CAUTION

MBAware

If you are doing a good deal of your online coursework through your corporate workstation, make sure there are no firewalls to prevent employees from viewing streaming video over Internet connections. If there are such firewalls, ask the computer tech people if you can have them disabled on your computer. Otherwise, you will not be able to view video streams at work.

Web Conferencing

One of the latest trends in educational technologies is *web conferencing*, which is a technology that allows students and faculty to collaborate over an Internet connection in real time.

Classes meet online in a special conference area that allows them to communicate with each other while simultaneously displaying PowerPoint presentations, text, graphics, and video clips. With the proper software and equipment, such as a computer microphone, speakers, and sound card, students and faculty are able to speak with each other during presentations as well as share and store files and links to online resources, conduct polls, and use a *whiteboard* to annotate their presentation or draw onscreen.

Online Term

Web conferences are when two or more people in separate locations communicate, with audio, video, and other presentation software, in real time over an Internet connection. Properly installed web conferencing software allows for video and text to be displayed during a conference, and for the participants to talk with each other, provided that they have a microphone hooked up to their computers with a sound card and speakers. Live polls can also be conducted during a web conference.

A **whiteboard** is an application that enables users to draw, erase, and point to elements on a computer screen in real time. Whiteboarding is utilized within web conferencing as an electronic chalkboard.

The only downfall to this kind of educational technology is that it is synchronous, requiring everyone to be online at the same time, which is amplified if students live in different time zones. Plus busy professionals who are frequently on the road will encounter difficulties accessing this kind of technology over dial-up and wireless Internet connections. However, web conferences can be recorded for later viewing if you can't make the live online gathering. Some of the leading web conferencing software vendors in higher education include CentraNow, Macromedia Breeze, Microsoft Office Live Meeting, HorizonLive, Elluminate Live, and Web-4M.

According to the MBA program director at the University of Florida MBA, Alex Sevilla, "The students using our web conferencing tool (CentraNow) speak very highly of it, and many of them understand what a quality product it is because they use it on the corporate side. My guess is that in three to four years, this won't be a competitive advantage for us because everybody will have some kind of web conferencing tool that works well."

Web conferencing technology is a trend that has been occurring for some time at major corporations that see it as a means for making dynamic online presentations to their employees, partners, and sales prospects worldwide and consequently saving dollars on travel costs. Most online MBA programs are in the early phases of adopting this technology or have no immediate plans of using web conferencing in their online courses. However, that might change in the near future as web conferencing software becomes more efficient and less costly.

The Almighty Discussion Board

Because most online students cannot take full advantage of synchronous (real-time) educational technologies such as the aforementioned web conferencing tools, the next best thing, and the most ubiquitous technology in an online course, is the *online discussion board*, which is an asynchronous communication technology that does not require real-time access. I discuss this topic more fully in Chapters 15, 16, and 17.

Online Term

An **online discussion board,** which is also referred to as a discussion forum or group, or message board, is where faculty and students in an online class post questions, responses to questions, and opinions, and enter into dialogues with each other asynchronously.

Basically, the discussion board is the heart and soul of most online courses. Every CMS has discussion board software. Essentially, discussion boards all work pretty much the same, with the professor opening up discussions by posting a thought-provoking comment, question, or challenge, such as an assignment to analyze and resolve a problem represented in a business case study. Students respond to the professor's post, hopefully intelligently and in a meaningful way that spurs more discussion among all students in the course. The initial post ends up becoming a long thread of responses and varied points of view that ultimately lead to a learning experience.

Instant Message

"A huge part of our courses is the discussion board, which is used to analyze cases. It works very well in our program because it is asynchronous. Our students are in 10 time zones. The discussion board is the single most used feature in Blackboard."

—Paula O'Callaghan, director of the Syracuse University iMBA program

Chatting Online

Live chat is another synchronous tool within your CMS that enables you to communicate with students and faculty in real time. Chat is pretty much limited to only text-based messaging that users type into a text field, so it does not have all the bells and whistles of web conferencing software. Live chat is used in those instances where students and faculty may want an immediate response to a discussion or

Instant Message

"Syracuse University introduced me to a whole new realm when it comes to digital convergence. I could communicate with my classmates via e-mail or real-time group chats. The Blackboard technology was a critical element to my learning experience at SU."

—Mike Venable, Syracuse University 2004 iMBA graduate

lecture. It is also frequently used by professors to hold live office hours at specific days and times.

Teleconferencing

The good old telephone is also frequently used in online MBA programs, especially for team-based projects where groups of students need to speak with each other to organize each other's responsibilities and deadlines concerning team assignments, which are common in online MBA programs (see Chapters 10 and 17). Phone-conferencing systems are used in online courses for real-time, voice-to-voice interaction among classmates and the instructor. Participants dial in to a special number and join a meeting by entering an ID code. In some cases, the phone conference is recorded and becomes available for review over the web.

Simulations

The use of electronic simulations is another learning tool that has been gaining in popularity in online MBA programs, as well as in on-campus MBA programs. Simulations provide an electronic representation of real-world business challenges that students can interact with repeatedly. The underlying goal is to make the right business decisions and ultimately learn something during the decision-making process.

The University of Phoenix, for example, has a set of custom business simulations that place students in real-world situations. The simulations are created in Macromedia Flash. Students role play as managers who must make a crucial business decision, such as pricing a new product, or developing a marketing strategy, or implementing a technology plan. They are provided with information such as marketing reports and financial data that will help during the decision-making process. The simulations are divided into cycles of time—week, month, quarter, year. Students input their decisions and are given feedback.

Simulations are often referred to as the premiere model for engaging students in effective problem-based learning environments. Visit www.phoenix.edu/simulations to see a demonstration of how electronic simulations work in graduate-level business courses at the University of Phoenix.

Problem-based teaching and learning is discussed in greater detail in Chapter 10.

Online Quizzes and Exams

The typical multiple-choice, fill-in-the-blank, and short-answer and long-answer quizzes and exams are included in many online MBA courses. In particular, quantitative courses rely heavily on quizzes that test your knowledge of calculation theories and concepts, as well as your ability to solve computational challenges with accuracy.

Many quizzes and exams are exactly like take-home tests, except they are conducted with the aid of spreadsheet and database software such as Microsoft Excel or Microsoft Access. Some CMS products, or other software applications, have equation editors that allow students to do math equations online. For online quizzes, the instructor may give you a specific date when the test will be made available through your CMS, and a password to access the quiz. Some online quizzes are timed and consequently shut down over a pre-established period beginning from the moment you log on to take it.

For final exams, you may be required to set up proctoring arrangements, meaning you'll need to be under supervision as you take the exam. Sometimes these can be arranged through testing centers, such as the Thomson Prometric Test Centers network, or at local colleges within your area.

In Chapter 16, I discuss quizzes, exams, and test-taking skills.

Grading

Grading is also conducted online. Your professor will clearly outline how your final grade will be determined. Like on-campus courses, your grade will be calculated by percentages aligned with specific tasks. For example, grading may be divided as 20 percent for quizzes, 20 percent for team responses, and 60 percent for the final exam. Or it may be 50 percent quizzes and exams and 50 percent written assignments. The CMS may have a grade book tool that faculty use to record and keep track of your grades (see the figure that follows). Your progress as you move through the course will be made public to you and you alone when the faculty releases that information to you through the CMS, usually displayed in a table with your point totals for each item and your overall grade.

Instant Message

"It did take some time to get acclimated to the online environment as a student. My initial reaction while reading the modules of my first course was to get out a highlighter and streak my notebook computer screen with it. Since that course I have found a balance of online reading and offline printing that works pretty well."

—Robert Breen, online MBA student, Arizona State University

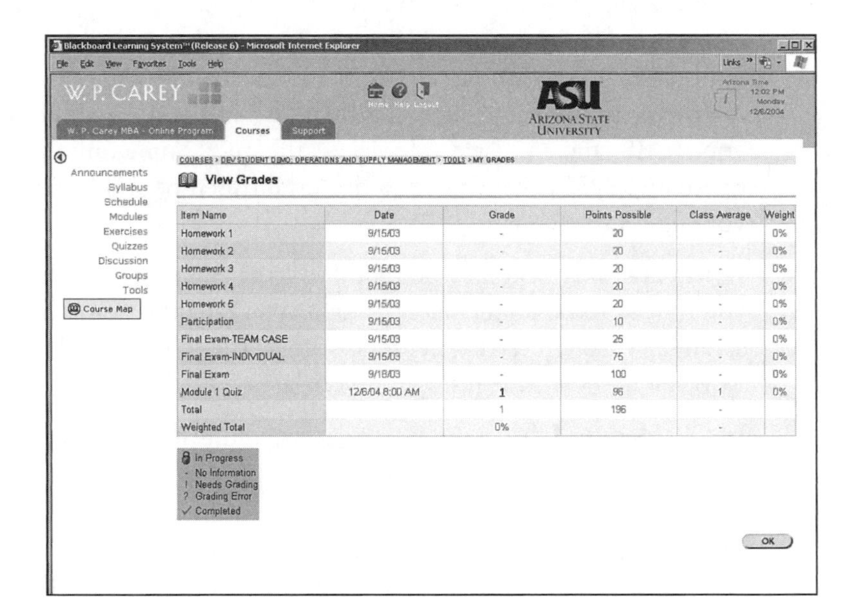

Example of a grading table inside an Arizona State University online MBA course.

The Least You Need to Know

- Depending on the school you attend, you will be introduced to a wide variety of educational technologies that will reside inside a course management system.
- The school will provide you with an orientation on how to use all the educational technologies that will be used in your online coursework.
- Basically, a professor's welcome message; a course syllabus; online and print-based textbooks, supplemental course materials, lectures, quizzes and exams; grading rubrics; and various communication technologies typically make up the overall composition of an online course.
- Some of the relatively new innovative advancements in online learning techniques include the use of electronic textbooks, web conferencing, and electronic simulations.

Chapter 10

Course Objectives and Learning Outcomes

In This Chapter

- Competency-based learning techniques in online courses
- Professional coaching practice at Capella University
- Bloom's taxonomy and Program Maps at the University of Phoenix
- Case studies and team projects in online courses
- Institutional course-development support

All these fascinating educational technologies in online MBA programs are really secondary to what should be foremost on your mind, which is what am I going to learn? What kind of skills will I have when I graduate? How can I apply what I am learning to my job and to my career-advancement goals? A course with all the latest technological bells and whistles is really no course at all if the eventual outcome is that you are no more knowledgeable than when you started. You will, however, definitely be poorer after you have paid your tuition, regardless of what you may or may not have learned.

Hence, this chapter is all about what online MBA teaching techniques and structures are the most effective for facilitating learning and gaining managerial skills, as well as how you might spot a school's ability to meet its mission to teach you the right stuff.

Competency-Based Learning

Competency-based learning and *learning outcomes* are two terms you may run across as you search for the right online MBA program. Both are particularly useful practices because each deals with the connection between the academic content of a curriculum and what a student has learned or can demonstrate as a skill.

Online Term

Competency-based learning is an education practice that measures and demonstrates what a student is capable of executing as a result of what he or she has learned. Related to competency-based learning are **learning outcomes,** which are the clearly stated capabilities or desired results of a learning experience.

AACSB addresses what it calls the "assurance of learning standards" in its documentation of "Eligibility Procedures and Accreditation Standards for Business Accreditation," stating that business schools should have "well-documented systematic processes to develop, monitor, evaluate, and revise the substance and delivery of curricula of degree programs and assess the impact of the curricula on learning." Additionally, AACSB identifies three broad capacities that students should develop at the Master's level:

- Capacity to lead in organizational situations.
- Capacity to apply knowledge in new and unfamiliar circumstances through a conceptual understanding of relevant disciplines.
- Capacity to adapt and innovate to solve problems, to cope with unforeseen events, and to manage in unpredictable environments.

The Council for Higher Education Accreditation also addresses the topic of learning outcomes, stating in its publication "Accreditation and Assuring Quality in Distance Learning" that over the past 10 years accreditation standards, in general, have changed to having a stronger focus on student achievement and that institutions are required to document their effectiveness in "meeting their educational mission and goals and that student outcomes are at an acceptable level."

Competency-based learning and learning outcomes emphasize practical knowledge that MBA students can apply to their work immediately. An example might be an accounting course where a student must demonstrate his or her ability to post a double-entry bookkeeping ledger, which, in essence, is a visible manifestation of knowledge gained. Another example might be based on a case-study teaching and learning method where a team of students analyzes a business challenge and comes up with a solution that includes a business and marketing plan that requires them to create a detailed financial section with spreadsheets showing income and cash-flow forecasts. How case studies are used in online courses is explained later in this chapter.

So, in general, how are schools building their curriculums to measure up to these kinds of standards? At Capella University, for instance, the entire online MBA curriculum has been converted to a competency-based learning environment. The same holds true for the University of Phoenix, which has a highly structured program that clearly states what MBA students will learn and how they will be continuously assessed on whether certain skill levels have been achieved as they move through each of their courses.

Capella's Coaches

At Capella University, part of the focus on competencies and learning outcomes revolves around an innovative Professional Effectiveness Coaching core. In addition to a business core, where students take core required courses, and a professional effectiveness core, where students study the best practices of effective management, Capella fosters a professional coaching environment geared toward applying what students learn in their courses to their jobs. The way it works is that students have the option of choosing a professional business coach who has been hired by Capella to provide objective one-on-one guidance to MBA students with relation to applying new behaviors on their jobs and helping them develop and implement plans to achieve career goals.

> **Instant Message**
>
> "We want to make sure MBA learners leave our program and then go back to the job and immediately have an impact. We try to build our projects around relevant problems that they can solve immediately."
>
> —Barbara Butts Williams, director of Capella University's Online MBA program

Capella students choose coaches by reviewing a list of coach bios and listening to audiotaped perspectives from the coaches online. The student then identifies his or her top three coach preferences, and based on the coach's load of students, a selection is made and then confirmed with the MBA student. The coach and the MBA student then establish an agreement for how they will work together, with the relationship intended to last as long as the student is actively enrolled in the program. According to Barbara Butts Williams, director of Capella University's online MBA program, "The intent of the personal coaching relationship is to help learners stretch their skills in key areas of performance improvement and apply what they learn right away, so they can demonstrate an impact on results within their organizations and help reposition themselves for success."

The Phoenix Model

At the University of Phoenix, online MBA students follow a straightforward course design that begins by clearly stating what the learning objectives are during each week of any given course within the program. The learning objectives align with a popular educational classification system commonly known by academics as *Bloom's taxonomy*, which has its roots in research conducted back in the 1950s by former University of Chicago Professor of Education Benjamin Bloom. Bloom's taxonomy has since been posthumously expanded and revised by numerous education professionals. At the University of Phoenix, it has helped faculty and instructional designers align learning objectives, course exercises, and course testing requirements in a way that allows online MBA students to demonstrate that they have mastered more than 50 business-related competencies.

Basically, competencies are reached through critical readings and exercises, including interacting with peers in discussion boards, and then the students are assessed through quizzes and examinations. An exercise within a course will have instructions that use verbs that fall within the six levels of learning identified by Bloom—knowledge, comprehension, application, analysis, synthesis, and evaluation.

Online Term

Bloom's taxonomy is named after Benjamin Bloom, an education professor and researcher from the University of Chicago who, in 1956, identified six levels of learning: knowledge, comprehension, application, analysis, synthesis, and evaluation.

So, for example, a student or team of students may be required to analyze, understand, synthesize, evaluate, apply, create, and develop a marketing plan based on one or more case studies and a required set of readings. Before, during, and after students work on their exercises and tests, they are required to discuss their work with their peers and faculty inside the course discussion board, where learning takes place from student to student and from faculty to student.

Program Maps

Online MBA students at the University of Phoenix are also able to see precisely what they should be able to accomplish within any course in the program through a relatively new online information service called Program Maps (see the figure that follows).

Program Maps are based on areas of learning called domains. Within each domain are subcategories of learning. Under each subcategory is a description of what is required of the student in a particular course inside a particular area of learning. So, for instance, a student can click on the Business Planning and Development domain and see a flowchart showing the following three subcategories within that domain: Strategic Planning, Marketing, and Business Research. When the student clicks on Strategic Planning, a description of what is required within a specific module of a specific course pops up. In this case, it's from week six of an economics course, and the result of the Program Map reveals that the student "will analyze a product or service offered by an organization and the market in which it competes, explore relevant forecasts, and recommend nonpricing strategies to enhance sales."

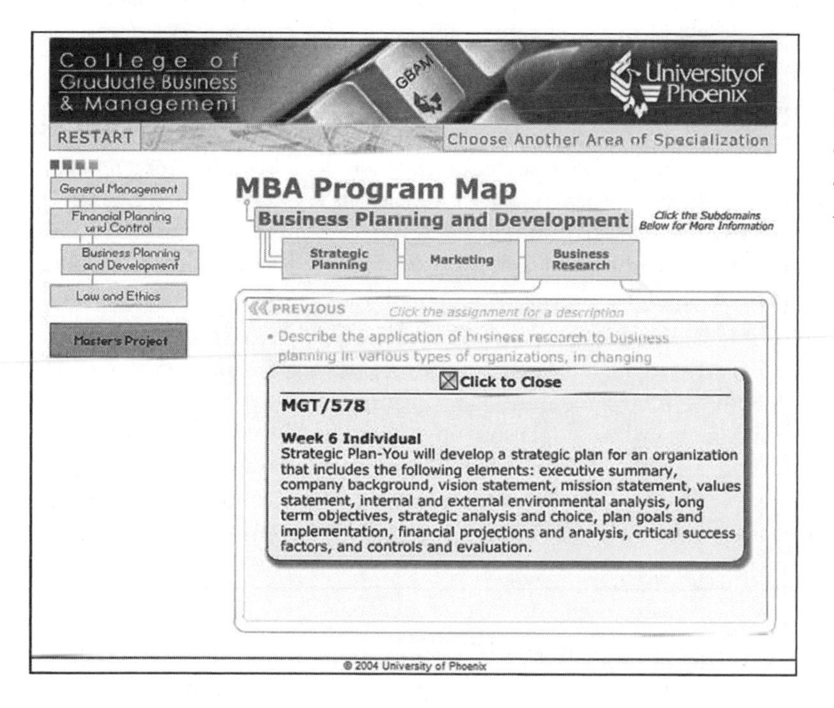

Example of a University of Phoenix Program Map, an online service that shows students what they can expect to accomplish in their online MBA courses.

Grading Rubric

For that final, all-important piece of the class—earning a grade—faculty will gauge how much a student learns and put a grade on a student's assignment within a course by using what's commonly referred to in online teaching parlance as a grading rubric, an example of which, from a University of Phoenix accounting course, is shown in the table that follows.

ACC/583 Rubric for Week One Assignment: Tax Research and Planning Paper

Criterion	Unsatisfactory	Satisfactory	Exceptional
Explain Role of Tax Planning in Business	Failed to explain the role of tax planning in the business environment, incorporating the four maxims of tax planning and six steps in tax law research.	Adequately explained the role of tax planning in the business environment, incorporating the four maxims of tax planning and six steps in tax law research.	In addition to meeting the requirements of satisfactory, assessed the challenges of integrating tax planning with an organization's strategic planning, goals, and objectives.
Evaluate Three Tax Research Sources	Failed to evaluate three tax research sources, or failed to compare the characteristics of the three to recommend the best resource.	Evaluated three tax research sources and compared the characteristics of the three to recommend the best resource.	In addition to meeting the requirements of satisfactory, assessed the limitations of the recommended resource.
Analyze the Role of Ethics	Failed to analyze the role of ethics in tax planning, focusing on evaluating the difference between tax avoidance and tax evasion.	Analyzed the role of ethics in tax planning, focusing on evaluating the difference between tax avoidance and tax evasion.	In addition to meeting the requirements of satisfactory, suggested ways to enhance the role of ethics in tax planning.

Other Competency-Based Teaching and Learning Styles

Examination and analysis of business case studies is another prevalent teaching and learning style that helps online MBA students develop the practical skills they need to become successful business managers. Also, virtual team projects is an important teaching and learning method used in online MBA curriculums. Both methods are geared toward building competencies that are aligned with learning objectives and outcomes.

Case Studies

What academics call case-based teaching has historically been an effective way for MBA students to participate in true-to-life simulations of a wide variety of business practices. A case study is usually a nonfictional story of about 10 to 30 pages in length written by a professional case writer who outlines all the details of a specific business situation, such as how company X faced the challenge of building a customer service department, or how company Y created an advertising campaign. Other cases are more holistic and might explore how a company rose to prominence within a certain sector and how senior management faced a wide variety of challenges during its early growth phase.

The most well-known publisher of case studies is the Harvard Business School, which, as stated on its website, believes that "the case method is by far the most powerful way to learn the skills required to manage, and to lead." Other well-known publishers of case studies include Babson College, Darden Business Publishing, Stanford Graduate School of Business, Thunderbird's American Graduate School of Business Education, and many others.

In some online MBA programs, students are supplied with digital versions of such case studies, supplied through a company called Xanedu. Xanedu aggregates and supplies copyright-cleared case studies from all the major case-study publishers, as well as other business-related articles from numerous newspapers and magazines through a partnership it has with the ProQuest online information service, into a web-based interface. Faculty members or course developers go into the Xanedu web-based system, search for relevant case studies and articles they

Instant Message

"I have had great success using the Xanedu research tools. It's a great resource in my job as a strategist and analyst."

—Robert Breen, online MBA student, Arizona State University

want their students to read and analyze, and, with the click of a mouse, create what's called a Course Pack of these preselected materials for students to access inside their online course modules.

Students are instructed to carefully review these materials and are asked a series of related questions by the professor inside the course's asynchronous discussion board. The students are asked what they would do in the situation or situations provided in the case study. They might also be given a variety of decisions to choose from and defend. Based on their answers, students can be divided into teams that must defend their positions through presentations and interactions with the rest of their classmates.

Guide on the Side

For a very detailed description on how the case method of teaching is used at the Harvard Business School, visit www.hbs.edu/case/hbs-case.html.

Team Projects

Working together as a group on a specific project is not uncommon in the business world, and therefore many online MBA programs have a strong emphasis on team-based learning assignments that often involve case studies. The course management system will have online tools that help to facilitate team projects online, such as private virtual rooms where team members can exchange files and communicate with each other both asynchronously and synchronously. Frequently team members will also be required to communicate by telephone at times during the process.

Typically a team project concludes with a presentation or paper that the team has jointly created. Sometimes a team project will take an entire semester or term. For example, a group of students might work on creating a full-blown business plan or on writing a research paper on a modern business evolution occurring on an international scale, culminating in a live face-to-face presentation at the end of the course (if the program includes a residency requirement). At Syracuse University, for instance, team project presentations are held during their last residency requirement, when they also hold final exams. If the school does not have a residency requirement, such presentations may be conducted with a web-conferencing tool such as described in Chapter 9, or as a PowerPoint presentation with audio components. Team project presentations are usually evaluated by both fellow students and the professor, who will give your team a grade based on the quality and depth of work performed.

Team-based assignments that conclude in a professional presentation obviously mimic the real world and can therefore easily be considered a competency-based learning technique based on specific learning objectives and outcomes.

One of the benefits of working in teams is that the team can establish great business relationships between students in which individuals bring out their expertise and share knowledge and practical advice openly, learning from each other as opposed to learning only from the professor or the work performed individually. One of the drawbacks of working in teams is that it can establish dislikes and friction between students, especially in situations where everyone is not pulling his or her weight equally. Chapter 17 discusses how to survive team projects.

Instant Message

"The main reason why we require team projects is because our advisory board of business people recommends them. We asked business people what they want MBA students to be capable of doing, and they said that it is very important that they be able to work in teams."

—Rosemary Hartigan, director of the University of Maryland University College online MBA program

The Infrastructure Supporting Course Development

Now that you know about the technologies used in online learning (from Chapter 9) as well as the competency-based teaching and learning techniques used in online courses, how do you get an idea about a program's ability to build and actually integrate the technology, teaching, and learning in an effective manner?

One way is to try to get a sense for how an online MBA program is supported by the institution. Does the program, for instance, have a teaching, learning, and technology staff, similar to what I mentioned in Chapter 9, actively assisting its faculty with the design and implementation of effective competency-based learning environments? Or are faculty more or less left on their own?

When you are talking to online MBA program administrators, simply ask them about the nature of their educational technology and online teaching support systems. Do they have a team of instructional designers who regularly assist faculty with course development? What kind of background and experience do their instructional designers have? Ask whether you can talk to their chief educational technology person to get a better sense for what their courses are like and whether their courses have incorporated competency-based elements. Again, you'll have to make a judgment call based on the response you get. A bit of frustration and hesitancy coming through the phone, or a sound bite that overly resembles an advertisement, may be a clue that the program is simply an online version of a boring experience.

For the most part, however, institutions that have a history of offering online degree programs also have adequate online education support infrastructures. Some of the more established providers of online MBA programs, such as the University of Maryland University College, Regis University, Athabasca University, the University of Florida, and Indiana University, have built efficient teaching, learning, and technology centers that have gone through the trial-and-error processes that are typically part and parcel of an institution's ability to provide effective online programs.

This does not mean, however, that smaller institutions are not capable of creating academically sound online learning environments. For example, Marist College, a relatively small AACSB-accredited private, nonprofit school in Poughkeepsie, New York, and the first college in New York State to gain approval to offer its entire MBA program online, is steeped in a unique collaborative culture known for its community building and personalized services. Marist has figured out how to transfer that culture to the online modality.

Basically the amount of knowledge and skills acquired in an online program should be no different from what's provided in its equivalent on-campus MBA program. "Online learning gives people a new approach or new modality (for teaching and learning), but it does not necessarily mean that the quality of the educational process is going to be anything less," says Tina Royal, director of technology training, Marist College.

Keep that quality factor in mind at all times as you go through the decision-making process of where you want to get your online MBA.

The Least You Need to Know

- Make sure the online MBA program you are thinking about enrolling in has incorporated competency-based teaching and learning techniques into its courses.
- Look for some innovative practices that a business school might be using that support competency-based learning.
- Find out how the program uses case studies and team-based projects throughout its curriculum.
- Try to get a sense for what kind of course-development support the institution provides to its online programs.

Part 3

Getting Started

The nuts and bolts of the application and financial-aid process are discussed in this part of the book. You'll discover that programs can be divided into low, medium, and high admission requirements and which way application trends are moving. You'll learn how to prepare for the GMAT and what you need to understand about essays, statements of purpose, interviews, resumés, and letters of recommendation.

The student loan process is reviewed, with information about the types of loans you need to consider and what forms you will need to fill out. Some information about scholarships and what military personnel can take advantage of is also presented. And finally, you get a complete overview of the technical requirements.

Chapter 11

Getting In

In This Chapter

- Low, medium, and high levels of admission requirements
- Information about application trends
- How to prepare for taking the GMAT
- Advice on admission requirements
- The University of Florida's admission process

To put it succinctly and in very general terms, some online MBA program admission requirements are more stringent and competitive than others. It's simply your job to find out what those requirements are and then decide whether the odds of getting accepted at any particular institution are worth the effort. After all, you don't want to waste your time going through all the paperwork, and possibly testing, of an admissions process only to find out you're not accepted.

This chapter provides an overview of admission requirements and some strategies for how you should meet them.

What's Required?

To give you an overall sense of admission requirements, the following examples reveal a spectrum of different admission processes that I have personally qualified as having either low, medium, or high standards. My personal definitions for these three categories, based on extensive research and interviews I have conducted as an education journalist, are as follows:

- **Low admission requirements.** These are schools that accept just about any applicant as long as the applicant has an undergraduate degree.
- **Medium admission requirements.** Similar to low admission requirements in that a high percentage of applicants get accepted, but you have to jump through more hoops to meet all the requirements.
- **High admission requirements.** These are more selective than most schools, requiring that you meet a longer list of more specific requirements than the "medium" programs. Schools with high admission requirements may reject anywhere from 25 percent to 60 percent of applicants. However, they typically have a prescreening process, whereby they will politely advise those prospective students who don't look acceptable not to apply, or to work harder at boosting their acceptability factors before they actually go through the application process.

The following examples should give you a better sense for how low, median, and high admission requirements are applied to online MBA programs.

Schools with Low Admission Requirements

Capella University, the University of Phoenix, and Jones International, three for-profit institutions, fit into this category of having low admission requirements. All three of these schools do not require prospective students to take the Graduate Management Admission Test (GMAT), nor do they stipulate that applicants need much more than a Bachelor's degree in order to be accepted into their programs. The University of Maryland University College (UMUC) also fits into this category, because it, too, does not require applicants to take the GMAT.

UMUC does, however, require all of its newly accepted online MBA students to take a one-credit MBA Fundamentals course (described in Chapter 15) that gets them off and running in the program. Also, students can opt out of the fundamentals course if they took the GMAT test and achieved a score of 600 or higher. With regard to its

Bachelor's degree requirement, UMUC stipulates that applicants' official undergraduate transcripts must indicate a cumulative grade-point average (GPA) of at least 3.0 on a 4.0 scale. Capella University stipulates a 2.7 cumulative GPA, and the University of Phoenix and Jones International stipulate a 2.5 cumulative GPA for their Bachelor's degree requirement.

In my opinion, the fact that these schools all have requirements that give every applicant with a Bachelor's degree a very likely chance of being accepted does not mean that their online MBA programs are any easier to graduate from than online MBA programs that have more stringent requirements.

Instant Message

"Our admission requirements are pretty straightforward. Students must have an undergraduate degree from an accredited university to be admitted. Student writing skills will be assessed to see if they need a remedial course. They must pass AMBA 600—MBA Fundamentals, which is, in part, a screening tool, as well as a method of orienting the students to online learning, MBA culture, and as a primer for the skills they need to succeed in the program."

—Rosemary Hartigan, director of online MBA program, University of Maryland University College

Schools with Medium Admission Requirements

Schools with medium admission requirements will stipulate that students must take the GMAT test, but not stipulate that a particular score must be achieved. They may also stipulate that applicants have a certain number of years of work experience, and a number of other general requirements, such as letters of recommendation, a resumé, an essay, and an interview. Some schools that fit into this medium category include Regis University, University of Massachusetts (UMass) Amherst, Florida State University (FSU), and Portland State University (PSU).

Regis University is a bit less stringent in its GMAT requirement, stipulating that two analytical essays can replace the test. UMass Amherst requires the GMAT and explains in its admissions overview statement that admission to its program is also based on "academic history, GMAT performance, motivation, aptitude for graduate-level work, and managerial experience." It also states that "no one academic background is favored in the selection of candidates," and that "candidates with full-time work experience are preferred." FSU states in its admission requirements that applicants should have "a general knowledge of accounting, finance, economics, and statistics. PSU states that "two years of full-time career-related work experience is preferred at the time of admission, but may be waived with a strong GPA and/or GMAT scores." PSU also stipulates that it wants applicants who have a "knowledge of introductory calculus and microcomputer applications, including word processing, spreadsheets, database software, and presentation software."

Instant Message

"We look at their transcripts, references, and writing and evaluate all that before we conduct an interview. We will then make a decision with them and basically let them know if they have a deficiency. Students have some choice. It is not likely that we will have a student applying for admission with poor writing skills, but they do have alternatives, such as enrolling in an online writing course or an online critical thinking course."
—Regis University MBA professor Ed Cooper

Schools with High Admission Requirements

These will have very similar requirements as medium schools but they will explain their admission requirements in more detail. In other words, you'll have to jump through a few more hoops to get recognized. Some schools that fit into this category include Indiana University, University of Florida, Syracuse University, Arizona State University (ASU), and Penn State World Campus. (By the way, these schools also have the highest tuition costs.)

In addition to your undergraduate GPA, Indiana University considers "your area of concentration, the balance of verbal and communications courses with quantitative and analytical courses, and the trend of your grades." Indiana University adds that "no matter what your academic experience or how unusual your background, we encourage you to apply."

University of Florida explicitly states that they are "very selective," with its admissions committee "interested in work-related responsibilities and accomplishments, career advancement and potential, managerial or international experience, and future career goals."

Syracuse University notes that admission into its iMBA program is "highly selective," adding, "historically one of the school's greatest strengths has been the diversity of its student body. We continue to seek candidates with diverse racial, ethnic, social, academic, and professional backgrounds and career goals."

ASU asks its applicants to "please include insights into your professional maturity, team participation experiences and academic potential" in their required "statement of purpose." They also "suggest you consider mentioning highlights of your personal background, formative events/circumstances, honors, community activities, and career-path experiences and aspirations."

Penn State World Campus seeks applicants with "coursework in accounting, economics, math, and statistics." Penn State also stipulates that "admissions decisions are based on the quality of the applicant's credentials relative to those of other applicants."

Instant Message

"We definitely look at what somebody has been doing in their career. How focused have they been? What kind of accomplishments have they been able to complete? How solid is that work experience and the direction in which they are heading professionally? Academically we clearly take a stronger look at students that have participated in peer institutions—nationally renowned four-year institutions, in addition to their GPA. And finally we require the GMAT for every single one of our students."

—Alex Sevilla, director of Executive and Professional MBA Programs, University of Florida

What Else About Admissions?

Many of the schools that I have talked with are not real specific about how many students apply to their program and how many ultimately get accepted. However, I think for the schools that have high admission requirements, which are typically lock-step cohort programs that can only accept a set number of students each term, the standard procedure is for the program's administrators to act as gatekeepers who advise prospective students on their good or not-so-good odds of getting accepted before they go through the entire admissions process.

At the schools that have medium admission requirements and are also lock-step programs with caps on the number of students they accept, it could become just as competitive as the schools with high admission requirements, depending on the school you are applying to. For example, FSU, which is a lock-step cohort program, received

167 prospective student applicants for the fall 2004 launch of its very first offering of online MBA programs, which consists of a general MBA and concentrations in hospitality administration and real estate finance and analysis. The program accepted 66 students, and 53 enrolled.

The reason for the competitive nature of FSU's program launch could be due to a number of factors, including the fact that it has a large alumni base of business undergraduate students who were initially seeking to enroll in the program, along with having relatively low tuition costs. For 2004, the cost was $18,695 for non-Florida residents, and $17,493 for Florida residents. Of the 66 students who were accepted into the program, 28 were FSU alumni, and 47 were Florida residents.

The bottom line is it all depends on the school. For those schools with medium to high admission requirements, you'll have to feel out the admissions process and your odds of getting accepted by talking to the administrators and/or counselors of the program before you start filling out forms, writing essays, and taking the GMAT.

Application Trends

Although no statistical data is available related to online MBA applicants, from a national perspective, some trends concerning the growth and decline in the number of applicants in traditional MBA programs can be inferred based on a recent study conducted by the Graduate Management Admission Council (GMAC; provider of the GMAT).

GMAC published a 2004 Application Trends Survey that tracked the percent change in the number of graduate business school applications for enrollment in the 2003–2004 school year and compared it to the number of applications in the 2002–2003 school year. The survey revealed that 78 percent of full-time, two-year business graduate programs experienced a decline in the 2003–2004 application cycle compared to 2002–2003. On the other side of this decline, however, 53 percent of Executive MBA (EMBA) programs reported an increase in application volume. Some educators see this growth trend in EMBAs, which are geared toward adult working professionals, as a positive predictor of future growth in online MBA programs that target a very similar student demographic.

Basically, prospective MBA students, in general, are increasingly seeking out programs that allow them to maintain their jobs while earning their degrees. This trend is likely to increase as more students are estimated to start entering the application pool in 2005. Also, as employers and prospective students alike become more cognizant of the availability and quality of online MBA programs, the competition could become stronger for getting accepted into schools with medium to high admission requirements. It could also mean that the schools with low admission requirements will continue to see an increase in the number of applicants to their online MBA programs.

The University of Phoenix (low admission requirements) is a perfect example of how this trend is already occurring; its fully online MBA program and FlexNet (part online and part face to face) MBA program have continued to grow substantially in the number of students enrolled over recent years.

At Penn State World Campus, "Online applications are increasing each year," says John Fizel, iMBA program director. "We are up about 25 percent each year, and we probably admit around 50 percent, or more, of the people who apply."

Stat

The U.S. Department of Education (based on population data projections) predicts an upward trend in the number of Master's degrees conferred that will start in 2005 and last through 2011. Source: "Application Trends Survey 2004," Graduate Management Admission Council.

Preparing for the Admission Process

If you are entertaining the possibility of applying to a school with medium to high admissions requirements, you will need to address three primary measures of applicant quality:

- GMAT score
- Essays and/or Statements of Purpose
- Interviews

Most schools will also ask for one or two letters of recommendation from professionals you have worked with or studied under, and they will suggest that these letters address both your academic and business acumen.

All these measures combined become your admissions packet that an admissions committee will review.

The GMAT

The first thing you need to tell yourself about the GMAT is "Don't worry about it." Taking this test, particularly for adult working professionals who have been out of school for a good number of years, is often the cause of a great deal of unnecessary anxiety.

"I tell applicants to approach the GMAT with confidence," says Penn State's Fizel. "You can do that in a number of ways. One is to recognize that it is something you have to do. Recognize that if you are a competent student, competent businessperson, competent individual in the professional business world, you can do well on the GMAT."

What's on the GMAT?

The GMAT is comprised of three components: verbal, quantitative, and analytical writing. The writing component was added to the test in 1994 based on the input of business schools and recruiters who emphasized that graduates should be skilled in effectively analyzing and presenting arguments, says Daphne Atkinson, GMAC's vice president of industry relations. For the quantitative component, test takers can expect arithmetic, basic algebra, and basic geometry questions. The verbal component measures reading comprehension and a person's ability to evaluate arguments and correct written material to conform to standard written English.

Instant Message

"If you were to pin me down and ask what does the GMAT really tell us in addition to it being a general aptitude and ability test, I would say that we have discovered that it is a good indication of somebody's ability to successfully complete an MBA program on the quantitative side."
—Alex Sevilla, director of Executive and Professional MBA Programs, University of Florida

Everything you need to know about the GMAT is available at GMAC's MBA.com website at www.mba.com/mba/TaketheGMAT. Atkinson adds that the test "is not a predictor. The GMAT does not attempt to say that its *raison d'etre* is to predict success in a career, but it was designed when used in conjunction with an undergraduate GPA, to give you a notion of the probability that someone will be successful academically. It measures constructs that have been validated for and predictive of success in the core requirements, which are often quite quantitative."

Getting Ready for the GMAT

To state the obvious, doing well on the GMAT will require that you prepare for it. "Take a few practice exams to allay the anxiety you may have," says Fizel. "It will improve your mental approach to the exam as well as increase your knowledge about the procedures and content. We find that preparation always improves scores. So if you just take your time, if you do it in a relaxed manner, most of the time you will do fine."

Atkinson says you may need to do more than simply take a few practice tests. She advises prospective test takers to start with a downloadable free software tool, located at the MBA.com website, called POWERPREP, which contains computer-adapted tests that will allow you to perform a diagnostic analysis of your strengths and weaknesses. POWERPREP features practice questions, with answers and explanations for each question, the ability to compute your score in real time, computer-based tutorials, and online help.

When you register for the GMAT, you may also choose to have a free CD-ROM version of POWERPREP mailed to you. It takes two weeks for delivery within the United States and four weeks for delivery to other locations.

"Understand what it is you are not getting right," says Atkinson. "That is the first thing. The second thing is to decide whether or not what you are not getting requires remedial help from outside. Is it that you forgot it, or is it that you did not learn it? If it is the latter, you may need to take a business math course, for example, at a community college during the summer term."

If you have simply forgot what you once learned, then you basically have two choices: Buckle down and study to refresh your memory, or pay for a test-preparation service to help you buckle down and study to refresh your memory. For the self-motivated, one way of studying is to purchase GMAC's most recent edition of *The Official Guide for GMAT Review*, which contains more than 1,400 multiple-choice questions found on the actual GMAT, along with explanations prepared by test authors. The guide also has analytical writing assessment topics, a math review, and test-taking tips. At the time of this writing, the guide was selling for $29.95, plus shipping and handling, via the MBA.com website. You can attack your study plan by combining this guidebook with the free POWERPREP tool; plus, for an additional $25, you can practice taking three downloadable GMAT paper tests. These are tests that are "retired" and out of circulation and include timed sections, an answer sheet, and a way to convert your raw score to the equivalent GMAT score.

You can find plenty of places online to get practice tests and web-based help for taking the GMAT, and many local and national companies provide face-to-face classes or have professional private tutors walk students through test preparation, both of which are typically pricey options. Depending on the instructional package and provider, face-to-face classes at some of the test-preparation providers can cost well over $1,000, and private tutors can reach to more than $2,000. GMAC does not endorse one method of test preparation over others, says Atkinson. "We do say that familiarity with the test is an important part of doing well on the GMAT."

Instant Message

"Our program is not designed for people who are good test takers; it is designed for people who are conscientious. It requires discipline and the ability to apply what you learn as opposed to being able to take a test."

—Rosemary Hartigan, director of online MBA program, University of Maryland University College

Following is a short list of additional GMAT-preparation alternatives, provided both online and face to face:

- **Test Prep Review.** Located at www.testprepreview.com/gmat_practice.htm, this free online service features self-assessment quizzes that keep your score and can reveal learning gaps. Also provides links to numerous online resources that can help improve your weak areas. The quizzes cover basic and advanced algebra, geometry, basic and advanced grammar, reading comprehension, and much more.
- **The Princeton Review.** Located at www.princetonreview.com/mba/testprep/default.asp, this company provides classroom-based, online, private tutoring, books, and other course materials for students who are willing to pay for GMAT test-preparation services. The Princeton Review has offices, where both the physical classes and private tutoring are conducted, across the country. The website has a search function that shows you where the closest office to your zip code is located.
- **Kaplan Test Prep.** Located at www.kaptest.com (click on the Business link), this company is similar to The Princeton Review in that it also provides classroom-based, online, private tutoring services, books, and other course materials for test preparation; it also has offices located across the country.
- **800score.com.** Located at www.800score.com/, this company offers a variety of software and downloadable test-preparation guides. Check out their free online Sample GMAT Math section.
- **Check with an institution nearby.** Most institutions have testing support service centers or academic resource centers on campus that provide classroom-based GMAT test-preparation courses to the public. Their prices are typically

competitive and worth researching. For example, the University of Baltimore, which has an online MBA program, provides a 14-hour live GMAT Quantitative Review course, held from 9 A.M. to 12:30 P.M. on four consecutive Saturdays, for $85. Many institutions have similar test-preparation services.

Another Point of View About the GMAT

As noted previously, not all online MBA programs require the GMAT, which, to me, is fine and good. However, schools that do require the GMAT might tell you otherwise. I personally have always believed that these kinds of tests are a waste of time, especially for people like me who are horrible test takers. Perhaps I am biased about this topic, but it goes back many years ago when I had to take the Graduate Record Exam. The night before taking that test I was so anxious that I could not sleep. The following morning I had to get up early and drive 1.5 hours to the nearest testing location. About one month before the test, I began a daily review trying to cram everything I learned as an undergraduate back into my brain. By the time I put pencil to paper on that fateful test day, I was frazzled. Needless to say, I did very poorly. Does that mean I'm not capable of being a successful student? Absolutely not. Does it mean that I'm a lousy test taker? Absolutely yes.

When you look at the big picture, there seems to be compelling evidence to support both sides of the test-taking issue. Some educators argue that the GMAT test can weed out students who would possibly disrupt the team and community building of an online course due to their lack of appropriate academic skills. Other educators argue that numerous adult, working professionals would contribute immensely to any MBA curriculum if only they weren't eliminated from the process because of a GMAT requirement.

Instant Message

"We know that with working adults, in particular—whether it is the GRE or the GMAT, or whatever—these tests are not good in terms of predictive validity relating to whether they will succeed. You find out very quickly if a person is going to succeed or not once they get into class. You set the bar, and they will show you that they can do it, or they will self-select out if they cannot do it."

—Craig Swenson, provost and senior vice president for academic affairs, University of Phoenix

Writing Essays and Statements of Purpose

As noted in Chapter 16, writing skills are very important as an online student. A small number of online MBA programs with medium to high admission requirements screen out applicants with poor communication competencies by having them submit an essay and/or a personal statement as part of their admission requirements. These essays/statements also serve as a means to qualify applicants in relation to their overall business skills and personal integrity.

At Indiana University, for instance, online MBA applicants are asked to "give examples of leadership and discuss career goals" in their personal statements. The University of Florida asks applicants to submit written essays to "convey one's unique background, personality, and ability to add to the diversity of the Florida MBA programs." Overall, however, most online MBA programs do not have this admission requirement.

Interviews

After reviewing application packets, a few online MBA programs with medium to high admission requirements invite applicants in for an interview. In the online world, these are typically held through a phone conference; however, if a student happens to live close by, these interviews can be conducted in person.

Paula O'Callaghan, director of Syracuse University's iMBA program, takes a personalized approach and interviews each iMBA applicant by telephone or in person. She adds that the iMBA admissions process is similar to what one might find in a good Executive MBA program. "In the online environment, you are dealing with people with a lot of work experience and very little time," says O'Callaghan. "It is almost embarrassing to turn them down. So I want to avoid that. These are people in their 30s and 40s. I don't want them to have to go through all this trouble only to get turned down."

Get Your Resumé Together

Most programs with medium to high admission requirements will ask for your resumé. It goes without saying that you should have a professional-looking, well-written resumé. Give it a good once over and make sure it looks good and is well written.

In particular, make sure you have a dynamite objective and mission statement right up front that relates to your goals and aspirations as a business professional in a very upbeat and positive way. If you don't have the time or inclination to do this, hire a professional resumé service to help you.

Letters of Recommendation

Most programs with medium to high admission requirements ask for two letters of recommendation. I don't mean to sound cynical, but has anyone out there ever seen a poor letter of recommendation? If you are not an idiot, you'll ask your favorite colleague, former professor, boss, and/or other high-level executive to write a letter that you know will shine brightly. So this requirement also seems to fit into a category of not being an accurate measure of a person's true capabilities. Nonetheless, you will find this criterion listed on many programs with medium to high admission requirements.

Instant Message

"There are reasonable rationales for every type of program, and there is no one program type that anyone should feel is better than or less than another. It depends on what your personal circumstances are, and what you are hoping to get out of a program. Regardless, program quality is critical."

—Daphne Atkinson, GMAC's vice president of industry relations.

Some programs are very specific about what kind of letters they want. For example, Portland State University points prospective students to the "Apply Effectively" section of GMAC's MBA.com website, which states that "meaningful recommendations provide specific information that demonstrates your ability to excel in both an MBA program and a business or professional career." It goes on to advise students to obtain letters of recommendation that "confirm or elaborate on your credentials, strengths, and aspirations."

A Google search using the term "letters of recommendation" will bring you lots of advice from career counselors about how to organize such letters and what kind of information should go in them. Here's a short list of suggestions for letters of recommendation in relation to business school applications:

- Try to have your letter writer focus the content of the letter toward what a business school would be looking for in a graduate candidate, such as self-discipline, analytical skills, communication skills, interpersonal skills, leadership skills, and intellectual strengths.

- Stress your ability to work well with others, your integrity, your reliability, and your energy and dedication to commit to a rigorous academic challenge.
- List all honors and awards you have received throughout your life, as well as any academic-oriented accomplishments you feel are worthy of noting.

Finally, my personal opinion is don't write your own letter for someone to sign and edit, which is a common practice. However, I do suggest you explain to any prospective recommendation letter writer that you would prefer that they focus their writing around some of the aforementioned topics. Also, be very gracious and appreciative when asking anyone to go to bat for you.

Transferring Credit Earned

Another aspect of the admissions process that could come into play deals with the prospect of transferring in previous credits earned. Some adult learners, for instance, may have started but never completed graduate-level courses in the field of business in the past through a different program than the one they are applying to.

If you earned such graduate-level credits at a regionally accredited institution and are applying to another regionally accredited institution, you may be able to transfer 25 percent or less of the total credit needed to attain the degree. However, regardless of accreditation status, every program handles credit transferability issues differently. How long ago you earned such previous credit as well as the nature of the courses you took are all taken into consideration in such circumstances. Basically, there are no guarantees that your credit will be automatically accepted.

UF's Point of View

Because the University of Florida (UF) has, in my view, one of the most selective online MBA admission standards in the country, I spoke with Alex Sevilla, director of its Executive and Professional MBA Programs, about UF's overall philosophy concerning the quality of students it accepts. I believe his response can be used as a basic guideline for getting accepted into any of the programs that have what can be considered high admission requirements.

First, Sevilla says, in addition to looking at an applicant's professional experience, academic credentials and GPA, every applicant, even if he or she is a senior vice president, must take the GMAT. "It's a valid assessment," he says. Second, to "maximize the learning environment for everyone" in the UF iMBA program, admitted students need to have the aptitude to understand statistics, economics, and the quantitative side of accounting and finance. "We would really be doing someone a disservice if we were to admit them into this rigorous iMBA program, without these quantitative skills, especially if they are keeping their job, working 50 to 60 plus hours a week, and trying to fit this into a very busy life," Sevilla says.

Sevilla also stresses that any student seeking admission into the UF iMBA program must have realistic expectations. "This is a tough program, and you have to have a commitment across the board, at home, at work, in your personal life and professional life—because you are looking at 15 to 20 hours a week." Finally, your overall expectations must be aligned with working hard and ultimately gaining knowledge, "not just a piece of paper that you are going to hang on a wall."

Of course, UF's iMBA program is not the only tough program out there. In fact, the vast majority of online MBA programs are very challenging and time-consuming, to say the least. Regardless of the admission requirements any particular program has, once you get accepted, be prepared to travel down a road that will require you to drive hard with a full tank of determination and brainpower.

The Least You Need to Know

- Online MBA programs have admission requirements that vary from easy to difficult, depending on your background and the specific program.
- As more people learn about online MBA programs, the competitiveness for getting accepted could increase.
- You must decide if it is worth your effort to take the GMAT based on the program(s) you are interested in and whether you can adequately prepare for this test.
- Depending on the program, you need to put forth your best and most intelligent effort at meeting all admission requirements.

Chapter 12

Paying for Your Degree

In This Chapter

- Tuition estimates
- Financial-aid options
- How to fill out the FAFSA
- Advice about employer reimbursement
- Information about tax issues

We have come to that familiar and dreaded place where the financial realities of getting an education bear down upon our bank accounts. We come to the stark realization that we must get creative and figure out how to meet those tuition payment deadlines. And then those familiar words stare us in the face: *financial aid.* But we haven't got a clue where to start. Plus, as an adult learner, your options are somewhat limited, especially when compared to the younger traditional-aged students who have many more opportunities for a wider variety of financial-aid packages than adult learners.

Fear not, dear reader. There is hope. But before we start to look at what kind of financial aid may or may not be available to you, we need to take a look at what this online MBA pursuit is going to actually cost.

Tuition

Chapter 1 briefly explained how tuition costs can vary greatly, and showed some example costs at several institutions. The table that follows features 12 examples of tuition costs of online MBA programs. It does not include application, graduation, technology, books and course materials, residency-related fees, or any other incidental fees that may apply.

It is provided to give you only a general sense about the cost of earning an online MBA. For information about tuition costs at schools not listed in this chapter, check out the specific school's costs online (see Appendix B). If you cannot ascertain the actual costs from a school's website, just telephone and ask for an enrollment counselor who can provide that information.

Tuition Estimates for 2004–2005 Academic Year

School	Cost
Arizona State University	$34,000
Capella University	$26,000
Indiana University	$39,600
Penn State World Campus	$40,752
Portland State University	$21,528
Regis University	$20,520
Syracuse University	$43,524
UMass Amherst	$22,200
University of Colorado at Colorado Springs	$18,070
University of Maryland University College	$25,026
University of Florida	$32,600
University of Phoenix	$24,525

Note that these 12 institutions charge the same tuition for both state residents and nonresidents. Some schools have in-state and out-of-state resident tuition rates for their online students. Also be aware that these prices are subject to change. Check with an institution's registration and/or financial-aid offices before coming to any solid conclusions about cost.

Guide on the Side

Remember, as a prospective student, you are a potential customer who is a valuable source of revenue for any school. If you call up a school and speak to an enrollment counselor, you do not have to give them your name or any other personal information. Just like many business inquiries, you can just ask about the cost and the processes of applying for admission and financial aid.

How Will I Pay for This?

To cut right to the chase, as a graduate student, if you can't pay for your education out of your own pocket, you are pretty much confined to the following four financial-aid options (unless you are in the military):

- A federal Stafford Loan, which can be either *subsidized* or *unsubsidized*
- A private loan, usually referred to as an alternative loan
- A scholarship (typically very limited availability, but they do exist)
- Employer reimbursement (getting more difficult as employers, in general, seem to be cutting back)

Online Term

A **subsidized** federal Stafford Loan is awarded to a student based on financial need, and it includes the provision of not being charged any interest while you are attending school and you continue to meet the basic eligibility requirements of the loan. An **unsubsidized** federal Stafford Loan is one that is not awarded to a student on the basis of financial need, and it includes being charged interest from the time the loan is granted.

The **Free Application for Federal Student Aid (FAFSA)** is a form in which students provide their income, asset, and tax information to be considered for federally funded financial aid, including government-backed subsidized and unsubsidized Stafford Loans for graduate-level students.

If you do attempt to obtain any sort of financial aid, make sure to time your application to correspond appropriately with your admissions application. For example, the Stafford Loan acceptance process typically takes about 30 days. However, it can take as long as 90 days (depending on the efficiency of your intended school's admissions process and whether all forms are completed correctly, for example). In contrast, private loans are generally processed more quickly (often in five or fewer days). The bottom line is to make sure that all of your financial-aid paperwork is processed well enough in advance of when classes begin.

Federal Stafford Loans

If you need to take out a loan to pay for your online MBA, consider applying for a subsidized or unsubsidized federal Stafford Loan. Stafford Loans are low-interest loans on which you can defer repayment until six months after you graduate. These loans are the biggest source of financial aid for all graduate students, and they basically come in two flavors: a Direct Loan or a Federal Family Education Loan (FFEL). According to the U.S. Department of Education, the terms and conditions of a Direct Stafford Loan or a FFEL Stafford Loan are similar. "The main difference, however, is that you receive FFEL funds from private lenders (such as banks, credit unions, or other lenders that participate in the FFEL program). Direct Loan funds come from the federal government to your school, which delivers the proceeds to you."

To qualify for a Stafford Loan, you must complete the federal government's *Free Application for Federal Student Aid (FAFSA)* form, along with any other forms the institution you are applying to may require.

Online MBA students can accumulate up to $138,500 in Stafford Loan debt over the duration of their higher education, which includes any Stafford Loans one may have received as an undergraduate. Only $65,000 of this amount may be in subsidized loans.

> CAUTION
>
> **MBAware**
>
> When applying for financial aid, ask your school's financial-aid office how, precisely, they determine whether you are officially considered a half-time student in order to qualify you for a Stafford Loan.

According to Ellen Blackmun, director of technology initiatives and distance learning at the Washington, D.C.-based National Association of Student Financial Aid Administrators, many adult students think that they can't qualify for Stafford Loans when, in fact, anyone can qualify for an unsubsidized Stafford Loan as long as they meet some relatively minimum eligibility requirements.

With unsubsidized loans, you are responsible for interest as soon as the loan is granted. You can pay that interest as it accrues, or you can defer that interest until after graduation. Deferred interest is capitalized, which means that it's added to the full balance of the loan you will ultimately be responsible for after you graduate.

You may qualify for a subsidized Stafford Loan if you demonstrate financial need, which is determined based on the information you submit on your FAFSA form.

Stafford Loan interest rates change every July 1 and have a cap of 8.25 percent. The interest rate for the 2004–2005 period is 2.77 percent for students while they are enrolled. During repayment and forbearance periods, the interest rate for the 2004–2005 academic year for loans disbursed after July 1, 1998 is 2.82 percent.

The one requirement that prevents some students from applying for these loans is that you have to be at least a half-time student, which is basically determined according to the way a school offers its courses. Generally, a half-time graduate student is someone who takes at least three graduate-level credits per term. For example, if you were enrolled in the University of Phoenix online MBA program, you could take one 3-credit, 6-week course at a time in succession, but they have to be no more than 29 days apart from each other in order for you to be considered half-time. If you were in the Regis University online MBA program, you would have to take at least one 3-credit, 8-week course over the duration of a semester, which at Regis lasts about 16 weeks.

Each school determines half-time status differently. The bottom line is that to qualify for a Stafford Loan, you must be committed to staying the course at least part-time without skipping semesters. Otherwise, you may have to immediately start paying back your loan. If you can't devote the time to earn your MBA under the half-time guidelines, you can always investigate private loan possibilities, which typically have no mandatory continuous attendance criteria.

For more information about Stafford Loans, visit www.studentaid.ed.gov.

Filling Out the FAFSA

Plain and simple, if you want to qualify for a Stafford Loan, you must fill out the FAFSA. Doing so is not as onerous a process as many adult learners, who have not gone to school in years, may believe it to be. If you are like me, you may have visions from your days-gone-past undergraduate years of physically visiting a financial-aid office and waiting in a long line for some hapless bureaucrat to provide you with the right paperwork and a list of mundane instructions. Today that's no longer the case. "The financial-aid process is not so much a people process anymore," says Blackmum. "It is a processing of applications online; and if you are planning to go to school online, I think it can be assumed that you have some capabilities on the computer."

So, dear reader, your job, if you choose to take it on, will be to eventually visit the FAFSA website at www.fafsa.ed.gov and begin the application process for getting a Stafford Loan.

Filling out the FAFSA online is the quickest way to submit this all-important document to the U.S. Department of Education's Central Processing System (CPS). The online process is also sophisticated enough to immediately identify potential errors and thus allow you to make the necessary corrections as you are filling out the form.

Before you actually begin filling out this form, however, you need to get a Personal Identification Number (PIN) that becomes your electronic signature. You can acquire your PIN by visiting www.pin.ed.gov/PINWebApp/pinindex.jsp and filling out an online form in which you supply your name, Social Security number, date of birth, mailing address, and e-mail address. After you submit this form, it takes approximately three business days to receive an e-mail notification with instructions on how to retrieve it electronically, or 7 to 10 days to receive it in the mail via the U.S. Postal Service. Your PIN will also give you access to return to the FAFSA website to check on the status of your application.

CAUTION

MBAware

If you want to practice filling out the FAFSA form, or have a guide to filling it out before or during the real deal online, you can download a pre-application worksheet in PDF format at www.fafsa.ed.gov/before012.htm. The worksheet is made up of all the application questions in the same order as you would see them on the web.

According to the U.S. Department of Education, the most common errors on the FAFSA happen in the sections related to income, and they strongly advise that you have your past year's income tax return on hand when applying. Also remember to save all the records you use to fill out the form. You might need them if you are selected for a process called verification; this process requires you to submit copies of your tax returns and/or wage-earning statements to the school.

After Applying for a Loan

First of all, if four weeks pass without hearing anything after you submit your FAFSA, contact the Federal Student Aid Information Center at 1-800-433-3243. Within four weeks, you should have received a Student Aid Report (SAR), which lists all the information you reported on the FAFSA. You are required to review this information to ensure it is correct. Your school will use your SAR as the basis for determining your eligibility and will process your Stafford Loan for the total loan amount that you are offered and notify you with a financial-aid award notice.

In the final stage of your loan, the school, if a direct Stafford Loan, or the lender, if a FFEL Stafford Loan, will generate a Master Promissory Note (MPN) for you to sign, either electronically with your PIN or by hand via snail mail. The funds will be disbursed through the school or the lender and will first go toward your tuition payments, with any possible funds remaining being sent directly to you by check or, if you so desire and have completed the necessary paperwork, by an electronic funds transfer.

MBAware

Be aware that every institution handles the basic processing of Stafford Loans differently through their various administrative systems. So your safest *modus operandi* is to contact the school's financial-aid office and have them walk you through the financial-aid process to ensure that you take the appropriate steps.

Private Loans

You should consider taking out a private loan only if you do not plan on being an official half-time online MBA student and/or you need to supplement a Stafford Loan. Private loans have higher interest rates and come in a wide variety of packages. They are available through the competitive lender marketplace, with many lenders offering benefits to students, such as low up-front fees and a variety of repayment incentives. So you'll have to shop around. Generally, the financial-aid office at your school will offer a list of lenders that you can consider, but they will not recommend any one lender over another.

Guide on the Side

Estudentloan.com features a LoanFinder online service that provides instant comparisons and online applications that match a student's specific lending needs with up to 12 private loan programs.

Scholarships

Generally speaking, online MBA programs do not offer a whole lot of scholarships, and if they do, they usually award relatively small amounts. This does not mean, however, that you should disregard this possibility.

At the University of Maryland University College, for instance, you could qualify for a number of scholarship awards made on the basis of academic performance and/or financial need that are offered on the institutional level.

Arizona State University (ASU) participates in a Future of Learning Online MBA Fellowship, sponsored by NextStudent, an education funding company that awards several $2,500 scholarships to ASU online MBA students. Potential recipients must submit an essay that "outlines their need for financial assistance and the direct affect the fellowship would have on improving their unique situation."

Bottom line with scholarships is that you have to ask the financial-aid office what might be available, because, typically, they don't promote these things unless asked. In short, you have to take it upon yourself to find whatever kind of financial assistance might be available to you. "Adult students have to be more proactive," says Blackmum. "They don't get the handholding (like traditional-aged students). They don't get the financial-aid nights that are held at high schools. They don't get any of this because it is assumed that if they are adults going back to school, they can do this on their own, which isn't always the case."

Employer Reimbursement

"Being more proactive" also applies to online MBA students who want to seek reimbursement from their employer. Employer reimbursement packages are starting to come of age in the world of online MBA programs as more employers learn that the online learning environment does, indeed, have its benefits. For one, online students don't have to take days off or leave early from their jobs to physically attend classes. Even in the flexible Executive MBA environment, spending Saturdays and/or early evenings on campus can often conflict with a busy professional's job responsibilities.

Nonetheless, prospective online MBA students seeking employer reimbursement must often (even today) prove to their bosses and human resources managers that the online environment is, indeed, a valid way to earn an MBA. A lot of employers are still in the dark ages about online degree programs, especially older executives who may not be so Internet savvy or cognizant of how education technology is changing the way people teach and learn.

In contrast, much of corporate America has adopted and created very sophisticated online learning environments for training employees and providing numerous professional-development experiences. In the corporate world, this is commonly referred to as e-learning. These Internet-based training and professional-development environments are not only effective from a teaching and learning point of view, they are also saving companies millions of dollars in (now unnecessary) travel costs. For example, because of e-learning, employees working for the same company but located in different regions no longer have to convene as frequently in the same physical space to learn and collaborate with each other.

Remember, therefore, employer reimbursement for an online MBA program will depend on where you work and what kind of perceptions of online MBA education executives within your company have.

Convincing Your Boss

If you find yourself having to explain what online education is all about to convince your boss or human resources executive to help pay your tuition costs, address the specifics of the program's curriculum. "The delivery model is not as important as the content of the courses," says Rosemary Hartigan, director of the online MBA program at the University of Maryland at University College. "If they (employers) look at our curriculum they will see that it has everything, if not more than, any MBA program has. We have plenty of students who have succeeded in the online environment, and they can best speak to its value. When you have graduates in big workplaces who are successful, then the credibility builds."

If your own initiative fails to convince your boss to provide reimbursement, you can always ask the school to go to bat for you. For example, Paula O'Callaghan, Syracuse University's iMBA program director, says that for students seeking employer reimbursement she will prepare what she calls a "briefing packet," which typically addresses issues about program quality, residency requirements, financial considerations, and how long the program will take to complete. "In most cases, the briefing packets have been successful."

Instant Message

"It used to be that 75 percent of MBA students had employer support. I have heard that it is more like 50 percent now. I have also heard that the amount of employer support has been reduced dramatically."

—Paula O' Callaghan, director, iMBA Program, Syracuse University

"The explosion of online degrees has certainly caught the attention of employers. Students may ask the online institution to provide letters of support or request the program directors of online programs to talk to their HR directors to increase their confidence in the quality of online programs."

—Venkateshwar Reddy, interim dean, College of Business and Administration and the Graduate School of Business Administration, University of Colorado at Colorado Springs

Help for the Military

In Chapter 3, I described how the Defense Activity for Non-Traditional Education Support (DANTES) program and the eArmyU program are helping soldiers earn their degrees through a variety of online degree programs. There is a huge amount of information (enough for an entirely separate book) about additional financial-aid and scholarship programs available to current soldiers, their spouses and dependents, and veterans.

If you are a soldier or veteran seeking to earn an online MBA, the first place you may want to start is an institution's veteran enrollment services office, if they have one. These offices will provide you with benefit assistance, counseling/guidance, credit-evaluation assistance, and tuition deferment programs. Many MBA program websites have special sections run by veteran service departments that are devoted to military students.

If the school you are interested in does not have a noticeable veteran enrollment service office listed on its website, make sure you tell whomever you communicate with during the admissions process that you qualify for military benefits, and they should be able to provide you with the appropriate financial-aid counseling services geared toward your special needs.

Finally, for almost everything you could possibly want to know about education benefits for military personnel, go to the Education section of military.com at www.military.com/Careers/Education.

Tax Credits and Tax Deductions

As a card-carrying online MBA student you can take advantage of both tax credits and/or tax deductions, depending on your situation. A tax credit allows you to reduce the dollar amount directly off the tax you owe. A tax credit is more valuable than a tax deduction, which is an amount that you can deduct from your taxable income.

The IRS has three categories concerning tax deductions for education expenses:

- **Tuition and fee deduction.** You can only claim this if you do not claim an education tax credit. Qualifying expenses must not have been paid with any other tax-free benefit. A maximum deduction of $4,000 if taxpayer's income does not exceed $65,000 ($130,000 on a joint return); $2,000 maximum if income is between $65,000 and $80,000 (between $130,000 and $160,000, joint return). You cannot claim this deduction if your filing status is married filing separately or if another person can claim an exemption for you as a dependent on his or her tax return.

- **Deduction for work-related education.** You can claim costs of education required to keep your job or to maintain or improve skills needed in your present work, but not if the education is needed to meet the minimum requirements of your position or is part of a program to qualify you for a new trade or business. If you are self-employed, you can deduct your expenses for qualifying work-related education directly from your self-employment income. This reduces the amount of your income subject to both income tax and self-employment tax.
- **Student-loan interest deduction.** You can claim a maximum deduction of $2,500 for interest paid on qualified student loans. Phases out as income rises from $50,000 to $65,000 ($100,000 to $130,000, joint return).

Like all IRS rules and regulations, deciphering what does and does not qualify for a credit or deduction can be an awfully confusing undertaking. You may want to consult with a tax counselor or the IRS itself for more information.

Lifetime Learning Tax Credits

You can qualify for an Internal Revenue Service Lifetime Learning Credit, which is determined by tabulating what you pay for "qualified tuition and related expenses" and the amount of your modified adjusted gross income (AGI).

Expenses that qualify for a Lifetime Learning Credit are tuition and fees paid directly to the school, including expenses for books, supplies, and equipment. You are allowed a Lifetime Learning Credit of 20 percent of the first $10,000 you paid for qualified tuition and related expenses. The maximum amount of credit students could claim for 2003 was $2,000 (20 percent of $10,000).

However, that amount may be reduced based on your modified AGI. The credit is gradually reduced if your modified AGI is between $41,000 and $51,000 ($83,000 and $103,000 in the case of a joint return). You cannot claim the credit if you are married filing a separate return.

Employer-Provided Educational Assistance

It's also important to note that you cannot use education benefits under $5,250 paid for by your employer as the basis for any other deduction or credit, including the Lifetime Learning Credit.

CAUTION

MBAware

As noted by the IRS, if you receive educational benefits from your employer under an educational assistance program, you can exclude up to $5,250 of those benefits each year. This means your employer should not include the benefits with your wages, tips, and other compensation shown in box 1 of your Form W–2. This also means that you do not have to include the benefits on your income tax return. Any amount over $5,250 must be included on your Form W–2.

Employer-paid education benefits that fall under the category of tax deductions include tuition, fees, and the cost of books, supplies, and equipment necessary for your education. However, meals, lodging, transportation, tools or supplies (other than textbooks) that you keep after you complete a course, and courses involving sports, games, or hobbies that are related to your work or are not course requirements, do not fall under the category of employer-paid benefits and are not tax deductible.

For additional information on both education tax credits and tax deductions, refer to the Internal Revenue Service's Publication 970, Tax Benefits for Higher Education, located online at www.irs.gov/publications/p970/index.html.

Consolidation Loans

If you happen to have multiple federal student loans that you have accumulated over the years, you can be eligible for a consolidation loan. Consolidation loans combine these federal student loans into a single loan with a lower monthly payment. Consolidation loans also offer flexible payment plans to meet the different needs of borrowers and can extend repayment deferment options.

Keep in mind, however, that consolidation loans increase the total cost of repaying loans, because you'll agree to a longer repayment period and consequently more interest.

For more information about consolidation loans, visit http://loanconsolidation.ed.gov.

Other Financial Considerations

Finally, rather than go into all kinds of budgeting strategies to pay for your MBA, I will say that the flexibility of an online education has some financial benefits that can perhaps justify your expenses.

First, if you are self-directed, disciplined, and organized, you should be able to accomplish all your coursework at times that are outside of your mainstream job and thus remain highly productive. Upon completion, if you work at a fair and just place, you may attain a higher-paying position.

Second, many traditional MBA students take off a year or two from their jobs, without salary. You don't have to. While earning your MBA online, you can immediately apply what you learn to your work. This, in turn, could obviously turn into a quicker financial gain.

Third, if you are in a fully online program with no residency requirements, you have no transportation costs (including those pesky parking fees and fines).

The Least You Need to Know

- Adult learners are relatively limited in their financial-aid options when compared to their younger traditional-aged counterparts.
- When applying for a loan, start with the federal Stafford Loan programs. You must be an official half-time graduate student to qualify.
- If you plan to take out a private loan, shop around for a loan from any number of financial institutions.
- Not many scholarships are available for online MBA students; nonetheless, always ask financial-aid administrators whether there are any scholarships you can consider applying for.
- As employers become more cognizant of online MBA programs, the likelihood of them providing tuition reimbursement increases.
- If you need to educate your employer about online learning, focus on the content of the curriculum and ask the program administrators to provide information that can help sway a tuition-reimbursement decision in your favor.

Chapter 13

Technical Requirements

In This Chapter

- Reliable computer systems and Internet services
- A primer on your software needs
- How to protect your data
- Some advice for buyers

You need to follow two primary "technology" rules if you want your online MBA experience to go smoothly: Get the fastest Internet connection available in your area; and purchase the most efficient, well-built computer system you can afford. If you follow these two rules, everything else will fall into place.

Of course, you will still have days when your computer seems to have changed its personality, or when your broadband Internet connection seems to have gone south. However, these nasty inevitabilities of living in the Information Age will be lessened if you follow these two basic rules.

In this chapter, I've provided some general action items and advice regarding hardware and software ownership and manageability.

Your Computer System

Most online MBA programs require that students purchase their own computer equipment (hardware and software). The programs do, however, list the minimum hardware and software requirements.

If specialized equipment is necessary, the school or program might facilitate a bulk purchase of requisite technology. For example, for the 2003–2004 academic year, the University of Florida's Internet MBA program used a portion of each student's fees ($2,550 of the total $37,000) for a new, fully loaded Dell Latitude X300 laptop for each student.

Instant Message

"Have access to a computer you will enjoy using. If you are going to spend hours of your free time in front of a computer, you want it to be as enjoyable as possible. While it wasn't necessary, I bought a new system that had nothing but my schoolwork and related programs loaded on it. When I traveled and needed to do work, I transferred necessary files. I also printed quite a bit of materials."

—Linda Couch, University of Maryland University College online MBA graduate

A System to Consider

For the record, and perhaps as a guide for you to consider when you make your hardware purchase—unless your computer setup already meets or exceeds the program's requirements—here's what the University of Florida students got. (I've added some defining details and recommendations for what I consider to be the optimal system for the online MBA student.)

- **Dell Latitude X300 notebook.** This is a thin, lightweight, and sturdy laptop, which are three important considerations for those who travel frequently and require a laptop.
- **Pentium M 1.2 GHz.** The Pentium M (for mobile) is Intel's latest processor, at the time of this writing, for wireless notebook computing. The 1.2 GHz (gigahertz) is the speed of the processor. The higher the GHz, the more powerful the processor. I would not buy anything less than a Pentium IV processor, with no lower than 600 MHz (megahertz).

- **512 MB RAM.** MB stands for megabytes, and RAM stands for random access memory. The higher MB RAM, the more powerful memory your computer will have. I would not go lower than 256 MB SDRAM (synchronous dynamic random access memory), which is simply another type of memory.
- **40 GB hard disk.** This is the part of your computer that holds all your data. The GB stands for gigabytes. Higher GB means more space to store all the files and software on your computer. For your purposes as an online MBA student, 20–40 GB is more than enough space.
- **4x DVD+RW.** The University of Florida supplies its online MBA students with DVD-based lectures, so this laptop features a DVD player with rewritable media, meaning it can both copy and record DVD video discs and CD-ROMs. Other schools will typically require only a CD-ROM drive that does not need rewritable media. The 4x in front of DVD is the highest DVD recording speed available; the other DVD recording speed is 2x. CD-ROMs come in different recording speeds, from 2x to 48x. I recommend 48x for CD-ROM recording speed.

> CAUTION
>
> **MBAware**
>
> Although I am a big fan of Apple computers, having been an avid Mac user for many years until finally being forced to convert over to what I consider the harder-to-manage PC environment, you'll find that some, but not all, online MBA programs will not even suggest that you purchase a Macintosh, listing only PC requirements.

- **Internal 56K modem.** This is for a dial-up Internet connection, which I don't recommend. However, if you are traveling, you'll need this for getting online in your hotel room. If you don't travel, I recommend nothing less than a cable-modem Internet connection, for which you'll need the next item on this list. DSL (digital subscriber line) is another Internet connection service provided by your local phone company, which is not as fast as cable modem but much faster than a dial-up connection. Both DSL and cable-modem services may not be available in your local geographic area, especially if you live in a rural community that is not close to a major city. If you can't get access to DSL or cable-modem, you can consider *broadband* access by satellite through such carriers as Direcway and Starband, but expect the cost to be significantly higher primarily because of equipment and installation fees.

- **Fast Ethernet adapter.** Without going into all kinds of esoteric computer lingo, this device enables you to hook up to a cable-modem service.

- **Built-in wireless networking capabilities.** Again, without going into all kinds of esoteric computer lingo, this will enable you to connect your laptop to the Internet through wireless technology, meaning you will not have to search for a phone jack in a busy airport while you're waiting for your next flight. Instead, by utilizing a *802.11 WiFi networking connectivity service* plan and a wireless network card in the laptop, for example, users can connect to the Internet through wireless networks located at an increasing number of "hotspots." Cellular phone service providers, such as T-Mobile and Sprint, provide WiFi networking connectivity service plans in addition to their customary cell-phone plans. Hotspots are basically wireless hub devices that are stationed in airports, hotels, cafés (all Starbucks have them), libraries, your local Kinkos, and college and university campuses all over the world. The owners of these hotspots can offer free or for-a-fee Wi-Fi wireless access service (most are free). At Starbucks, you'll have to have a T-Mobile account in order to use their WiFi service. Without T-Mobile you'll have to purchase a day pass T-Mobile account. Many airports offer free Wi-Fi access, with hotspots located in certain terminals, waiting areas, or inside airline club lounges.

Online Term

Broadband allows for more types of data to be transmitted over channels simultaneously, such as coaxial and fiber-optic cable channels that have a wider bandwidth than traditional copper telephone line channels (which means data can travel faster). Internet users with broadband access can view web pages more quickly than Internet users with dial-up Internet access.

An **802.11 WiFi networking connectivity service** is a specification that allows your computer to connect to the World Wide Web via high-frequency radio waves. If you and your laptop, for instance, are in an area where a wireless hub device is installed, and you have an 802.11 WiFi networking connectivity service plan and a wireless network card installed in your laptop, you can go online without having to plug into a modem.

- **Optical mouse.** An optical mouse does not have all those moving parts, which means you don't have a ball to clean. You can also get an optical mouse that is wireless, which would eliminate that tangling cable annoyance.

- **Windows XP Professional.** The latest Windows operating system for PCs is highly recommended.
- **Office 2003 Professional.** This is that important Microsoft software package that includes Access, Excel, Outlook, PowerPoint, Publisher, and Word. For most online MBA programs, Office 2000 will suffice, which can be purchased from most software vendors for considerably less money than Office 2003.
- **Video card, sound card with speakers, and a microphone.** You'll need all these hardware components to participate in web conferences if your program uses this kind of technology, as well as for viewing and listening to other audio and video streams. You can eliminate the microphone if web conferencing is not in the picture. For more information about web conferencing, see Chapter 9.

To reiterate, this list can be considered an optimal computer system, so it's not something that every online MBA student must have. For instance, you may not need a laptop, wireless access, or an optical mouse. All you need to really be concerned about is that you meet the necessary technical requirements stipulated by the program and that you're comfortable and happy with whatever hardware and software you have.

Add On a Printer

A printer was not listed in the University of Florida package, but you are going to need one. My recommendation for this is pretty straightforward and somewhat biased: Purchase a used black-and-white laser printer, preferably a Hewlett-Packard Laser Jet 4.

Guide on the Side

I purchased a Hewlett-Packard Laser Jet 4 for $250 from an accountant more than four years ago and have abused it on a daily basis, printing thousands of pages for all the research I do in my work as a professional education writer. Before I purchased this printer, the accountant abused it for about two years, printing out reams of tax forms. I have not really performed any maintenance on this printer since I bought it. The only thing I do is purchase a new cartridge every few months.

Because your printing requirements as an online MBA student will be limited pretty much to journal articles, case studies, and a variety of other business-related documents (e.g., spreadsheets, research-related web pages, PDFs, and various research-oriented tomes), you really do not need a color printer. For that occasional paper-based presentation with the spiffy graphics that you want to have printed in full-blooming color, it might be more economical to go to your local copy center (e.g., Kinkos) instead of investing in a color printer that has relatively costly ink cartridges. You'll find all kinds of used black-and-white laser printers in your local classifieds as well as through a Google search or at eBay.

Your ISP

As mentioned previously, I strongly recommend that you buy either a cable or DSL Internet service provider plan, both of which are considered broadband Internet access. Neither ties up phone lines, and each is many times faster than a dial-up Internet connection. Your local cable television company should have broadband cable access, and your local telephone company should have DSL access. These services are not available everywhere yet, so, depending on where you live, you may be stuck with a dial-up connection, in which case you have my deepest sympathies.

Cable and DSL access do have some drawbacks, however. For one, both are always on, making them vulnerable to hackers. The cable and DSL providers, however, have started to tackle this problem by providing their customers with new software and services that protect and prevent any possible outside intrusions into their customers' computer systems.

Additionally, in relation to cable access subscribers, when lots of people on the same street or in the same small neighborhood have cable access, you can experience slowdowns when everyone goes online at the same time of the day. With DSL, you have to live close to a telephone switching station to really experience high-speed Internet access.

Software Needs

First and foremost, you'll be supplied with a student account that includes a special username and password that you will use to access your course management system over an Internet connection. To access the Internet, you will obviously need to have an Internet service provider (ISP) account.

In addition, you'll need to purchase the obligatory Microsoft Office package, if you don't already have it, and you'll be supplied with some additional software packages that are typically free, such as the multimedia *plug-in* players, web browsers, e-mail clients, Adobe Acrobat Reader, and compression utilities such as WinZip for the PC and StuffIt for the Mac. You'll be able to download these from the school's web pages that feature technical requirements. You'll also typically get a CD-ROM loaded with all the software you need to install. When downloading software from a web page, be aware of the following:

Online Term

A **plug-in** is an application that complements the capabilities of a web browser. Once installed on your computer, plug-ins are activated to display multimedia files.

- Make sure you have virus and personal firewall protection because anything you download could possibly be infected. The two most common virus and personal firewall protection software packages come from Symantec (Norton Anti Virus) and McAfee. You'll also need to watch out for spyware and adware (more on these later in this chapter).
- If you don't have a "temporary files" folder on your desktop, create one for downloading the software installers, which are self-extracting .exe extension files, into this folder. After you have downloaded the .exe extension file, click on it and follow the directions until the software is installed on your desktop. To save on disk space, you can delete the .exe extension file after you have finished the installation process.

Hopefully, you won't have too much trouble downloading all of the software you will use. It can be a relatively time-consuming process for the downloads and installations to fully take place, so be patient. Overall, however, it is a simple process that requires only a few mouse clicks to complete.

Multimedia Plug-Ins

Plug-ins basically expand your computer's ability to play audio and video files from an Internet connection. Four plug-ins you may need are Windows Media Player, RealOne Player, Macromedia Flash or Shockwave Players, and QuickTime. If you want to experience all the sights and sounds that many schools provide online, you'll need some, or all, of these plug-ins installed on your computer. You'll also need a video card and sound card with speakers. If you don't have these plug-ins on your computer yet, the table that follows lists where you can go to download the latest versions. (Also noted are the minimum system requirements for each to operate on your computer.)

Multimedia Plug-ins with Latest System Requirements

Plug-In and Website	Minimum Requirements
Windows Media Player www.microsoft.com/windows windowsmedia/9series/player.aspx	Windows 98 Second Edition, 233 MHz Pentium II processor or equivalent, 64 MB RAM, 100 MB disk space
RealOne www.real.com	Windows 98 Second Edition, 350 MHz Pentium II processor or equivalent, 64 MB RAM (128 MB on Windows XP or later), 52 MB disk space
Macromedia Flash or Shockwave Players www.macromedia.com/ downloadsspace	Windows 98 Second Edition, 600 MHz Pentium III processor or equivalent, 128 MB RAM, 347 MB disk
	Mac OS x 10.2.8 and later, Macintosh 500 MHz Power PC G3 Processor, 128 MB RAM, 280 MB disk space
QuickTime www.apple.com/quicktime/download	Windows 98, Pentium processor-based PC or compatible, 128 MB RAM
	Mac OS X 10.2.8 or later, Macintosh 400 MHz Power PC G3, 128 MB RAM

Browsers and E-Mail

You'll obviously need to have a web browser for connecting to the Internet. Most schools recommend that you use the latest version of Microsoft Internet Explorer or Netscape, and you'll be asked to configure your browser to accept cookies. Other browsers, such as those provided by the dedicated Internet service provider companies such as AOL, CompuServe, and Earthlink, are typically not recommended. For e-mail services, the Microsoft Outlook or Express or Eudora e-mail clients are generally recommended.

Adobe Acrobat

You'll need to be familiar with the Adobe Portable Document Format (PDF), which is the standard format for displaying and printing documents, including colors, graphics, typefaces, and photos, on any computer platform. Some of the required readings in your courses will be provided in the PDF format, and you'll need to install the free Adobe Acrobat Reader application in order to view and print them. You can download Adobe Acrobat Reader for free from www.adobe.com/products/acrobat/readstep2.html.

Compression Utilities

If you work on a PC, you'll more than likely need WinZip software (see www.winzip.com). If you work on a Mac, you'll need the StuffIt software (www.stuffit.com). Both are known as compression utilities because they crunch large amounts of data into smaller packages. They often come in handy when downloading software, which is usually formatted in data-compressed files, as well as for attaching large files, which are more reliable if compressed, to more easily transmit over an e-mail correspondence. Both are relatively inexpensive software utilities.

Protecting Your Data

Protecting and backing up everything that resides on your computer is becoming more and more important these days as viruses, *spyware*, and *adware* become more commonplace; power surges continue to fry machines; and hard drives consistently crash. You'll need two things: software that identifies malevolent digital bugs, such as the earlier-mentioned Norton Anti Virus or McAfee software packages, as well as a means to back up all the files on your computer on a fairly regular basis (in case you ever lose data).

Online Term

Spyware is software that watches where you travel in cyperspace. Unbeknownst to the user, it tracks your clicks and typically uses that information to send you unsolicited e-mails. **Adware** is software that generates advertising messages that pop up all over your computer screen while you are surfing the web, or, in some cases, when you are not surfing the web. Spyware and adware software are often secretly installed on people's computers when they download freeware, or when they click a button at an unethical website that then installs spyware and adware on unsuspecting visitors.

The Norton and McAfee software offer some, but not complete, protection against the newer malevolent spyware and adware buggers. Two popular programs for spyware and adware protection, both of which have free basic versions that you can download, are Lavasoft's Ad-aware (www.lavasoftusa.com) and Spybot Search and Destroy (www.spybot.info). For an excellent overview and more tools you can download for protection against the nasty underworld of spyware and adware, visit the Anti-Spyware Guide website at www.firewallguide.com/spyware.htm. Another good spyware site is SpywareGuide.com, which, according to its home page, "was created to provide an all-inclusive and updated resource on spyware applications, what they do and how they're used."

Because all this stuff can wreak havoc on your computer, you would be wise to invest in a backup protection strategy. My personal preference is an external hard drive that you can quite easily plug into your USB port, install the hard drive software, and then just copy all your files to it. They come in all shapes and sizes, and a wide variety of price ranges. To do some online shopping, type "external hard drive" into the Froogle shopping service. Costs will range, on average, from $80 for a 40 GB hard drive to about $160 for a 120 GB hard drive, and everything in between and above.

Where to Buy It All

Of course, you might not need to get an expensive laptop and the very latest and greatest software packages. Your current computer system may be more than adequate, and you may already have older versions of software that will more than do the job required of you as an online MBA student.

However, if you need to do some shopping, have I gotta deal for you .... Did you know, for instance, that as a matriculated student you can take advantage of some pretty good computer hardware and software deals? Most schools, for instance, other than the virtual institutions, have retail outlets on campus where students can purchase their computer software and hardware at substantial discounts. As an online student, you are entitled to these discounts, except you'll have to pay for shipping costs (unless you happen to live close by and can pick up whatever you purchase). Also you can, obviously, comparison shop at national chain and local computer stores, as well as surf around the web for the best buys you can find.

Guide on the Side

About.com Guide Mark Kyrnin's PC Hardware/Reviews website, located at http://compreviews.about.com, has lots of reliable information about the technical side of how to buy a desktop or notebook computer and where to get the best value for your dollar.

For software deals, in addition to buying from your school's retail outlet, you can take advantage of educational discounts offered only to students at JourneyEd.com. You must provide proof of your academic status.

This concludes my spiel about technical requirements. As always, when it comes to anything that requires a purchase, *caveat emptor.*

The Least You Need to Know

- Your computer setup will have to meet some hardware and software requirements, and your best bet is to buy a state-of-the-art computer system and the best broadband Internet service plan you can find in your area.
- You'll need a workhorse printer for much of your reading materials. Finding a used black-and-white laser printer could be your most economical and reliable way to print course materials.
- Take the necessary safety precautions when downloading your required software, and always have a system backup plan in place (in case you ever lose data).
- Just like an on-campus student, you can take advantage of computer hardware and software student discounts offered by your school's retail outlet.

Part 4

How to Be a Successful Online Learner

This could very well be the most important part of this book because it shows you all the ropes of being an online student. You'll be shown how to build a good home-study environment and introduced to what you can expect by way of support from your friends and relatives. Also the important issue of time-management is discussed.

The details of the student orientation process are provided, with some examples of both an online and on-campus orientation process for two online MBA programs. The importance of your online profile, your presence and participation factors, and netiquette skills are presented. And finally, you learn how to communicate online with loads of advice from a real online MBA student.

Chapter 14

Setting Yourself Up for Success

In This Chapter

- What you need to be a successful online student
- Time management and workload considerations
- Tips for surviving family matters
- How to avoid computer-based syndromes
- Advice on how to control your academic fate

In addition to going through the entire process of choosing, getting admitted, registering, sending in your first tuition payment, and making sure that all your computer hardware and software is properly set up and ready to go, you have to understand what's really going to be required of you to succeed in this new online education environment. You're going to need a good plan and support system in place to keep you on track.

Just like any traditional MBA program, you are embarking on a highly demanding educational journey. To use a worn-out cliché, "Be prepared." This chapter helps you understand what you need to be prepared for.

Three Qualities for the Online Learner

The three qualities that it takes to be a successful online learner are:

- Self-directed
- Disciplined
- Organized

You need to be self-directed primarily because there will not be any professor looking you in the eyes; there will not be a classroom meeting that you have to physically attend to keep you on track each week. You will be left to your own devices to figure out the most appropriate times, within the structure of the course or courses you are enrolled in, for entering the virtual classroom space, reading the assignments, doing the exercises, taking the quizzes and exams, writing the papers, and participating in the online discussions. In short, you have to be motivated and committed.

You need to be disciplined, which sounds obvious, but perhaps more so in the online environment where managing your time is of the utmost importance. Especially if you are doing the majority of your coursework from home, where it is easy to put off or delay an assignment after you have already put in a full day of work or after a family dinner or social event. Basically, you have to consistently push yourself to put forth the mental effort required of the academically challenging work typical of any MBA program.

Tied into being self-directed and disciplined is the need to be highly organized. Time management definitely comes into play. There will be times when your coursework will cut into your sleep. You'll want to limit that scenario as much as possible by devising a strict schedule and sticking to it. In the early phase of your online learning endeavor, you have to experiment with balancing your studies with your job responsibilities and family and social life. However, the sooner you can figure out a solid schedule for effectively dealing with all of these facets of your life on a daily basis, the sooner you will start moving in the right direction.

It's Not as Easy as You May Think

Essentially it should now be perfectly clear in your mind that online is no easier than on-campus and that you need to be motivated, energized, and committed to do your best.

First and foremost, you'll have lots of reading to deal with, from textbooks to case studies and journal articles, and all the discussion-board posts and e-mails. Unlike listening to a lecture and taking notes in a physical setting, reading becomes the primary method for disseminating information in the online format.

Second, you'll be required to meet all the assignment deadlines, and take all the required tests, quizzes, and exams. In many cases, these assignments will require that you apply concepts and theories you are learning in the course to your actual work environment, which can be a difficult and frustrating task if you are working in a nonreceptive workplace. Additionally, depending on the course, you'll be required to conduct research and write an intelligent paper or case study on a particular topic of interest.

Instant Message

"I found this (online learning) to be a more difficult way to obtain an MBA compared to a full-time (on-campus) student because with a full-time program you have the constant camaraderie with your classmates and you have more direct contact with the faculty."

—Mike Venable, Syracuse University iMBA graduate

And last but not least, team projects may pose a serious challenge, as students and faculty work to find the best way for everyone to work together, despite time-zone differences and various personalities and skill levels between cohorts.

Depending on your background, you may find some courses to be extremely difficult. For example, if you do not have accounting skills and are not particularly fond of accounting, in general, you'll have to push yourself to read what you may consider a very dry accounting textbook. Also when and if you run into a difficult computational challenge, it could be hard to get the assistance you need via e-mail or a discussion board, as opposed to being able to walk into a faculty member's office or classroom for such help.

Other students find the soft-skills courses that are typically part of an MBA program, on subjects such as leadership and teaming, for instance, to be less interesting and too subjective, and therefore arduous and less meaningful to them. These students instead prefer coursework that requires statistical-like analyses to explain theoretical business concepts.

Instant Message

"The accounting and statistics courses have been the most difficult for me. Accounting has been difficult because it centers around factories, which I have no experience in. However, one of the most relevant courses I have taken has been a (Microsoft) Access course."

—Joy Futrell, online MBA student, East Carolina University

Help! My Time Has Been Eaten Up

One thing that every online MBA graduate will tell you is that the single most challenging part of their studies was managing their time. However, because more than 90 percent of all online MBA students are working professionals, they do frequently commiserate with and offer each other moral support for coping with the challenges of balancing their work, family, and social lives, usually in a special discussion board outside of the course that is reserved for this kind of discourse. Also as students get to know each other online, or through their team projects, or through a residency, they form stronger bonds and communicate and support each other via the telephone when necessary.

Still, the issue of time management is indeed a challenging one, especially when you consider that an online MBA course alone customarily takes anywhere from 10 to 20 hours of time each week. If you enroll in a program that has accelerated courses that typically take anywhere from 6 to 8 weeks to complete, you could possibly spend an average of 25 hours per week on your coursework. Combine that with your job and other responsibilities and the prospect of earning your MBA can easily become a daunting task.

In the long run, most online MBA students wind up using weekends and evenings for accomplishing their academic responsibilities.

Instant Message

"The biggest challenge is simply finding the time when I'm awake enough to remember what I'm studying."

—Jodie Filardo, online MBA student, Arizona State University

"The time you are going to have to spend on assignments is considerable, and it means changing the way you organize your life. I've had to be more rigorous about the time I leave work, get up earlier at weekends, and cut down radically on my social life."

—Christopher Hodges, online MBA student, Syracuse University

Super Moms and Dads—*Not!*

As someone who has worked out of his home for about five years and is married with two children—one in elementary school and another in middle school—I can tell you firsthand that juggling your work life with your family life at the same moment and time, simply because you work from home, is neither feasible nor possible. The same holds true for juggling your studies from home and your family life.

As you surf around the web and read stories about online learners, you may run across the Mom who claims to be feeding her baby with one hand while typing out a homework assignment. This is hogwash. In that particular scenario, either the baby or the homework will not get the appropriate amount of attention. In short, trying to be that super Mom or super Dad who manages to provide adequate attention to his or her children and MBA studies at the same time is indeed another challenging proposition you'll face. I can tell you what has worked for me. Here are six important tips for surviving family matters:

- Make sure your work environment is separate from the rest of the house, and to enter it one has to go through a door. When that door is closed, nobody is allowed to enter.
- Conduct your studies during hours when your children are either sleeping or not at home.
- Make it perfectly clear to your children how important your work is and that they are not to disturb you unless it's an emergency.
- You and your spouse or partner must come to a solid agreement regarding who is responsible for what and when regarding all domestic and child-rearing issues.
- Make sure your friends and relatives are very aware of your schedule and that they know when not to call on you. Turn off the phone if you have to. One thing I have invested in is caller ID, which allows me to see who is calling me and thus answer only those calls I know are important, such as the call from my aging mother who may need my help, instead of the call from my daughter's girlfriend.
- Practice patience. If your kids are like mine, they will, on occasion, break the rules and knock on your door or simply walk into your work/study environment and start talking to you. Stop what you are doing and give them your undivided attention. For dealing with this kind of innocent interruption, it helps to remember what it was like when you were a kid.

Robert Breen, an online MBA student at Arizona State University, who is a married father of two children, age six and two, and vice president of strategic planning and financial analysis for a temporary labor firm in Tacoma, Washington, sums it up well: "I attempt to be the best Dad and husband I can be, and I spend the wee hours studying my MBA materials," Breen says. "I don't enjoy very much free time."

Other In-Home Study Considerations

As noted earlier, it is important that you have a private area of your house, preferably with a door that you can close for privacy when doing your coursework. However, I also realize that this kind of setup may not be feasible within the confines of your home. If this is your circumstance, you have to find a quiet corner of your home to put your workstation—which, by the way, should be only your workstation. In other words, and for a long list of obvious reasons, I strongly suggest that you do not share your computer and Internet connection with anyone else in your household.

Also because you'll obviously be spending a great deal of time in this space, you want to make it as comfortable and aesthetically pleasing as possible. Personally, I like having a window nearby. I also like being within easy reach of a coffeemaker. Finally, I have a sofa in my study for taking those absolutely necessary naps. Or, if you are like Ernest Hemingway, all your greatest work can be accomplished in the upright position, for Hemingway always wrote standing up.

A Word on Partners and Friends

If you live alone or are single, consider yourself fortunate to have a general lack of disturbances and an overall quiet home study area to do all your coursework. However, unmarried students also typically have plenty of social and familial challenges to deal with and must also perfect a balancing act when it comes to devoting the majority of their time to pursuing their MBA.

Jennifer Skipton, online MBA student at the University of Colorado at Colorado Springs, for instance, says she is in "a long-term committed relationship" and has the support of her partner, who is also a student. She adds that her "friends understand and are proud of me, but they complain a little when the books come before the bike ride or the volleyball game."

Christopher Hodges, a single online MBA student at Syracuse University, adds, "I sometimes wonder whether my parents and friends appreciate the extent of the workload and time commitment. I suspect they think I exaggerate! I think, however, that true friends will realize why they can't see you as frequently as before without it having a negative impact."

The Support You Need

Every online MBA graduate will tell you that they would have never been able to effectively complete their degrees without the support of their spouses, partners, relatives, employers, and/or friends. "Your family makes a huge sacrifice in this endeavor," says Syracuse University iMBA graduate Mike Venable. Regis University online MBA graduate Katherine Porter explains how her husband was "100 percent onboard" while she pursued her degree. "I had his commitment because he knew it was important to me to finally finish that graduate degree. I was completely honest with him and made him part of the process. He knew it was a two-year commitment and that we would be sacrificing free time for two years. He knew well in advance when I would be in class and when I would have breaks. He knew how much it would all cost. He knew what I thought I might gain from the investment of time and money. Other family and friends, co-workers, neighbors, you name it, all were supportive as they found out what I was doing. You'd be surprised how enthusiastic and willing to help everyone is when you share such a big undertaking with them."

Instant Message

"Get support for your MBA from your spouse or significant other and family. This is a big, big deal and requires a lot of time that could otherwise be spent with them. Before signing up, make sure everyone in your immediate family understands the commitment and sacrifice they will be undertaking and that they support it."

—Robert Breen, online MBA student, Arizona State University

Avoiding Computer-Based Syndromes

As an online student, you are going to be sitting in front of a computer for long periods of time. If you also happen to use computers frequently on your job, the possibility of developing a repetitive stress injury or computer-related syndrome increase. A repetitive stress injury can occur when an action performed repeatedly causes an overabundance of stress on joints, muscles, and/or tendons. Advanced cases of a repetitive stress injury can cause a permanent disability.

One of the more common forms of repetitive stress injury that is caused by excessive typing and mouse maneuvering at a computer is carpal tunnel syndrome; some other related injuries include tendonitis and bursitis.

Computer-related repetitive stress injuries are known to be the result of poorly designed workstations. According to the U.S. Department of Labor, the following basic design goals should be considered by computer users when setting up their workstations:

- The top of your computer monitor should be just below your eye level when your head is straight upright.
- Your head and neck should be balanced and in line with your torso.
- Shoulders should be relaxed.
- Your elbows should be close to your body and supported.
- Your lower back should be supported.
- Your wrists and hands should be in line with your forearms.
- Make sure there is adequate room for your keyboard and mouse.
- Your feet should be flat on the floor.

Some other tips to take into consideration include making sure that your wrists do not rest on any support device or are tilted in any way, but instead are in a straight line with your forearm. Also, it is strongly advised that you take rests and breaks frequently, at least every hour, by getting away from your computer for at least 5 to 10 minutes or by looking away from your computer screen and stretching your arms and legs.

Guide on the Side

The U.S. Department of Labor has a special website devoted exclusively to the proper ergonomics of computer workstations at www.osha.gov/SLTC/etools/computerworkstations. Also, an award-winning website that has everything you could possibly want to know about repetitive stress injuries is located at http://eeshop.unl.edu/rsi.html.

Controlling Your Academic Fate

Finally, the following tips, many of which are just common sense but worth repeating, are general rules of thumb for controlling your academic fate as an online learner and increasing your odds for success:

- Don't procrastinate or let the work pile up. It is the kiss of death in any online course.

- Keep a running up-to-date calendar of everything you need to do academically, socially, and work related.
- Eliminate superfluous behaviors, such as watching television.
- Make sure you know exactly what is required of you in your online course at all times and do not be afraid to ask for clarification from your instructor if there is something that you do not understand. In short, read the syllabus carefully and know what all your assignments are and when they are due as well as how you will be assessed for the work you perform.
- Think before responding to any online discussion-board posts. One of the beauties of online learning is that you have the time to provide valuable insights to the overall learning environment of the entire class. One method frequently used by smart online learners is to first use a word processing program to write a response to a discussion-board question, then reread it and further analyze the response before copying and pasting it to the board. This method can be cumbersome, but it will make your comments more meaningful and substantial, which can in turn affect your grade, not to mention gain the admiration and respect of your peers and teachers.
- Make yourself fully aware of the library services available to you and seek out any information literacy training the institution may provide to its online students.
- If you have had problems writing clearly in the past, get help in changing this as soon as possible. Many schools have online writing labs and services you can take advantage of prior to taking your first class.
- Fully understand the rules of plagiarism. Adult learners, in particular, who have been out of school for a long time and may be a bit rusty on their writing skills, need to review what can be construed as plagiarism.
- "Have a backup plan in case your Internet connection goes down and you need to 'meet' with your professor or classmates (online)," says Dawn McAvoy, online MBA student, East Carolina University. "Technology is great, but only when it works. You can't wait until the last minute to do an assignment, because if something goes down and you can't submit it, you may be out of luck."
- Take a break. Yes, this is a demanding road you're taking. If you don't take a nap at the rest stops, you could fall asleep at the wheel and wind up in a serious accident. In fact, it's a good idea to take several breaks from the grind every day. For me, looking at a *National Geographic* magazine or paging through the local newspaper is a refreshing alternative from the computer screen. I also take naps regularly. It's amazing what a 10-minute snooze will do for your energy level.

- Try to study during the day if at all possible. Nighttime is often not the right time for studying.
- Get the fastest Internet connection available in your area. Also it's a good idea to have the best computer you can afford, over and above what may be required. Any additional cost will more than pay for itself in time savings and increased productivity.

To sum things up, my last piece of advice with regard to setting yourself up for success is a cliché often used when discussing effective business practices: "Work smarter, not harder." In other words, always reevaluate what you are doing and change your plans and strategies accordingly to ensure the greatest success is achieved within the parameters of your professional, educational, familial, social, and spiritual well-being.

The Least You Need to Know

- To be a successful online student, you need to be self-directed, disciplined, and organized. You also need the full support of family and friends.
- The environment where you do your coursework should be private and comfortable.
- Because you will be working at a computer for many hours, take the necessary precautions to prevent the possibility of repetitive stress injury.
- Don't procrastinate, know what's required of you at all times, take advantage of academic services, make sure your writing skills are up to speed, have a decent computer with a fast Internet connection, and rest as needed.

Chapter 15

Getting Oriented

In This Chapter

- A look at the format of an online course
- The importance of an online profile
- What you need to know about communicating online
- The relationship between technology and learning

At most institutions, your very first course will be a non-credit-bearing or one- or two-credit orientation course taught by an educational technologist who will introduce you to the functions of your course management system and how, in general, courses are taught online. This is a very important first step in the process and is mandatory before you can be considered a bona-fide online MBA student. Every institution handles this process differently.

In this chapter, I show you what some of these orientation courses are like and how you should definitely take this opportunity to learn how to communicate online effectively as well as work with the technology to your best advantage.

Learning the Ropes of Online Learning

Previous chapters covered some of the educational technologies used in an online program, how to make sure all these technologies are installed and working on your computer system, and basically what you need to know to get started on the right footing from an organizational and time-management perspective. All these are also in some way related to the orientation process. The orientation process includes getting acquainted with and playing with the technology as well as doing some readings, assignments, exercises, and tests that are part and parcel of an online course.

Even though many online MBA students are not newcomers to some of the technologies used in online courses—perhaps having used such things as e-mail, listservs, web conferencing, file sharing, and audio and video streaming technologies in their workplaces—they may not have had any firsthand experiences with moving through an actual higher-education online teaching and learning environment.

As online learning, in general, has progressed over the years, orientation processes that familiarize students with educational technology have grown in sophistication. There are basically two methods used for providing these orientations: an on-campus orientation or a completely online orientation. Following, I explain the components of an on-campus orientation at Arizona State University (ASU) and an online orientation at the University of Maryland University College (UMUC). The information in both of these examples is provided as a general overview of what an online learning orientation process would customarily entail at most institutions.

Guide on the Side

It is imperative that you fully understand how to use all the technology you will be accessing online before you officially start taking your core required courses. You cannot expect your professors to help you with technology-related issues, nor your fellow students to have patience with you if you can't master the technology. In short, students who may irritate the flow of the coursework by being technologically inept will not be tolerated.

ASU's On-Campus Orientation

Online MBA programs that have residency requirements will conduct orientation sessions at the first residency. In this scenario, students are ushered into computer labs where educational technologists go through all the steps of how online courses are conducted.

For the W.P. Carey MBA - Online Program at Arizona State University (ASU), for example, this kind of orientation begins with live lectures and lab sessions where the parts of the online course interface are explained and simulated in detail.

Students begin by logging in their pre-assigned username and password in the front-page interface of their Blackboard course management system (see the figure that follows).

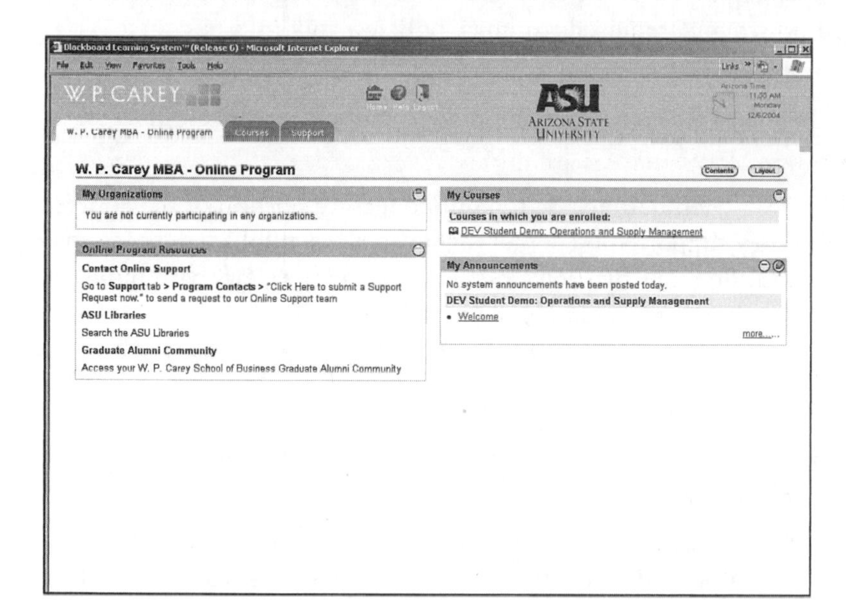

Example of ASU's front page interface after logging in to the Blackboard course management system.

They are then taken to a new front page showing four primary sections they can access:

- **My Organizations.** Where students get to know their fellow students, faculty, and support staff by posting their profiles and entering into non-course-related discussions. This is also the place where administrative and program information and announcements are supplied and discussed.
- **Online Program Resources.** For linking to the alumni community, the ASU library services and any other program resources, such as Xanedu course packs (see Chapter 10), as well as for linking to online support services.
- **My Announcements.** Where announcements are posted for all the courses and organizations a student may be participating in.

- **My Courses.** Where students link to the actual courses they are enrolled in. Each course is made up of nine standard sections:
  - *Announcements.* Reminders about what's required of you as well as links to exercises, quizzes, and exams.
  - *Syllabus.* Information about the overall course, including faculty introductions, grading scheme, required readings, policies, and links to course materials and external resources.
  - *Schedule.* Due dates for completing modules, readings, exercises, quizzes, and exams.
  - *Modules.* At ASU, modules include the online lecture portion of the course, comprised of text supported by digital media, such as graphs, tables, animations, video introductions by professors, and video interviews with industry experts. See Chapter 9 for a sample of an ASU module.
  - *Exercises.* Interactive online exercises that enhance the learning of module concepts.
  - *Quizzes.* Can come in a variety of formats, including multiple choice, fill in the blank, and short and long essay.
  - *Discussion.* In most cases, the heart of the class where students and faculty interact with each other, by posting questions and answers, usually asynchronously, inside an online forum. See later in this chapter under "Presence and Participation" and Chapter 9 for more information.
  - *Groups.* Where team interaction via e-mail, discussion forums, and file sharing takes place. See Chapter 17.
  - *Tools.* Where students can view their grades.

Depending on the program, the format of your online courses will be similar, but not exactly the same as the ASU model. Other course management functions may come into play, such as live chat, instant messaging, online surveying and polling tools, a course-evaluation area, a calendar tool, and various audio and video streaming components.

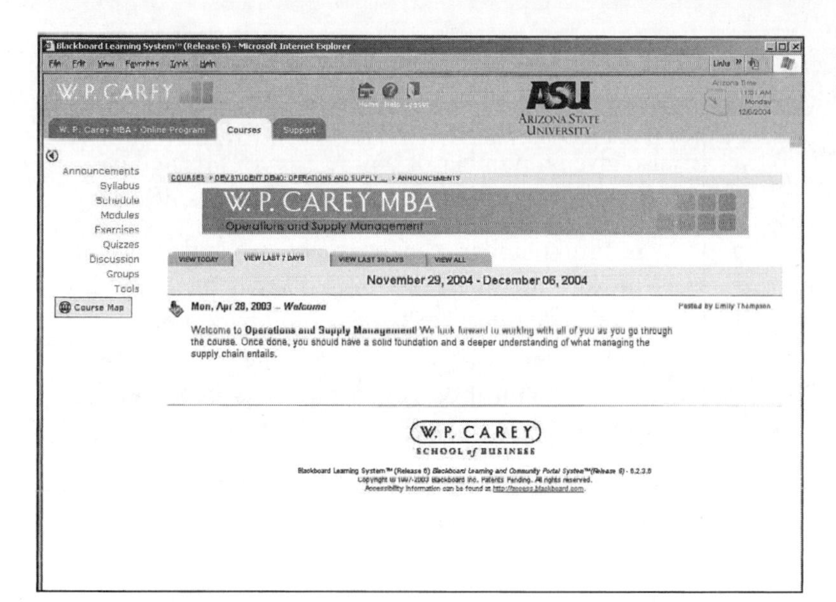

Example of an ASU course interface.

UMUC's Online Orientation

Online MBA programs that do not have residency requirements will conduct orientation sessions completely online. These orientation courses are comprised of new students just like yourself. Similar to a face-to-face orientation, the course will be facilitated by an educational technologist or manager who will introduce everyone to the technology of online learning. In addition to taking this course online, students have the option of communicating by telephone with technology support professionals who can personally walk them through any questions about the technology they might have.

An excellent example of a thorough online orientation can be found at UMUC, where all online MBA students must first pass a 13-week, 1-credit, online MBA Fundamentals course before they can move on to the real deal, so to speak. According to Rosemary Hartigan, UMUC's online MBA director, the MBA Fundamentals course "gives students the opportunity to see if they will like working online. Sometimes students decide that they don't have the time, and sometimes they decide that they want to go to the face-to-face mode (which is also offered by UMUC)."

UMUC describes the MBA Fundamentals course as serving three key purposes:

- Acquaint students with the online environment and technologies used in the MBA program
- Help students improve their research, writing, and analytical skills
- Ensure that students have a foundation in basic management concepts

Online Term

The **theory of constraints** was created by Eliyahu Goldratt, a physicist and business consultant who developed a management practice and philosophy that identifies and measures multifaceted systems and facilitates continuous improvement by limiting or eliminating constraints that prevent businesses from reaching goals.

In addition, students are given assignments, with due dates, in statistics, financial accounting, financial decision making, and the *theory of constraints.* They are also given a number of online exercises related to research, writing, critical thinking, and teamwork.

A faculty member teaches the course and is available to answer any questions students may have. By the end of the course, students should have a good understanding of both the academic requirements and the technical skills necessary to succeed in the MBA program.

As noted on the MBA Fundamentals course syllabus, upon successful completion of this course, students should be able to …

- Use accepted business practices to prepare a presentation.
- Critically assess the arguments presented in scholarly activities.
- Explore the concept of plagiarism and techniques to avoid it.
- Write a research paper on a current management issue supporting a recommended course of action incorporating scholarly research.
- Build a simple business model for a new product or service.
- Perform basic descriptive and inferential statistical analyses.
- Employ the basic tools of corporate financial accounting.
- Apply the theory of constraints concepts in an organizational setting.

As you can see, much of what's required of you to become an online MBA student, except for the scholarly stuff, is pretty much identical to what will be required of you to be a successful business manager, which leads me to your online profile.

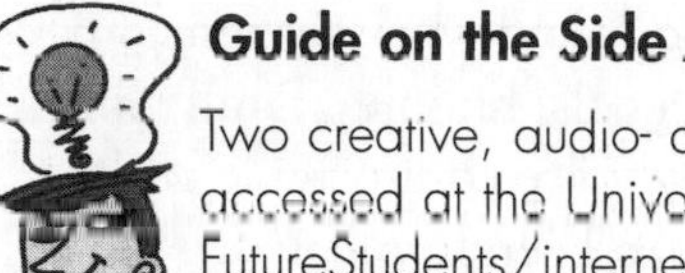

Guide on the Side

Two creative, audio- and video-streamed demos of how online courses work can be accessed at the University of Florida's course demo at www.floridamba.ufl.edu/FutureStudents/internetdemo/index.asp and at Drexel University's eLearning demo at www.drexel.com/demo/. Also course management system provider WebCT features examples of exemplary online courses in a wide variety of subjects at www.webct.com/exemplary.

Your Online Profile

Most orientation courses start with the typical icebreaker activity of having students submit short biographies as a means of introducing themselves to their classmates and the instructor. This exercise will customarily be repeated in many of your regular courses as well. Although this may seem like a trivial pursuit, it really is an important step that you need to think through before typing away. In short, you want to make an intelligent and honest impression.

Especially if you are in a completely online program, your profile will be that all-important first impression that your professors and fellow classmates will come to know you by. Typically, a special section of the discussion board or a unique area reserved especially for student profiles will be built in to the first required assignment. In many cases, you also have the option of posting your photo in this section of the course.

According to Karen Sangermano, distance MBA program director, Graduate School of Business Administration, University of Colorado at Colorado Springs, "Students post their profiles so that they can get a sense of who their fellow students are; where they work; what they do; where they live; are they married, single, have kids? Most students have gotten to the point where the first thing they do is post their profile, because they know it's beneficial to other students and they want to see it from other students."

Sometimes your profile plays an important role in who you wind up collaborating with in any class. For example, people with similar occupations will frequently form bonds based on the similar challenges they face at work. Or people of varied backgrounds, such as a marketing person and an accountant, will seek advice from each other related to their areas of expertise. Overall, a well-written, detailed profile often becomes the catalyst for community building and sharing in an online course. So in addition to the typical resumé-like explanation of your skills and work responsibilities, it is beneficial for you to open up about your career goals, hobbies, family life, age, challenges you face at work, and anything else that you are comfortable with sharing. Also as you move through the program, it's wise to keep it updated.

Presence and Participation

Your profile helps to establish what online educators refer to as your "presence" in a course. This presence is further bolstered and identified by your effort and ability to participate in online discussions, which in many online courses will become part of your grade evaluation. In other words, you have to be actively engaged in all those online discussion threads that your professor kicks off with a challenging business-related question based on a textbook, article, or case-study reading you were assigned. Being actively engaged, however, does not mean that you just agree or disagree. It means that you contribute something meaningful and substantial to the discussion forum on a regular basis, which will obviously require some writing and communication skills, which, as a prospective or current business manager, you should already have for the day-to-day operations of your business. Online learner skills are discussed more in Chapter 16.

Rochester Institute of Technology (RIT) Professor Anthony Trippe, who teaches online computer programming courses, says that 30 percent of his online students' grades are dependent upon the number of "significant" messages a student posts in the threaded discussions portion of his online courses. "A significant message is at least 300 words and related to a course topic," he says. "They can't just post something like 'Yes, this is interesting.'" To get the full 30 percent, students must post 3 significant messages each week of the 10-week course. "I give a feedback message to each student at the end of the week," Trippe adds. "I encourage them to interface with each other and share experiences."

Guide on the Side

Jump in with all your typing fingers and learn how to communicate online, starting with the discussion board and student profile sections of the orientation session, where you can learn the ropes of what it takes to be a successful online student.

Trippe claims that every course usually has what he calls his "backrow buddies." These are students who need a little push to start participating more frequently in online discussions. "They would not say anything if I threw a rock at them," jokes Trippe. "So, in the first two weeks of class, I feel it is an important part of my job to send them a message and get them engaged."

Mercy College, which offers online Master's of Science programs in business-related areas, such as organizational leadership, direct marketing, and Internet business systems, has come up with some criteria for determining whether a discussion-board message is actually effective and worthy of receiving full credit. A worthy message should be …

- related to the course material.
- concise, not more than one screen length.
- one that encourages responses.
- one that expands concepts or connects ideas in new ways.
- timely.
- logical.
- grammatically correct and written clearly.

Source: Sloan Consortium Effective Practice, "Defining Effective Participation," located online at www.sloan-c.org/effective/details3.asp?LE_ID=18.

Online Term

Netiquette is a term that came of age with our adoption of the Internet. It refers to the practice of being civilized in both asynchronous and synchronous online communications. The short definition is practicing etiquette on the Internet.

For additional help in this area, see Chapter 16, where I discuss writing skills, and Chapter 17, where I review the art of working with your online peers. I've also provided some information about *netiquette*, next, that you should be cognizant of when communicating online.

About Netiquette

In any social situation it's always a good thing to be polite and respectful. The same holds true for the online world, and then some. The written word can be more powerful than the spoken word, and the fine nuances of language can be more easily misinterpreted in an e-mail or discussion-forum message than it can in a face-to-face meeting. Hence, the word *netiquette* has come onto the Internet scene. A simple Google search on this term will bring up numerous sites that outline the rules of proper online communication. For now, here's a short list that you can paste on the wall next to your computer:

- Don't use uppercase.
- Format your messages in a way that is easy to read.
- Respect copyrighted materials.

- Keep your emotions in check.
- Don't use smileys inappropriately.
- Don't be overly brief and don't be overly verbose. In other words, find a middle ground.
- Always address people by their name in an e-mail correspondence, and always conclude your message with a polite "thank you" or "best regards," etc., and your name.
- Proofread your message for spelling, grammar, and clarity before sending it off.
- Do not criticize another person's opinion.
- If you are asked to critique someone's work, do it in a professional manner and support your critique with valid resources.
- Try to respond promptly to any of your fellow classmates' questions.
- Try not to send and share files that are larger than 1 megabyte.
- Stay on topic.
- Don't assume that everyone you send a message to will respond to you.
- Don't assume that a short response from a professor or student is a sign of curtness or disrespect. Most of the people you will encounter as an online MBA student are extremely busy people.

I have a simple rule that I try to follow when communicating electronically with anyone. I respond to messages and interact with people in the way I would like them to communicate back with me. In other words, show respect, don't offend, and be precise and straight to the point.

Final Notes on Technology

One piece of solid advice that I think needs to be said here is don't be intimidated by technology. During the early years of online learning, it was quite common for students to drop out of an online program because they simply could not get a handle on how to use the educational technology. Even today, many students struggle with navigating through their online courses because they lack basic computing skills. Couple that with the isolation of working online, and some students begin to feel disconnected and subsequently lose all their motivation.

First, if you lack basic computing skills, take some continuing-education courses at your local college or university before thinking about enrolling in an online MBA program.

Second, the best way to overcome any technology ineptness factors is to simply pay close attention to the orientation process and repeat it over and over, if necessary, until you feel comfortable. Also, every school has a friendly technical support service in place to help you with technological challenges. Don't be afraid to use these services often. After all, you're paying for such services through your tuition dollars.

Finally, remember that the technology is really secondary to the learning that will occur in an online MBA program. The goal is for you to gain business knowledge and skills through your coursework. Most schools have figured out how to teach without letting the technology get in the way of learning by creating and fine-tuning their orientation and support processes and putting more emphasis on the interactions that customarily occur between students and faculty in any online MBA program.

The Least You Need to Know

- You will be required to go through an online learning orientation process that will teach you the ins and outs of how online courses are conducted.
- In addition to learning how to use the educational technology of your courses, you need to learn how to effectively participate in your online coursework.
- It's important that you learn how to communicate effectively in your online courses. In addition to posting a well-written and thorough online profile of yourself, you need to contribute meaningfully to the online discussions required in your courses.
- Don't let technology intimidate you. If you lack basic computer skills, find a way to rectify that problem as quickly as possible so you can focus on learning and not technology.

Chapter 16

Online Learner Skills

In This Chapter

- Skills needed to be a successful student
- A student's point of view on online communication
- Online resources for online learner skills
- Tips to help increase your online learning skills

Being a successful online learner requires a set of skills that differs from the skills required to be a successful traditional on-campus student. The online environment also presents a unique set of challenges not seen in the face-to-face classroom environment.

Many of these skills and challenges discussed in this chapter hearken back to the two previous chapters in which I explained how online learners need to be self-directed, disciplined, and organized and be ready to put forth their best effort during the online learning orientation process. All those characteristics will ultimately form the foundation of your success.

However, when you get down to the bare essential skills and challenges of being an online MBA student, some interesting points of view come to the surface. And that's what this chapter is all about.

Communicate, Communicate, Communicate

In the online learning environment, having strong communication skills can make a real difference in how much you ultimately get out of your overall MBA education. Unlike the face-to-face classroom, there is no back of the class in an online course. In the online discussion forums and team exercises, for instance, everyone will be quite aware of your lack of participation, including, obviously, the professor, who will grade you on your discussion contributions and ability to work with your course teammates.

According to the director of the Penn State iMBA program, John Fizel, "If you are completely undisciplined, you are found out a lot faster in an online program than you may be typically in a regular (face-to-face) program. You can't hide online, especially if it is a collaborative, team environment."

"In Blackboard we have tools that can tell us who has logged in to what parts of the site and how long they were there, so the instructors know who is engaged," says Paula O'Callaghan, director of the Syracuse University iMBA program.

In short, online student interactions via the discussion board, e-mail correspondence, or telephone are a vital part of your learning experience. Conversations about every course assignment, reading, and team exercise are occurring each and every day on numerous levels. And the faculty member, in fact, typically takes less of a directive role in these conversations, acting more as a facilitator to get meaningful discussions going and only intervening when and if the conversation takes a wrong turn.

"A huge part of our courses is the discussion board, which is used to analyze cases," adds O'Callaghan. "It works very well in our program because it is asynchronous. Our students are in 10 different time zones. The discussion board is the single most used feature in Blackboard."

Instant Message

"Online discussions force students to talk the language and use the vocabulary that they may not have ample time to do in a classroom setting. You will see, particularly in a strategy course or a marketing course that has its own language, that by the end of the sixth week, the students are really talking the talk."

—Ken Sherman, associate dean, University of Phoenix Graduate Business Program

As you communicate with fellow students and your professors online, keep in mind that you have plenty of time to think through your responses before making a post live, and remember that your colleagues have plenty of time to review and go back over what you posted. So when making a contribution to a class discussion, make sure it's an intelligent, meaningful, clear, and concise contribution and not something that you hastily typed up just to be recognized as a participant. You can refer back to Chapter 15 for more information about online communication skills.

To give you an idea of how discussion board posts can be graded by faculty, the following point-system criteria is used by Bill Pelz, a veteran online professor of psychology at Herkimer County Community College in upstate New York, who is also the recipient of the 2003 Sloan-C Award for Excellence in Online Teaching:

- **0 points.** The post adds no academic value to the discussion; no new information is presented.
- **1 point.** The post contains at least one usable fact or piece of information; however, the fact or information is available from the textbook.
- **2 points.** The post contains at least one usable fact or piece of information not available from the textbook.
- **3 points.** The post makes a substantial academic contribution; material is included that is not available just by reading the textbook and some issue or concept is clarified.
- **4 points.** The post contains documented information that contributes greatly to the understanding of some issue under discussion; the new information is explained and applied such that the reader gains insight into the material being studied.

Source: Sloan-C Effective Practice, "Applying Research on Presence to Guide Online Discussions," by Bill Pelz, available online at www.sloan-c.org/effective/details3.asp?LE_ID=35.

So as you can see, earning the highest level of recognition for your discussion posts requires a good deal of effort on your part.

Communicating with Faculty

You will also find that faculty members are more than willing to communicate with you outside of the formal class discussions on education-related issues and even on a personal level if you just put forth the effort to form a relationship with them. Don't take the approach that you are imposing on faculty by calling them on the phone or sending them an e-mail outside of the course discussions. Professors love to talk, and they love to teach. They do, however, get an extraordinary amount of e-mail and are required to enter into numerous discussion forums every week, especially if they are teaching multiple online courses. So don't be offended if their written responses are relatively short in length.

A professor's online style may be much different from his or her offline style. "A faculty member may say something short online and that may be interpreted as being curt," says Emily Thompson, senior coordinator of instructional structure and systems, W.P. Carey MBA - Online Program at Arizona State University. "We walk students through this process. Just because a faculty member does not say 'Hi, how are you?' first, does not mean that he or she does not care about how students are doing."

> **Instant Message**
>
> "I've been surprised by how much the faculty inspired me to learn about an area which I knew little of and/or to produce excellent work."
>
> —Christopher Hodges, Syracuse University iMBA student

Most professors will have office hours when you can call them on the telephone for a more in-depth and personal dialogue. The truth of the matter, however, is most students don't take advantage of these kinds of value-added services, when, in fact, they should. Ironically, the same thing happens in the on-campus environment, with students rarely visiting with their professors during office hours.

Rosemary Hartigan, director of the University of Maryland University College online MBA program, who is also an online professor in the program, explains how students sometimes "don't think of their online faculty members as real human beings, so they don't try to establish a relationship with them. Some students are perfectly happy not having that kind of relationship. They will turn in their assignments and that's enough for them. But for students who want to build relationships, they need to put forth the effort. I'll send out e-mails, and some students will respond back to me personally, but most won't. They will just take the information and not respond back."

The bottom line is that you have to take more of an active initiative to speak with your online faculty members by simply calling them on the phone during their prescribed office hours. This way you will get the full benefit of their expertise and knowledge over and beyond just the online course environment.

A Student's Point of View

Finally, Dawn McAvoy, an enterprising student in the East Carolina University online MBA program, provides the following nine tips about effectively communicating in the online learning environment:

- It is important to remember that online communication is a lot like face-to-face communication minus the benefits of body language. It is important to be a little more direct, I think, because subtle cues can't be conveyed through body language; and if you want someone to get your point, you may have to be a little blunter. But do it in a nice way.
- Try to get a feel for people's style and communicate accordingly. Chatty people (like me!) tend to be chatty online, too; but when you are in a group with more focused people, they may get frustrated. In a face-to-face session, you get verbal cues that someone is ready to move on that you may not get online.
- Try to learn to type halfway decently. If you are really slow or make a lot of typos or misspellings, it can frustrate people. It can also convolute the point you are trying to make.
- If you think you misunderstand what someone is saying, repeat it back to them in a slightly different way so you make sure you really are getting their point (much like regular communication, but I think it is easier to misunderstand online).
- Be yourself. When I first started in some of the online class forums, I tended to be rather formal and stiff; as I got more comfortable with the whole idea of taking classes again (I'd been out of college for 10 years), however, I loosened up. Now I'm probably closer to my normal face-to-face self.
- If you have a group project, let people know what's going on. If you are going to miss a deadline the group set for something, let them know in advance if at all possible. Many online students have jobs and other responsibilities, so they completely understand if something comes up once in a while—just let them know.
- Speak up! If you don't understand something—let the people you are working with know.
- Be willing to share your experiences and insights. Chances are, you have a lot to offer your classmates via your unique perspective on things.
- Let other people finish their thoughts. Talking is so much faster than typing, so it is important to give people time to type everything out before commenting.

McAvoy's tips are loaded with common sense, which, in the back-and-forth of any kind of communication, can often be lost in emotion. When the heat and excitement of an online discussion starts to rise, take a deep breath and remember that you can give yourself as much time as you like to respond in a meaningful and insightful manner that will gain the respect of your colleagues.

The Other Skills You'll Need

Of course, you are going to need more than just communication skills to succeed as an online MBA student. To reiterate from earlier chapters, this is an academically rigorous and challenging pathway you are taking. A necessary skills inventory includes good typing skills, good reading-comprehension skills, basic computer and Internet skills, a solid ability to use a number of important programs, an ability to write at the graduate level, a keen understanding of how to conduct research and avoid plagiarism, some math skills that you may not have used in quite a while, and test-taking skills.

Typing Skills

This may seem apparent, but you'd be surprised at how many business managers are not the greatest typists, primarily because they have administrative assistants who do their typing for them or they are typically so busy with the day-in, day-out management cycle that they don't spend all that much time in front of a computer. In short, you'll be a typing machine in the online environment, so you'll need to know how to type fast and accurately.

Instant Message

"The biggest liability faced by some students might be poor typing skills. This can quickly be remedied with some practice using any one of the off-the-shelf typing software packages available.

—Tim Bzowey, Athabasca University online MBA student

"Learn to increase your typing speed for online chat sessions if you are really slow."

—Dawn McAvoy, East Carolina University online MBA student

Reading-Comprehension Skills

This, too, might seem apparent, but much of what online MBA students have to read requires more than just reading. Case studies, for instance, require that you become adept at identifying and analyzing information presented in cases and coming up with solutions that could resolve a variety of related business issues and challenges.

Because as an online MBA student you'll be reading a great deal more than you may be used to, and you have time-management challenges to begin with, you may want to brush up on your reading speed and comprehension skills.

Guide on the Side

A provider of software solutions for enhanced reading, ReadingSoft.com, out of Switzerland, has a fun and informative online reading speed and comprehension test on its website, located at www.readingsoft.com/quiz.html.

Basic Computer Skills

How efficiently you can work on a computer and navigate the Internet are important skills that every online student needs to have. In addition to being able to copy, paste, delete, and save files; download and install software; attach files to e-mails; and search online; probably the most important skill, overall, as it relates to technology-related skills, is knowing how to be highly organized on the computer. All the correspondences, weekly course assignments, and special projects you may be working on will get hefty and unwieldy if you don't practice good file-management skills.

For the Internet side of things, use your Favorites folder wisely. Know how to organize all those web pages you visit as you do research throughout your coursework into related categories and subcategories. Know how to succinctly label the websites you save in these categories and subcategories.

The same holds true for Word and PDF documents and e-mails. Good folder management, in tandem with creative category labeling, can save you an extraordinary amount of time when you need to go back and review your research, correspondences, and assignments, which will happen frequently.

Software Skills

You will have to be skilled at using three primary programs: Microsoft Word, Microsoft Excel, and Microsoft PowerPoint. You may also be required to use

Microsoft Access. How you master these programs will depend on your course assignments and the way you adapt to the online learning environment, as well as your level of creativity, especially for PowerPoint presentations.

You'll use Word for writing papers and other research-based documents. But you may also use it for writing, editing, and proofreading your discussion board and e-mail communications prior to actually sending them off through cyberspace. You'll use Excel for the obvious spreadsheet and financial-analysis stuff that is so common in the world of business, as well as for other data-control-oriented exercises, such as inventory allocations and tabulations and production analysis functions. PowerPoint will come in handy for team projects, when you or the team as a whole will be required to present to the class, either live at a residency or online inside a web conference.

Instant Message

"The single most important software skills would be the use of the Excel spreadsheet package. Use of this data tool is pervasive in MBA courses."

—Paula O'Callaghan, director, iMBA Program, Syracuse University iMBA program

As an online student, you will be exchanging all these files you create on a frequent basis with your classmates and professors either through your course management system's file-exchange function or via e-mail attachments. Often, for team projects, for instance, you will have a separate area on your course management interface for group collaborations in which files are shared by only the members in your team. You may go back and forth with editing and proofreading each other's work, so you'll need to know how to use the edit tracking feature in Word.

Using Excel can be a daunting task. I have yet to meet anyone who knows all the Excel commands that exist today. It is, indeed, a powerful program, and the sooner you can master it, the better off you will be. Excel is really a multifaceted application that is also used for list management, charting, applying formulas, and much more. There are also Excel add-ins that provide another set of tools, such as special statistical, linear algebra, matrix, accounting, interactive graph functions, and much more.

Guide on the Side

An interesting website with everything you could want to know about Excel and taglined "The Ultimate Excel Portal," is the Excel Nexus, located at http://vertex42.com/ExcelLinks. Of course, the most logical cyberspot to visit in relation to getting all kinds of information and tips for using Microsoft products is the Microsoft Office website at http://office.microsoft.com.

Using PowerPoint can be another daunting task. Like Excel, many features of this program can make you go batty. As a graphic designer in a former life, I can offer you some tips about designing graphically pleasing PowerPoint presentations:

- Use standard typefaces that can be found on most PCs, such as Arial, Times New Roman, Century Schoolbook, and Courier New. And do not use more than two type styles.
- Contrast background with text. In other words, use dark-colored text with a light background and light-colored or white text (usually referred to as reverse type) with a dark background.
- Try to keep your font size to no smaller than 24 point and absolutely no smaller than 18 point.
- Try to use as much blank space (also known as white space) around the content of your slides as possible.
- Don't get too fancy on the graphics and/or tables you use. Try to keep them as basic and simple as possible.
- Use bullets wherever possible.
- Never use all uppercase. To emphasize key points, use bolder typefaces and larger font sizes.

Finally, I have one personal pet peeve about PowerPoint presentations: Please do not write long sentences on your slides and then read them word for word to your audience. This is a surefire way to put your audience into a hypnotic state. Write only short phrases—not full sentences—that hit on the main points of your presentation, and prepare like you would for any public-speaking engagement.

Guide on the Side

For more tips and guidelines on using Word, Excel, and PowerPoint, visit the University of Kentucky Human Resources Technology Training website at www.uky.edu/IS/Training/tips.html.

Basic Writing Skills

As an online MBA student and as a business manager, you obviously need basic writing skills to compose effective business plans, letters, memos, and reports.

As someone who writes and edits for a living and who once taught freshman English composition to college students, I have come up with my own set of very basic writing tips:

- Don't be afraid of writing. Writing is actually a very simple process. Many people develop unfounded paranoia about their writing abilities, going back to some high school or early college experience when a teacher red-inked a paper they were initially so proud of composing. I've run into so many people who repeat a self-prophesying "I can't write," when all they need to do is say the reverse of that and add "writing is easy" to their vocabulary to conquer their writing fears in an instant.

- Understand logic. From years of editing other people's work I have found that the most common writing errors are related to logic. The grammar, punctuation, sentence structure, and clarity problems can be easily reconciled with some remedial studying and homework. One book I strongly recommend for a remedial writing refresher is *The Elements of Style*, written by William Strunk, Jr. in 1918—the full contents of which are freely available online at www.bartleby.com/141/.

  With my freshman composition students, I would ask them if they felt their papers followed a logical progression of thought. In other words, did one paragraph lead to the next and so on until they reached their conclusion? Did they follow the rules of *inductive* (from specific to general) and *deductive* (from general to specific) *reasoning?* For example, in a writing assignment, you might induce that a company is unethical based on your reading of a number of specific cases in which that company performed unethically. Or in another writing assignment you might deduce that if a business has been accused of performing unethically, and that business is brought to a court of law in which its executives are found guilty of unethical business practices, that business will either fold up or be restructured. In other words, the premises of an argument, if true, will lead to a valid deduction or conclusion. Writing clearly requires that you repeatedly read your essays and papers with a keen eye to the overall logic of what you have composed.

Online Term

Inductive reasoning is the process of using specific observations, situations, cases, etc. to draw a general conclusion. **Deductive reasoning** is the process of using generalizations to draw a specific conclusion.

- Does your writing flow? Pay attention to how your sentences and paragraphs are tied together to produce a smooth-flowing piece of writing. Some of the tricks of the trade for this include using transitional statements such as *nonetheless*, *therefore, thus, hence, for example, for instance*—but try not to overuse these. Another is to tie your second sentence to the sentence that precedes it. For example, the following three sentences are all tied together and thus provide a smooth train of thought:

Three of the company's top executives were accused of "cooking the books" for their personal financial gain, resulting in their shareholders' losses. These unethical accounting practices led to the company's demise. Furthermore, a jury found that the company's accountancy firm obstructed justice by shredding documents related to these unethical accounting practices.

Graduate-Level Writing Skills

Most online MBA programs require, in addition to remedial writing skills, graduate-level writing skills. This basically means that you will need to understand how to quote and cite whatever sources of information you use in your writing assignments. Additionally, you'll have to understand how to avoid plagiarism. Some programs also require that you follow the guidelines of a particular writing and citation style, such as the *Chicago Manual of Style*, the American Psychological Association (APA) style, or the American Medical Association (AMA) style.

If your academic writing skills are rusty, which is definitely not unusual for the typical online MBA student, most programs will politely ask you to take advantage of the school's online writing lab, called an "OWL," and/or various other writing tutorial services that the school may provide, which are quite common today.

Guide on the Side

Purdue University's online writing lab (OWL), located at http://owl.english.purdue.edu, is a top-notch website that has been serving students all over the world since 1993.

In Chapter 7, for instance, I highlighted the University of Phoenix's Center for Writing Excellence. Other schools have very similar services, such as UMUC's "Online Guide to Writing and Research," located at www.umuc.edu/prog/ugp/ewp_writingcenter/writinggde/welcome.shtm. The UT TeleCampus provides students with access to SMARTHINKING, an online tutorial service with real-time and asynchronous tutoring in writing and a full range of study resources, including writing manuals. Students interact with live tutors, submit questions or papers and get help within 24 hours, or they can schedule a session with a specific tutor. There is also a Grammar Center for answering quick questions and a Brainstorming Center for students who need help with topic ideas for papers.

Information Literacy Skills

Information literacy is an important competency that online students need to develop quickly. The prevalence of Internet-based research has brought about a stronger emphasis on information literacy instruction today. A relatively new field of distance-education librarianship has evolved that is geared toward showing students how to find dependable information for their research and studies.

Online Term

The Association of College and Research Libraries (ACRL) defines **information literacy** as a "set of skills needed to find, retrieve, analyze, and use information .... It includes the technological skills needed to use the modern library as a gateway to information. It enables us to analyze and evaluate the information we find, thus giving us confidence in using that information to make a decision or create a product." For more information, see www.ala.org/ala/acrl/acrlissues/acrlinfolit/informationliteracy.htm.

The amount of free information easily accessible over the Internet has caused concern among librarians regarding the reliability and validity of such information. Additionally, higher-education libraries have been rapidly growing their subscription-based, full-text electronic archives, which have become increasingly available through mass digitization of information by publishers and information aggregators. The end result of all this is that a vast sea of digitized information presents itself to students conducting business research, and it's easy to drown in this deep expanse of intelligence.

Distance-education librarians will explain how people have become overly reliant on "Googling" for all their information needs, which is not considered scholarly research because such popular search engines do not access information from proprietary databases designed and licensed by academic libraries.

In short, any search-engine research is very limited in its scope, and students need to learn how to use alternatives by taking advantage of their school's academic library services. This is where online information literacy skills training plays an important role in the overall online educational system.

At UMUC's online library, for instance, students can take advantage of a host of innovative services provided by a large professional library staff. The UMUC Information and Library Services website at www.umuc.edu/library/library.html—much of which is available to the general public—is a good example of what you should expect from an online library service.

Guide on the Side

I highly recommend that every person who searches the web for information visit a truly great website provided by the University of California Berkeley library, titled "Beyond General World Wide Web Searching." This service is available for free at www.lib.berkeley.edu/TeachingLib/Guides/Internet/BeyondWeb.html, and it features an extremely thorough online tutorial about how to find information on the Internet.

First and foremost are the electronic resources that registered students can log in to with their student ID username and password to access the library's more than 125 proprietary databases, which includes periodical indexes, reference materials, and electronic books. This is the kind of library service that you can expect from any online MBA program. Students use such databases to find articles from magazines and major U.S. and international newspapers; information from papers published in scholarly, peer-reviewed journals on a wide variety of topics; statistical data; and transcripts of television and radio programs. Getting access to all these resources is worth its weight in gold because, first of all, as a matriculated student, you get access to all this valuable and costly information for free. Secondly, many of your assignments will require that you include such resources in your research.

The UMUC library also provides technical support if students have trouble logging in and getting access, online guidance on how to search databases, and 24-hour telephone and live "Chat with a Librarian" support services. An Online Tutorials section covers how to use the web for research, including special online tutorials on how to search for company, financial, and industry information in the library's databases, which online MBA students will frequently use during their individual and group projects and assignments.

All graduate students at UMUC must take a noncredit course called "Library Skills for the Information Age," which, as noted on the UMUC website, is designed to familiarize students with online library and information resources—material that is critical for twenty-first-century managers." In this self-paced online tutorial, students learn to use a variety of electronic retrieval systems. The course is designed so students take a pretest, six modules with self-assessment questions and quizzes, and a post-test. "The purpose of the course is to alert students to the many resources, databases, and research opportunities that are now available online."

Overall, my advice is to take advantage of any library services being offered as soon as you are considered a registered student with a valid student ID username and password. It will be beneficial for all your coursework, and you will learn a lifelong Internet-based research skill that will serve you well in both your personal and business life.

Quantitative Skills

The quantitative-oriented academic side of online MBA programs is often the most challenging for many students. Most programs require that you have at least a basic knowledge of algebra and statistics. However, many adult learners have what can be considered "math anxiety," because they have either not used algebra and/or statistics for years or they have bad memories associated with their math education experiences as undergraduate or even high school students. UMUC's Hartigan explains that some students perceive math courses as being "too theoretical or impractical, although anyone who has worked in business understands how loud numbers can talk, particularly if they have dollar signs attached to them."

Guide on the Side

Many, but not all, online MBA programs require you to take the Graduate Management Admission Test (GMAT) as part of their admission requirements. The GMAT has a quantitative section that measures basic mathematical skills. Questions on the GMAT require knowledge of arithmetic, elementary algebra, and commonly known concepts of geometry. However, preparing for this test may not be enough to prepare you for the quantitative-oriented coursework of a typical online MBA program.

Hartigan says that to combat such negative attitudes, students enrolled in UMUC's MBA Fundamentals course—which is UMUC's online orientation that I covered in Chapter 15—must go through two modules that cover statistical concepts and some basic financial accounting concepts. Hartigan adds that the professors who teach quantitative-oriented subject matter in the UMUC online MBA program explain to students that they cannot approach quantitative assignments like they approach reading. "Students think they can spend an hour or so reading a math problem and they will be able to figure it out. Not so. There is no way around going over the material very carefully numerous times until you absorb it. You just have to be willing to put in that time, unless you are a math genius, particularly if the material is new to you. Students also tend to expect that they should be able to plug numbers into a set formula. This does not help to solve problems. However, one professor (who teaches quantitative courses) did say that part of students' problems with math relates to having inadequate Excel skills."

Another area where math comes into play for an online MBA student is in any accounting courses, which are core to all MBA programs. In particular, students who were not business majors during their undergraduate years find accounting coursework to be the most challenging. The iMBA program at the Penn State World Campus helps to rectify this by providing all its students with an optional self-paced online course that highlights fundamental accounting skills that students take prior to enrolling in their first-term "Accounting for External Reporting" course.

Instant Message

"As an accounting major, I've seen most of the material before, albeit 15 years ago. Even so, I found that my work experience in the intervening years made my learning experience much more vital and relevant than that first time around."

—Robert Breen, online MBA student, Arizona State University

So the bottom line with regard to quantitative skills is to simply take advantage of any remedial math courses and/or tutorial services that most schools offer to their online MBA students.

Test Taking

Another important skill that you may or may not have relates to taking tests. The academic community lumps testing under the single term of *assessments*. An assessment can mean an exam, text, quiz, or survey. Exam results quantify a student's overall knowledge about any given subject or subjects. Tests are more like diagnostic tools in that they measure a person's level of understanding about a subject. Quizzes are typically used as a means to provide feedback to students about their understanding of any given subject. With quizzes, students answer a series of questions and then get immediate results. Surveys are diagnostic tools that measure a group's level of understanding of, or their opinions about, a subject.

Depending on the program, you may take all, some, or none of these assessments either online or at a residency. Most assessments require that you complete them within a certain time frame. An online assessment, for example, might automatically shut off within one hour after you start taking it. Some students are not good at taking assessments under time pressures, be they online or on-campus, giving rise to anxiety. Other students and faculty dislike exams and tests and believe that they are not valid measurements of a person's true intelligence, but they really enjoy taking online quizzes that provide immediate feedback about their knowledge, skills, and/or ability to make wise decisions under pressure, which brings me to the conclusion of this chapter.

Take This Test, Please

If you want to take a fascinating online assessment that measures your level of information technology knowledge and skills (ITKS), computer knowledge and skills, word processing, spreadsheets, databases, presentations, and web development—all of which are important in the world of business—go to www.unt.edu/slis/apppacket/ITKS/ITKSassess.htm and play with the ITKS online diagnostic tool from the University of North Texas (UNT) School of Library and Information Sciences (SLIS).

See whether you score the recommended standard score of 75 percent to demonstrate "satisfactory readiness" in each of the aforementioned areas. If you score lower than 75 percent, you may need to take some remedial action. The ITKS diagnostic tool is currently used as a measure of entry-level requirements for UNT's SLIS Master's degree program, but it's generic enough to give you a good indication of your information technology capabilities as they relate to the business world, as well as good practice for getting used to taking online assessments.

Ten Tips and Tricks for the Online Student

School district instructional technologist and former online graduate student at the University of Phoenix Mark Evans says he did not expect "too many bumps in the online road" when he enrolled in his first online graduate-level course in 2000. After all, he's an avid computer geek and Internet-savvy professional who is "firmly entrenched" in all that is new and cutting edge in the world of education technology. Or so he thought.

Evans claims that at the end of his first week as an online student he felt "panicked, confused, and overwhelmed," as it quickly became apparent to him that "this virtual schooling was not going to be easy. I struggled to work within a synchronous and asynchronous environment while juggling my teammate's schedules, multiple assignments, and my day-to-day job. Finally, after the first course, I realized I had to make some changes."

To help himself, and his fellow classmates, Evans came up with the following 10 tips (condensed version) for the online learner:

- Read everything twice. Read everything twice. It's very easy for a student in an online environment—pressed for time and anxious to complete homework—to scan through postings, lectures, and assignments without really reading or, consequently, retaining anything. By reading each posting twice, a student has a better chance of understanding the true message being communicated.

- Wait to reply. An immediate response to a posting or message that a student finds upsetting or challenging can often result in a war of words rather than thoughtful discussion or meaningful discourse. You may send something thinking your words are humorous or satirically funny, but others may misinterpret them. Take the equivalent of a "Count to 10 and breathe" break before hitting the Reply button.

- Reference it. Perhaps print it. The temptation in an online classroom is to print everything you're assigned to read, from e-mails and postings to websites and lectures. Only print reading assignments that are to be referenced later or if the assignment is somewhat lengthy. However, if you're "paper-trained," you may need to have the tactile sensation of holding what you read in your hands, so feel free to print your reading assignments.

- Talking in class. Instant messaging (or live chat) can bring spontaneity of real-world conversation to you and your fellow online colleagues. If you are allowed to use chat software, it's important to keep a log of your conversations for posting to your classroom. For example, when my teammates and I chatted about projects, we copied our conversation to the class folder. This allowed absent team members to follow our train of thought as we developed our ideas and processes.

- A place for everything and everything in its place. In an online course, information comes at you fast and furious and, before you realize it, you're buried under a deluge of data and piles of printouts. Organize both your printed and computer files the same way. The naming structure you have on your hard drive should mirror what you have in the real world. This method of organizing my coursework saved me time, eased my frustration, and helped me focus more on the course.

- Getting personal. Title the subject line of postings with personal and requirement data. Simply put, make it easy to know who sent the posting and why. Is it an assignment, a comment, a question to the professor? Above all, use your subject lines for quick identification by others of your postings.
- Make your message meaningful. Make an effort to include more details, rationale, and opinion in your online discussions. Cite the specific portion of the discussion to which you are referring. This enables those in your class to follow the conversation's path, and contributes to a more intelligent discourse. Otherwise, postings have little meaning, and the students and facilitator have to "hunt" around for shifts in discussion topics.
- Better safe than sorry. For complete and accurate documentation, anytime you send an e-mail or posting, send a copy to yourself. This provides proof that the e-mail is delivered through the school's system, and shows when the e-mail was sent. This is critical for assignments due by a certain time. Send a copy of important messages to yourself at an alternate e-mail address (such as a Hotmail or Yahoo! account) to ensure that you have a complete set of records in case something happens to the program server or network. If you have all of your information stored in a separate account, you can continue working without interruption.
- Be your own guide. If your professor does not seem to be an effective classroom leader, you can help by communicating clearly and effectively with him or her. Keep e-mails to one question or one topic; multiple questions in a message may be overlooked in a response. Make use of all methods of communication provided by the professor: phone, e-mail, chat software, etc. If you do contact him or her by phone or chat, follow up with an e-mail or posting afterward stating what you asked and what you believe the answer was. Do not wait for the situation to become unbearable before asking for help or clarification. By asking questions immediately, you may never have problems.
- Ready, set, go. Maintain an accurate calendar and schedule. At the start of each course, enter all assignment due dates in your planner. Then determine how many days you will need to complete each assignment. For instance, if an assignment is due on Thursday that you believe will take three days to complete, mark your planner to work on the assignment on Monday, Tuesday, and Wednesday. Remember to allow time for personal and employment-related events. If possible, allow an extra day or two for technology glitches, team members running behind on projects, and other unforeseen delays. Don't forget to set aside time for studying, reviewing, and researching.

So there you have it—just about every skill requirement for becoming a successful online learner has been covered in this chapter. If you are like most adult learners, you already have many of these skills but perhaps not all of them. Fine-tuning those areas where you may be lacking shouldn't take you longer than one semester or quarter. You may, however, find it a bit more challenging to tackle what's covered in the next chapter on how to be an effective team player.

The Least You Need to Know

- How to communicate effectively and efficiently is one of the most important skills you can have in the online learning environment.
- Other skills you'll need to be a successful online learner include typing, reading comprehension, basic computer, software, writing, information literacy, quantitative, and test-taking skills.
- If you are lacking in any of the skill areas, always take advantage of any remedial online courses or tutorials a school offers to help increase your online learning skills.
- Take the initiative to visit websites and use online diagnostic tools that can identify your strengths and/or weakness and help you gain insight into online learner skills in general.

Chapter 17

Working with Your Peers

In This Chapter

- How schools facilitate team projects
- How schools ensure your participation in team projects
- How students and administrators regard team projects
- How team projects can be beneficial

Most online MBA programs emphasize teamwork and frequently put students into revolving groups, usually of four to five people, to work together on a variety of assignments, such as case-based projects, research reports, and business plans. Cohort-based programs with residencies often have these team projects culminate in their face-to-face sessions, where students present their collaborative work that they have conducted primarily online during a semester or quarter, and where they get evaluated by their peers and faculty to ultimately tabulate a final grade.

Programs without residencies conduct team projects completely online. Either way, students are required to learn how to work with their classmates, which at times can be a challenge for a variety of reasons, especially in the online environment when team members are located in different time zones and need to synchronously connect online.

In Chapter 10, I introduced the notion of how team projects are good examples of competency-based learning techniques that are based on specific learning objectives and outcomes. In this chapter, I go into the details of how some schools facilitate team projects and how you can be an effective team player. Real-life examples and advice are included throughout.

Instant Message

"Students expect group projects at this level, and Blackboard has a feature for group file exchanges, so groups have their own private place in Blackboard where they can work on papers and pass around drafts without having to e-mail them. They can also have their own chat rooms and discussion boards, which is important when students are in different time zones."

—Paula O'Callaghan, director, IMBA Program, Syracuse University

Team Projects in General

Basically, working in teams is what most businesspeople must deal with on a daily basis, particularly those who work within large corporations. When it comes to online learning, the goal for many business schools is to parrot real-life business team endeavors as closely as possible with the aim of teaching students how to become better team players.

One of the themes that consistently comes up when talking about online MBA team-based projects is that they can be both invigorating and disgruntling to students. Overall, however, there is a growing trend in the world of online MBA programs whereby business schools are becoming more adept at facilitating active and highly organized team projects that students can find to be quite beneficial to their overall business education.

Stat

The University of Phoenix sponsored a study (the results of which were published in March 2004) in which 467 online military students responded to a 27-question survey about their online learning experiences. According to the summary report of the survey, "About half of the students surveyed appear to like learning teams, as measured by *satisfaction* with, *importance* of, and *value* derived from the team approach (51, 47, and 49 percent respectively)."

Team Innovation Example (Penn State)

I have talked extensively about team projects with more than a dozen online MBA program administrators, almost all of whom double as professors who facilitate team projects in their online courses. Some of the most innovative team-based projects I came across were from the Penn State World Campus program, now in its fourth year of providing a lock-step cohort online MBA curriculum.

Penn State's online MBA program consists of eight terms. At the end of the third term, which is about nine months into the program, students meet face to face for their first week-long residency. A second week-long residency is held at the end of the final term. The entire program takes 24 months to complete. Both residencies are team-based.

As noted on the Penn State online MBA website, "In the first residency experience, students work with a prominent U.S. firm and its executives; integrating financial, organizational, cultural, and strategic themes as they dissect the operations of the firm and provide a perspective on future operations. In the second residency experience, the capstone requirement of the program, students integrate knowledge and skills attained from all previous courses to develop and implement strategic plans in an international business environment. Guest speakers from business and industry take part in each residency experience."

A Team-Based Integrative Experience

Penn State Program Director John Fizel explains how corporate America, in general, looks toward MBA programs to develop managers "who can work in all functional areas of business." The iMBA program integrates that philosophy across its curriculum, including its two residency requirements. At one of its recent first week-long residencies, for example, a group of approximately 60 students were given the opportunity to interact with high-level executives at QVC, headquartered in Philadelphia.

Prior to the residency, student teams prepared by conducting an analysis of the company using information that is publicly available. At the residency, students toured the company's operations and questioned executives from different functional areas of QVC about their roles in the business and within QVC's overall mission and vision. The students then combined this public information with the information they gleaned at the live meetings and came up with an integrative company analysis that examined the financial, organizational, cultural, and strategic aspects of the company.

During the week, the teams made several presentations before iMBA faculty and each other and participated in a poster session related to the QVC project. The culminating assignment for each team was to use their company analysis as the foundation for offering a document that outlined strategic alternatives for the future operations of QVC. These documents were 75 to 100 pages and shared with the company.

This kind of team project "integrates everything they have learned and immediately puts theory into practice with a company outside of their own," says Fizel. "Students develop the skills to work in all functional areas of business by completing this broad and in-depth analysis."

International Teamwork

For the second and final week-long residency in Penn State's iMBA program, students come to the Penn State campus and participate as teams in an international business electronic simulation exercise. Each team takes on the role of a mock business competing in the international marketplace. The electronic simulations allow the teams to integrate production, marketing, finance, and people skills.

Working an average of 60 hours over the entire week, the teams tackle a series of questions and challenges concerning such issues as overseas and domestic operational plans, marketing strategies, distribution channels, organizational strategies, internal costs, profitability, and more. "Students again see the integration of business functions but now extended to a global marketplace," says Fizel.

Instant Message

"A crucial part of our program is where international students who don't know each other's cultures have to work on team projects. In this kind of environment, we are actually preparing our students for existing and future organizations (that customarily collaborate on business solutions online). You cannot do this in the traditional classroom."
—Venkateshwar Reddy, interim dean, College of Business and Administration and the Graduate School of Business Administration, University of Colorado at Colorado Springs

More Perspectives on Teams

Other variations of team projects include small groups of students coming together completely online without ever meeting face to face. Some completely online team projects might have students take sides in a business debate inside a special group-based discussion board, for instance, arguing back and forth about a company's strategic adaptability, or lack thereof, over the long term of a business cycle. Other team projects will assess various segments of a business enterprise, through the examination of case studies.

For example, one team might do an evaluation of a human resources or marketing case and another team might collectively critique that evaluation. Again, all these types of team-based projects usually culminate in teams working together to write a paper or create a PowerPoint presentation. Overall, the added value of such team assignments typically comes from the rich discussions and give-and-take learning and sharing that takes place between students. "You get a lot more input from a lot more people when they do team projects," says Penn State's Fizel.

Ensuring Participation

Still, not all team projects operate as smoothly as both students and faculty may want them to, so business schools usually develop rules for teams that ensure, for instance, that everyone carries his or her own weight instead of having the bulk of the burden of team projects fall on the more enterprising students in any particular group. This is accomplished through such things as team charters and team work plans.

At the University of Phoenix, for instance, students must fill out a "Learning Team Charter." The charter lists team members' names and contact information (phone, fax, and e-mail), each team member's skill inventory, learning team goals, ground rules, and a conflict-management section that asks what potential conflicts might arise among or between team members and how members will deal with such conflicts.

Instant Message

"My advice in terms of working with your peers in team projects is that you have to lighten up a little bit and communicate. The communication is critical."

—Rosemary Hartigan, director of online MBA programs, University of Maryland University College

Similar to a University of Phoenix Learning Team Charter, the University of Maryland University College (UMUC), requires students to develop an official work plan for their team projects. The plan sets forth very clearly who is suppose to do what and outlines responsibilities and deadlines for turning in assignments. The work plan is submitted to the course professor for approval, and all contributions to the team project must be posted inside a special group section created in the course management system. If a problem arises, the professor has the work plan for evidence as well as the ability to see who met their responsibilities inside the online group section.

In general, team project agreements are known to be very successful with regard to cutting down on team problems, as such agreements enforce accountability.

Another form of enforcing accountability is often accomplished through team project peer evaluations. At Arizona State University, for instance, at the end of a team project students anonymously rate their fellow teammates by completing a special online peer evaluation form in an area of the course management system that is only viewable by the professor of the course. Professors will use the evaluations, particularly in relatively large team projects that occur over the time period of an entire course, as a guide for tabulating a percentage that is worked into students' overall grades.

Instant Message

"Communicate and let your team know where you are going to be at all times. If you are going away for two days, don't just disappear. This can be the cause of problems with new students in courses with team projects. Seasoned students, however, will let everyone know if they are going away on vacation."

—Ken Sherman, associate dean, University of Phoenix Graduate Business Program

Comments and Advice from Students

In researching this book I communicated with about 20 online MBA students and alumni and asked them a number of questions related to team projects. What follows are some of the questions I asked and their comments. These are provided to give you a general feel for how online MBA students reacted to and adapted to team projects. I think you'll find an interesting mix of observations and advice that could prove to be helpful when you are put into a similar team situation as an online MBA student.

What Are Team Projects Like?

The obvious primary and general question was what were your team projects like? Overall, the responses were both emotional, in relation to working with teammates who did not pull their weight, to fairly straight forward, in relation to how teamwork was organized and accomplished.

From Linda Couch, online MBA graduate, University of Maryland University College:

> **Learning about international business.** "We had team papers, for the most part. During the finance module we also had problems to solve. But most of the work involved writing papers that had varying degrees of difficulty and complexity. The most complex one was in our international business module. We were given a list of pairs of countries. Then we had to identify a real company that was not doing business in one of the pairs of countries. We first split into sub teams, and each sub team studied one of the countries with respect to political climate, economy, infrastructure, trade, labor market, legal system, etc. We wrote interim papers for different sets of criteria for each country. Then each sub team evaluated that country with respect to bringing out our chosen company's product to market into that country and wrote a paper analyzing the opportunity. Then the sub teams compared notes and decided as a team which one of the countries was better suited for the product. We wrote our final paper to recommend one country and supported our recommendation."

From Christopher Hodges, online MBA student, Syracuse University:

> **Working on a team from across an ocean.** "I've sometimes had to reassure students from the U.S. that it will be possible to function effectively with my being based in Spain provided that they remember to build in the six-hour time difference, which, in fact, works to their advantage because it effectively gives the team a 30-hour day. They can post something last thing at night U.S. time that I can work on in the European morning and have ready by the time they get up. Organizing the work between team members seems to depend on the number and complexity of assignments. For a larger number of shorter assignments, a team member will usually take responsibility for preparing a draft of an entire assignment on which the other team members will give feedback before final submission. For more complex assignments, the members prepare different sections and then an 'editor' will put them together to create one document. The assignments range from Word documents to PowerPoint presentations, including one that required a voiceover commentary. The content varies enormously between modules and professors. Some use more case studies than others."

From Katherine Porter, online MBA graduate, Regis University:

> **A differing point of view.** "Thankfully, I had precious few team projects, maybe four total. My experience has been that team projects in school generally turn

into one or two people doing all the work and everyone else benefiting from it. In checking with friends who had completed their MBAs—all in traditional programs—those who were in team-based programs, and those who just had to work on projects in teams on occasion, all agreed that the team concept was a distraction, that it helped unqualified/undeserving students graduate, and unfairly burdened the real go-getters. So, I made a concerted effort to find a program where team projects were not a focus. Though the schools with team-based projects will argue that teamwork is a part of life and professional work, I think during school it is important to focus on mastering the concepts and subjects yourself. You can later contribute to a team according to your strengths and weaknesses as discovered during school."

From Jennifer Skipton, online MBA student, University of Colorado at Colorado Springs:

Improving communication skills. "As far as what the projects were like, they were somewhat challenging given that everyone has different ideas. Only twice have I come up against someone who didn't bother to contribute and seemed to just 'hide' in the background, but we were able to overcome that and managed to entice that person to participate. Usually when doing projects, we meet once—online or through e-mails—and plan what needs to be done and break up into tasks for everyone, with timelines provided. Second, we all submit our work to each other and then meet again to discuss our findings. Finally, one last meeting is held to kind of summarize and write up our paper. Everyone takes turns on who completes what portion of the assignments to ensure all are involved. Basically, to do online courses you have to plan ahead. One of the first things we all seem to do at the beginning of the semester, when teams are first assigned, is to let everyone know our contact methods, work schedules, and finally, any vacation plans that will make it difficult for us to contribute. We all do this so that we all get a good understanding of what challenges, personally, everyone is up against, and this way we can work around things."

Any Advice for More Effective Teams?

Some of the other questions asked of these students centered around providing advice in regard to collaborating effectively and actually getting the work done. There was an immediacy factor emphasized, with recommendations to move away from the online environment to live chat or phone conversations for more personal, easier-to-comprehend interactions and to quickly resolve any disagreements or workload questions and strategies. There was also a strong emphasis on respecting cohorts under what could be trying and challenging circumstances. Following are some observations and advice related to working sensibly as a team member.

From Linda Couch, online MBA graduate, University of Maryland University College:

- Our teachers forced us to start by creating a team web page. This perhaps sounds like a waste of time, but it accomplished several things. First, it forced you to figure out how to work together before you had something very difficult to do. Second, the web page included contact info, so you had everything you needed if/when you needed to reach someone. Third, we were asked to include codes of conduct—e.g., when people will check e-mail, how people will offer criticism, or how we would resolve conflicts. It created a sense of being a team right away.
- Especially at first, use the most "intimate" form of communication possible in order to build a relationship and establish working methods. The order of communication preference should be face-to-face meeting, phone conversation, chat room, e-mail.
- Ask people to identify their strengths and weaknesses, or likes and dislikes. This helps make it easier to distribute workload and figure out how to function best as a team.
- Force different teammates to take leadership roles. In an online environment, it is much easier to "disappear" and hope someone else will do the work.
- Enable real-time communication vehicles such as chat room and teleconference capabilities.

From Christopher Hodges, online MBA student, Syracuse University:

- Establish the ground rules for teams at the start of the term, covering communication, timing, working arrangements, and a detailed agreement regarding how the first assignment is going to be handled.
- Remember that things take longer when undertaken virtually, so plan accordingly.
- Take the initiative to keep in touch, come up with ideas, and generally keep the momentum going.
- Keep team members informed of what you're doing, especially if you can't meet a deadline.

- Mix calls with e-mails.
- Always give feedback on other team members' work, even if it's to say "job well done" and you don't have anything to add.
- Address problems quickly. Call team members if they are not maintaining communication to find out what's going on. Consider dropping a member, even if that person's name appears on the assignment, which makes organizing work much easier for the remaining members.
- When the problems start early, consider warning the team member that he or she will be dropped from the team and the professor informed accordingly.

From Katherine Porter, online MBA graduate, Regis University:

- Always take the high road. You might feel confident that you're in the right, but it's a big world and you don't own it, so don't take any bait, and never lower yourself to another's level. In fact, give some thought to why someone might be baiting you or slinging mud. (Did you inadvertently cause offense?)
- Keep an open mind, especially with online communications it is easy to misunderstand someone. Ask forgiveness when you've been a jerk. Better yet, don't be a jerk to begin with.
- Start every interaction respecting others, respecting them as humans, classmates, and professionals. Resolve to learn something from everyone. If you approach interactions with that intent, you're more likely to succeed in every way.

Final Note on Teams

Yes, indeed, team projects can be multifaceted, dynamic, and valuable learning experiences, but also somewhat controversial and troubling at times. Being open-minded, conscientious, unselfish, and a good worker bee, so to speak, should serve you well. Team projects have been known to create excellent networking opportunities for students, so don't take them lightly. Under the right circumstances, you could be interacting with and learning from high-level, knowledgeable businesspeople, which is an aspect of being an online MBA student that is truly valuable, beyond what you might learn from your professors and the overall curriculum itself.

The Least You Need to Know

- Most online MBA programs require a certain number of team projects. If a program has a residency requirement, a team project will culminate at the live meeting. Fully online programs have fully online team projects.
- There are a good number of team project variations, including business analysis projects, debate-oriented projects, and case-based study projects.
- To ensure participation by all team members, most team projects have rules and regulations that are outlined in a contract or charter that all participants must agree to and follow.
- Online MBA students advise that being active, reliable, and a skilled communicator are very important in regard to succeeding in a team-based learning environment.

Part 5 Your Career Evolution

What will your pathway to business success entail? Does your current or future employer(s) have an understanding of what it means to be an online MBA graduate? How can you tally a potential return on investment from earning your MBA? These questions, and more, are answered in this part of the book. Also how to market your unique skills is explained, and there are some notes about the MBA job marketplace, in general.

Better yet, you'll get to read 14 MBA student profiles from 8 online MBA programs. These students provide a treasure trove of valuable insights and advice that you can take to the bank. Overall, these profiles are a special added value and must-read part of the book.

Chapter 18

Your Pathway

In This Chapter

- How to deal with employer perceptions
- Resources and strategies for determining your ROI
- Resources for networking
- What a recruiter might do
- How to sell yourself

Although most online MBA graduates are already gainfully employed, a good number of them are also actively seeking new pathways to carry through the knowledge and skills they have gained during their education. It's not unusual, for instance, for online MBA graduates to experience high levels of frustration with nonreceptive employers. These graduates find that their enthusiasm to make a difference at their jobs, which was generated through their online education experience, is not so readily heeded by their bosses. Consequently, many online MBA graduates do keep their eyes open for other opportunities. I heard of one enterprising student, for instance, who made four upwardly mobile job moves during his three-year online MBA experience.

Other students have found that their online education could bring them immediate rewards, resulting in promotions before they actually graduated. These students work for progressive companies that have a keen sense of how technology is changing the workplace. In fact, as more of corporate America utilizes web-based technologies in its day-to-day business activities, executives are increasingly seeing online learning itself as a skill-builder that teaches people how to communicate effectively in the online environment.

No matter what your situation, you are going to ask yourself how this new degree will affect your career. In short, the online MBA graduate is really no different from the traditional MBA graduate. The same rules apply for finding work; however, the job-seeking online MBA student may face a few hurdles that the traditional online MBA graduate does not face.

All this relates to your career advancement, or what many people refer to today as career switching, career enhancement, or even lifelong learning. This chapter contains some tips, advice, and perceptions from some experts in the field of career development, and some general information that can help you evolve to the next level of your professional life and beyond.

Potential Employer Perceptions

Even though your degree will not stipulate that you earned your MBA online, any prospective employer you talk with during a job-hunting expedition could easily find out that you did. If, for instance, a graduate earned his online MBA from a school in California and applied for a position in New York, where he happens to live, his resumé would show a discrepancy between his place of residence and where he went to school. Plus, during an interview process, when and if the conversation turns to education history, "online" will more than likely come to the forefront.

Instant Message

"What I have found most rewarding is that the mix of academics and real-world discussion with peers from around the world has provided not only an understanding of the fundamentals but also of the applications. I am often able to leverage a classmate's experience by recalling some of our online interactions. As a result, I believe I am a more valuable colleague and coach."

—Tim Bzowey, online MBA student, Athabasca University

One problem that can arise is a potential employer's perception of online degree programs. As mentioned in Chapter 12, some executives are not fully aware of how online education can be considered a learning and skill-enhancing experience on equal footing with a traditional MBA.

Online MBA graduates who find themselves in a circumstance where a potential employer's perception is misinformed have to become educators themselves. For instance, if you're in a potential employer's office that has an Internet connection, you can easily do an online demonstration of your program's features and curriculum. Or you can keep printouts handy of your program's curriculum that outline the courses you took as an online student. You can also refer prospective employers to the professors and deans of the program you graduated from, who are always more than happy to assist graduates with career advancement.

Perhaps most importantly, if there was something that you learned as an online student that you immediately applied to your job, make sure you have that recorded in some way that can be shown on a resumé or report or referenced through a colleague or letter of recommendation. For example, online MBA student at Athabasca University Tom Kiley, who works as a senior manager of organizational effectiveness for a financial group in Toronto, notes that his experience as an online learner "has broadened my understanding of key business concepts and sharpened my analytical skills. I have been able to directly apply this learning to workplace initiatives, heightening my personal contribution to key department projects—early payback on the investment in the MBA program." So the basic message to all online MBA students is, if you've already experienced what Kiley refers to as "early payback," be sure you have that as proof of how online learning is really no different from on-campus.

Nonetheless, if you are an experienced business professional, you will more than likely not have to deal with a scenario in which you will have to explain your formal education to a prospective employer. If you only have a few years of professional work experience under your belt, the formal education part of your resumé may be a more important factor.

Instant Message

"Not only have I used elements from each class thus far in my day-to-day work life, but also I have been promoted from director and general manager to VP of economic development. I believe that the concepts learned in my coursework have enabled me to be prepared for my new position."

—Jodie Filardo, online MBA student, Arizona State University

The ROI Factor

In typical business fashion, MBA students frequently talk about their return on investment (ROI), or, in other words, what is their degree really worth? They look at the cost of their education as a profit or loss statement that is ultimately figured out by the salary increase they hope to obtain after graduation. What MBAs can expect to earn depends on many factors, including the program they graduated from, the geographic region where they are seeking a new position, and, obviously, the type of new position they are pursuing.

Start with the Occupational Outlook Handbook

To get a sense for what your MBA degree might be worth in relation to where you want to live and what kind of position you're hoping to land, you can start with the *Occupational Outlook Handbook*, updated every two years by the U.S. Department of Labor Bureau of Labor Statistics. The handbook has a seemingly endless amount of data on occupational and employment trends on a national level. If you are someone who has grown into a kind of information technologist from your online MBA schooldays, which you should be by the time you graduate, you can sift through and decipher the valuable information provided in the handbook entirely over the Internet at www.bls.gov/oco/home.htm.

According to Margaret Dikel, an Internet consultant for employment, career counseling, and career-transition services, MBA graduates can start with the handbook to get a sense for national trends on various jobs that are listed under the federal government's *Standard Occupation Classification (SOC) System*, which is a hierarchical structure of both broad and detailed occupational definitions.

For example, a search on the 2004–2005 handbook website showed that the 2002 medium salary on a national scale for marketing managers was $78,250, and that the industry employing the largest number of marketing managers was in the computer systems design sector. You can then compare that national data to what's happening at a state level by going to any state government website and reviewing all the data it typically provides under what's referred to as Labor Market Information, or LMI, which includes wage and salary statistics, what professions are growing, what local companies are hiring, and much more. "Nationwide trends are one thing, but what is happening in your state or even in your region can be completely off kilter from what you see across the nation," says Dikel, who also is the creator of a terrific web directory of employment and career information called "The Riley Guide," located online at www.rileyguide.com.

The Riley Guide, which has links upon links to all the top resources for jobseekers, also has a special section titled "Employment and Industry Trends" located at www.rileyguide.com/trends.html. Here, among many other links to resources, are links to the government agency websites of all 50 states. Each state website has different levels of LMI data, and to sift through and interpret all this data can be daunting at times, because each state presents their LMI data differently. Nonetheless, these sites provide more localized information, often down to the county and city levels, that can help you make a decision that reflects upon your MBA ROI goals. Going back to our marketing manager job, for instance, the average annual salary in the state of Michigan for this position in 2002 was posted at about $95,000; in Arizona, it was about $73,000.

Online Term

The **Occupational Outlook Handbook** is a nationally recognized source of career information designed to provide valuable assistance to individuals making decisions about their future work lives. Revised every two years, the handbook describes what workers do on the job, working conditions, the training and education needed, earnings, and expected job prospects in a wide range of occupations.

The **Standard Occupation Classification System** is used by federal, state, and local government agencies to classify workers into occupational categories. There are 820 occupation classifications in the system listed within 23 major groups, 96 minor groups, and 451 broad occupations.

More ROI Strategies

In addition to digging up LMI data to see what you may be worth in a specific field or sector and geographic region that you have historically worked in, Dikel suggests that graduates take a look at how they could transfer into new industry sectors where their worth might be higher than what they realize. "How many ways can you take your MBA, plus your previous qualifications and skills, and apply them across industries?" she asks. "A lot of times we tend to focus on only our industry or field. Now that you have these added qualifications, you should think of what we call transferable skills. How can I take my knowledge of, let's say, mechanical engineering, for instance, and recombine it and move it into a different industry sector or a different career path that might be growing?" In this particular example, the mechanical engineer could seek out a new career path as a financial analyst, a senior research associate, or an international sales and marketing agent for a major manufacturing company.

Networking Online

One way of putting in motion more opportunities to move into a new career path is to start networking. Dikel has a special section on her web directory titled "Network, Interview, and Negotiate" in which she provides plenty of advice and links to outside resources that can help MBAs fine-tune their networking skills. In an article titled "Networking and Your Job Search," which Dikel composed based on "everything good" that she has read or heard, she explains that networking is frequently referred to as the best method to obtain a new and rewarding position.

In particular, Dikel has some very sound advice for how to network over the Internet. One thing she stresses is to make sure your online persona does not work against you. She writes that "a lot of Internet oldie-moldies need a reminder that there are real people behind the electrons, and real people make real decisions based on your electronic communication blunders." As an online MBA student, one thing you should have in your favor is that you have learned how to present yourself quite well online, so online networking should be an ideal way for you to get things started in the right direction.

The following is a list of advantages of online networking (by Dikel):

- There are thousands of discussion groups and community forums covering hundreds of subjects.
- You can "break the ice" before meeting someone in person.
- You can listen, engage, or be engaged as you wish. No one can see you sweat, and you don't have to feel like a wallflower wince no one can see you standing off by yourself.
- Many recruiters are lurking the lists to find potential candidates.

The following is a list of disadvantages of online networking (by Dikel):

- Networking online is just as difficult as networking in person! In fact, it may be harder because you can't really establish a true personal relationship online.
- First impressions count even more. Be careful with your first public posting.
- Your online behavior matters more than you think. Don't be a jerk!

Dikel also provides links to mailing lists, chat rooms, websites, and business-related forums where working professionals can network. To read her full article about networking online, go to www.rileyguide.com/network.html.

Finally, for links to websites with job listings and more, see Dikel's "Job Listings: Places to Start Looking for Opportunities" at www.rileyguide.com/jobs.html.

Instant Message

"Networking does not have to be a carefully choreographed process of meeting and greeting people. It's much better done on a more informal basis, but remember that networking is always a two-way street. It must benefit both persons to be most effective, so as you ask your network for help, be prepared to return the favor when asked."

—Margaret Dikel, Internet consultant for employment, career counseling, and career transition services

The Recruiter's Vantage Point

To get a sense for what human-resources departments and recruiting divisions at large companies might think about online MBAs, I talked with Debra Besemer, president and CEO of BrassRing, an award-winning international company that provides recruitment software, talent consulting, and recruitment process management services to companies throughout the world. Major corporations, such as Baxter Medical, RR Donnelley and Unisys, that have access to large databases of job candidates use BrassRing's software to help them find the right professionals to fill their executive job openings.

According to Besemer, employers often search for MBAs based on the quality of the institution they graduated from. "Most employers have their favorite institutions," she says. "They go to their executives in management and do a profile of where those people earned their degrees, and those tend to be the schools that they recruit from over and over." So in short, at some large corporations, where you graduate from does, indeed, make a difference.

Besemer's advice to prospective MBA students, be they online or on-campus, is "don't try to take a quick path from a less-than-stellar institution." She adds that job recruiters today frequently use software, such as what BrassRing provides, that allows them to segment by school all the resumé searching they do electronically through large databases, such as Monster.com and CareerBuilder.com, as well as through their own internal databases. If a recruiter has a negative or positive bias toward any given MBA program, he or she can automatically eliminate or add to their database of job candidates based on the institution they graduated from.

Market Your Unique Skills

No matter what your circumstances may be, if you are seeking a move up within your company or a new position someplace else, you have to market yourself. For the online MBA student, you can reveal that you have the right stuff to be a valuable asset to any organization. In particular, your experience working on virtual teams as an online MBA student could be perceived as a valuable skill with a modern mid-size to large corporation where virtual teaming is commonplace.

John DePolo, director of global staffing with RTI International, says that although many management-level employees do need to be good in front of people in terms of making presentations and having a professional appearance, they may also need to have a good "virtual presence." Online MBA graduates can obviously bring their virtual skills out into the forefront of their interviews and on their resumés. The ability to get things done in a virtual team through the power of one's ideas, presentation skills, and logic should be stressed as part of an online MBA graduate's self-marketing strategy, says DePolo, who also previously owned a private practice that provided strategic recruitment consulting services to Fortune 100 companies.

Instant Message

"So much of business today is done online, that learning those sills through an online degree program should be valued in the marketplace. Where we used to have face-to-face meetings, we now use instant messaging and e-mail, as well as web conferencing."

—Debra Besemer, president and CEO of BrassRing

Basically you need to sell yourself, and adult, working professionals are frequently the kind of people who need to be reminded of this. According to Andrea Davis, vice president and co-founder of FlashPoint, a human-resource consulting firm in Indianapolis, "Most people don't like selling themselves. They may think that their experience should speak for itself, that 'you should know I'm successful because otherwise I would not have been promoted to the next job.' Well, they should also be able to explain how, why, and what they actually did. Don't just let the MBA listing on your resumé speak for itself. Be able to talk about it."

Davis further explains that at your current job, this notion of selling yourself in order to move up the career ladder can be even more difficult because "your employer may have a hard time seeing beyond where you have been," with the company. So "you have to do a better job of always coming back to saying 'Here is what I am learning, or let me work on this project while I'm in the online program so I can strengthen my skills.' You need to be doing that the whole time. I do think many people have the false expectation that they are going to get this MBA and be promoted immediately. That's not going to happen if your employer does not see how your education is bettering your performance or improving your skills."

Job Outlook for MBAs

So what's the job market look like these days for MBAs? A quick content analysis of the literature on job prospects for MBAs, in general, reveals a mixed bag of opportunities. Most recruiters will tell you how the market for MBAs fluctuates. Two or three years ago there were all kinds of articles about how MBAs were in high demand; one year ago the tone of many of the articles stressed a very poor marketplace for MBAs; and currently there seems to be a movement that says the demand for MBAs is coming back. You'll find the pundits on this topic to be both positive and negative.

Guide on the Side

Check out the MBA Career Opportunities section of MBA.com at www.mba.com/mba/AssessCareersAndTheMBA/Default.htm#MBACareerOpportunities. This site contains a searchable database of articles from Vault and WebFeet, two excellent sources for industry and career profiles.

To perhaps oversimplify regarding the demand for MBAs, in general, it really depends on the economy. As the economy fluctuates, so do executive- and management-level job prospects. My personal feeling is that it's no use getting caught up in the job outlook and economy picture. Instead look at your degree as a long-term investment that will sooner or later get you ahead, but also know how to connect the dots, so to speak. "Figure out a way to connect your experiences throughout your career," advises Davis. "The work you have accomplished, the results you have achieved—somehow connect that to the learning you have gained in an MBA program. Putting MBA on paper is not going to show how that has made you a better candidate. It may get someone to take a second glance, but what is that connection?"

The Least You Need to Know

- Know how to explain what your online MBA curriculum consisted of and how it was a learning and skill-enhancing experience that is just as valuable as earning a traditional MBA.
- Understand that some recruiters and employers might eliminate you from their job-searching criteria based solely on the school you graduated from.
- Use Internet resources such as the online Occupational Outlook Handbook and state government websites to find out what positions might be available in a specific geographic region as well as for finding data about average salaries.
- Learn how to find networking opportunities, many of which can be found and facilitated online. Make sure you know how to communicate skillfully online and how not to create an online persona that may work against you.
- Make the connection between what you learned and what you accomplished in your work and always stress that connection with your current employer or any prospective employer in order to move up the career ladder.

Chapter 19

Profiles of 14 Students from 8 MBA Programs

In This Chapter

- Student backgrounds
- Online learning experiences
- How students chose their programs
- Advice from students
- Examples of Career Advancement

One of the best ways to learn about the career and education evolution of online MBA students is to directly ask them about their experiences learning online, as well as how they have applied what they learned to their jobs. So to get a sense for what the students in these programs are experiencing, for this chapter I created a 10-question survey that was sent to more than 50 online MBA students and alumni through the administrators of online MBA programs at the following eight institutions, listed in alphabetical order:

- The W.P. Carey MBA - Online Program at Arizona State University
- Athabasca University
- East Carolina University
- Regis University
- Syracuse University
- University of Florida
- University of Maryland University College
- University of Colorado at Colorado Springs

The questions I asked these students covered a lot of areas, such as their backgrounds, including their personal lives; how they found and decided to attend the program they enrolled in; what advice they had to offer to new online MBAs; what their overall experience has been like; how they worked in teams; and how their education may be helping their careers.

Many of their quotes are in other chapters of this book. What follows are the stories of 14 of these students provided in greater detail. I believe that much of what they have said can be applied to many of the online MBA programs at similar institutions.

Also, in general, the information these students provide can possibly give you ideas for formulating questions to ask programs as you conduct your search.

Finally, you will see that all of these students have very positive things to say about their online MBA experiences. They are all hard-working, positive people who have learned how to make the most out of the online learning environment, and they have gladly shared their perspectives on how to succeed.

W.P. Carey MBA - Online Program at Arizona State University (ASU)

The ASU program kicks off with a first-year, five-day orientation held on the campus of Arizona State University in Tempe, Arizona. Team-based learning is used extensively to practice effective team participation in the workplace. The program is designed to provide a general MBA degree to individuals who want to develop and/or improve their management skills, irrespective of functional work area.

Robert Breen

Age: 40

Employment status: Vice president of strategic planning and financial services for Labor Ready, a provider of temporary manual labor to the light industrial and small business markets, based in Tacoma, Washington.

Robert Breen, who earned a Bachelor's degree in accounting from Western Washington University, is also a licensed CPA in the state of Washington. He is married and has two young children. He lives on a small island in Puget Sound and takes a car ferry to work each day, "which allows me a good deal of study time," he says.

The last time he attended any college classes was back in 1989, so he admits that he was "a little rusty" going into the ASU program, which he started in January 2004. He says that he initially looked into attending a local Executive MBA program, but "ruled it out after weighing the classroom time commitments. I learn best in independent study and find the classroom for me is a really inefficient, low-bandwidth mode of learning."

Instant Message

"I took on the challenge of the MBA partly because of boredom. I had been doing the same job for a number of years, and I wanted to find a way to advance myself and seek new challenges. My boredom has been cured, and I have many new ideas on ways to add value to my job."

—Robert Breen

Why ASU?

Breen says the fact that ASU had more stringent admissions requirements than other schools he looked into was an important factor because "it gave me comfort to know that my cohorts in the program would be top-notch and that the degree would be worth something when I finally got it. I also like the reputation that ASU carries in the business community and the fact that it does not export the teaching of its online program to other universities, but uses its day and evening MBA professors to teach the online sessions."

Experience as an online learner ...

Like most of the students profiled here, Breen considers himself computer savvy. Plus, his background in accounting obviously helped in the Microsoft Excel skills area and on the quantitative skills side of earning an MBA. It took him a little while to get used to the Blackboard CMS, but overall he adapted quite well, calling it "a rich and robust learning environment that raises the bar in distance-learning software."

He adds that the team-based format of his courses were "great. It helps that I constantly communicate by e-mail with colleagues at work who are spread out throughout North America and the UK, so I am used to working in a virtual community."

Advice ...

Breen has some strong advice regarding time management, saying things such as "don't procrastinate," and that "it's easy to put off studying, especially in the online format." He adds, "Don't underestimate the time requirements."

Career advancement factor ...

Not long after enrolling in the ASU program, Breen was promoted from director of financial analysis to his current VP position, "due in no small part to the pursuit of an MBA and the requisite commitment to self-improvement."

Jodie Filardo

Age: 48

Employment status: Vice president, economic development, Yavapai College in Prescott, Arizona.

Jodie Filardo has a Bachelor of Arts degree in economics from Stanford University. Her employment history includes holding positions as a chief information officer, chief financial officer, programmer analyst, and software engineer, along with being a private consultant. She is married with three children, one teenager and two adults. She holds "many, many" board positions on various nonprofit organizations. The last time she attended college was 27 years ago. As an ex-programmer she did not struggle with the online learning technology and says she did not need any "adjustment time."

Why ASU?

Filardo explains that in addition to being familiar with ASU because she lives relatively close to its campus, her research found that many ASU faculty were recipients of teaching awards, were published, and provided consultant services for major corporations both in the United States and abroad. "I am interested in the international perspective," she adds.

Experience as an online learner ...

"My favorite elements of the coursework are the one-on-one access to and feedback from our highly qualified faculty, coupled with the group projects with my diverse team members," says Filardo. At the time of this communication, she was working on a class project with a group of five fellow students: one consultant, one college recruiter, one accountant, and two engineers. "The consultant and I tend to deliver more of the experienced-based examples," she says. "The engineers tend to deliver more help on the math. From the accountant we got an up-close-and-personal look at the SBC strike. Our college recruiter tends to be emotionally supportive to the group, as I do."

Advice ...

"The best advice for achieving success online is to stay on top of your assignments," says Filardo. "By doing some work each night, the course load is manageable, although rigorous."

Career advancement factor ...

Filardo claims that thus far she has experience many "work-enhancing elements," from the ASU program. For instance, she was introduced to an Excel add-on tool that does regression analyses, called StatPro, in a statistics course. "That's been helpful on the job," she says. Additionally, through an organizational behavior course, she has "applied several of the analytical tools presented to help me diagnose some personnel problems at work."

Instant Message

"I think I'm realizing that when we're taught new tools, I'm trying to apply them to my current situation. This past weekend at a constituent deliberation meeting I used managerial economics in explaining the effect of tariffs on the quantities of products produced domestically versus internationally."

—Jodie Filardo

Athabasca University (AU)

In 1994, Athabasca University's (AU) Centre for Innovative Management (CIM) logged on with the world's first fully interactive online Executive MBA program. Today, the AU MBA, which is provided fully online without any residency requirements, is Canada's largest Executive MBA program. The program has a strong focus on networking and peer support. Students discuss current work issues with professors and fellow students, thereby obtaining a broad spectrum of feedback.

Tim Bzowey

Age: 37

Employment status: Executive with an insurance division of a diversified financial services company.

Tim Bzowey earned a Bachelor of Arts degree with a major in economics from the University of Saskatchewan. He has a 20-year background in sales and sales management that involves approximately a decade in a small business environment and just over a decade at one of Canada's largest publicly traded companies. He is married with three young children, all under 11 years of age.

He's a lifelong learner, having taken approximately one continuing-education course every year since he earned his undergraduate degree in 1991. He did not consider himself computer and Internet savvy, but he does say he is "an average user of both." He adds that there was very little adjustment for him to adapt to the AU MBA program, saying that he is "used to working independently and in groups."

Why AU?

Bzowey explains that he was familiar with AU, having taken courses there in the past. Plus, "I needed flexibility in student time and place due to travel and the potential for relocation. In fact, I was relocated across the country during my MBA program." Another contributing factor was that his employer "strongly encouraged" him to choose AU, and they provided the funding for it.

Experience as an online learner …

Like many online MBAs, Bzowey's biggest challenge was "balancing the commitment of school and work. Study time varies but would average 20 hours per week. Some weeks it could be as low as 10 hours, and other weeks it could be as high as 30 hours." He particularly enjoyed an optional residential elective that he participated in for one week in Germany, saying that it "was the learning experience of a lifetime." He admitted that sometimes the group projects weren't always the best. "Like anything involving a wide range of individuals, some groups are more productive, engaged, and interesting than others." He adds, however, that new groups are created for every eight-week course, and thus new and better group dynamics often emerge at frequent intervals.

Advice …

Bzowey stressed that family and employer support play a major role in his ability to maintain his commitment to the program and his work. Without such support, he says, "I would not finish the program. I can assure you that statement is neither a platitude nor an exaggeration. Everyone sacrifices for the candidate to meet his or her commitments. It is hard to be fully prepared for the nature of the commitment required."

Career advancement factor ...

Bzowey says that he was recently transferred to a new role at his workplace "where many of the principles I learned are now being utilized day to day. In fact, I accepted the position, in part, because it contained many elements that were directly applicable to my learning experience."

Tom Kiley

Age: 47

Employment status: senior manager, organizational effectiveness, RBC Learning Services, which is part of RBC's training and development Centre of Expertise.

Kiley earned an Honours Bachelor of Arts degree in history from the University of Western Ontario. Most of his career has been in training and development within the banking and financial services sectors, and he holds the Certified Human Resource Professional (CHRP) designation. He is also a member of the Human Resource Professional Association of Ontario, Canada. He is single with no children, and he enjoys traveling to Europe, which he does frequently.

Instant Message

"Overall I have found the online MBA program immensely challenging and rewarding. Successfully completing any MBA requires focus and discipline. In this regard, the online MBA program is no different from programs offered through traditional channels."

—Tom Kiley

Why AU?

Kiley says that two of his co-workers completed their MBAs at AU and "were very satisfied with the program. Their favorable experience influenced my decision to apply to Athabasca. He adds that, when he applied, he was traveling frequently though his work, and that "the online, asynchronous learning approach at Athabasca offered me the flexibility that I needed."

Experience as an online learner ...

Kiley found the program "immensely challenging and rewarding," and one that required "focus and discipline." He says that "one of the greatest strengths of the Athabasca experience lies in the diversity of participants, who are experienced managers from all over North America and around the world."

Advice ...

The volume of work was in the range of 20 to 25 hours per week, and "the demands of making high-quality written submissions to group discussions renders written communication skills a key success factor."

Career advancement factor ...

He says it's too early to establish a direct correlation between career enhancement and the MBA, adding that the experience thus far has broadened his understanding of business and sharpened his analytical skills.

East Carolina University (ECU)

The mission of the East Carolina University College of Business is to be a highly recognized regional business school in the Southeast United States. This fully online MBA program is designed for both business and nonbusiness undergraduates. The degree is completely self-contained, requiring no prerequisite coursework or business experience and is available to qualified students holding baccalaureate degrees in any business or nonbusiness field.

Joy Futrell

Age: 39

Employment status: Area director of four-county program for a mental-health-care center.

Joy Futrell earned her undergraduate degree in finance from East Carolina University in 1987. She has held positions in sales and as an accounting technician and finance officer. She is married with two young children who are "very active." She teaches Sunday school to third and fourth graders. She says that her husband is "very supportive. He assists (actually I assist) with cooking, cleaning, and transporting the children to their various events."

Futrell says that she was not computer and Internet savvy when she enrolled in the program but is now. "It is amazing how much it has increased my computer knowledge."

Why ECU?

Futrell lives in a rural area where there are few choices close by for obtaining a graduate-level education. "I didn't want an online degree from a college I had never heard of and didn't know anything about," she says. "I wanted to ensure that my degree would be from a well-known school and that I was doing the same work to earn my degree as students enrolled in the same classes on campus. I felt that East Carolina University could give me that opportunity."

Experience as an online learner …

She says that "finding the time to do the work" has been one of her biggest challenges. "Many nights I begin my schoolwork at around 9 P.M. when everyone else has settled in for the night. Life is so busy between the demands of my job, my family, and school. I attend many workshops out of town, and it is usually with my books in tow."

Advice …

Futrell claims that students have to realize that although online programs are flexible, "there are still numerous deadlines to meet," and it's easy to skip assignments "when no one is there to make you complete them. Because of this you have to be really motivated and committed to the program. Also, she says it's very important that students understand the computer hardware and software requirements. Plus, "your computer needs to be somewhere in which it is accessible to you at all times."

Career advancement factor …

Futrell says that her current job requires an advanced degree and that she was granted an exception because she enrolled in the ECU MBA program with an estimated graduation date of spring 2007.

Dawn McAvoy

Age: 34

Employment status: Public information officer/marketing director for a community college.

Dawn McAvoy earned a Bachelor of Arts degree in English and Linguistics from the University of North Carolina at Greensboro. She has worked as a technical writer, in business development for an environmental services firm, and in the telecom industry as a proposal manager, marketing manager, and product manager. She is single and lives in a remote area of North Carolina.

The last time McAvoy took any classes was in 1992. In particular, her work in the high-tech telecom industry has made her highly computer and Internet savvy, and she has experienced computer-based training, so "online learning didn't faze me too much. I was initially concerned about taking classes outside my comfort zone, such as accounting and statistics online, but have done so and did well."

Instant Message

"A huge benefit of online instruction is that as long as I have my laptop and Internet access, I can travel when I feel like it, not when classes aren't in session."

—Dawn McAvoy

Why ECU?

McAvoy says she conducted research online and selected ECU "because of accreditation, proximity to home, and cost. Compared to other online programs, ECU is very affordable to in-state residents. At this point in my career, I am not as concerned about going to a big-name B-school as I am earning the credential from an accredited program."

Experience as an online learner …

"I really enjoy my online coursework," McAvoy says. "All the faculty I've worked with have been great. Of course, some are better than others in adapting their material for online delivery. I've had online classes that actually scheduled time to meet online once a week during which time the professor may call on you for a response, and I've had online classes that consisted of nothing but reading the book and taking exams."

Advice …

McAvoy had lots of great advice. See Chapter 16, where she offered nine tips about effectively communicating in the online learning environment.

Career advancement factor …

McAvoy explains that being enrolled in the program has "certainly helped" her career and sees it as being necessary to increase her odds to possibly move up the career ladder. "The coursework has exposed me to functions I understood before, but not intimately, and I feel that it can only make me a better, more successful employee in the long term. If nothing else, I will be more empathetic to the folks in accounting."

Regis University

The purpose of the Regis University Online MBA Program is to produce exceptional leaders. The fully online program claims to be the largest "multimedia" online MBA program in the nation. It is one of the first programs to provide students with multiple, flexible learning formats, including video, audio, and textbook instruction. Regis University is one of 28 Jesuit colleges and universities nationwide—others include Georgetown, Boston College, and the University of San Francisco.

Katherine Porter

Age: 49

Employment status: vice president of marketing for POD, an IT solutions provider and systems integrator.

Katherine Porter provided the most in-depth answers of all the students who responded to the survey. She earned her Bachelor of Science degree in Computer Science from the University of New Mexico in 1983. She has held important technical positions in the defense industry, which included working on a NATO project.

She is married and does not have any children. Her computer and Internet skills helped make online learning a "natural" transition for her. Her responses revealed that she was an active learner who took her education under full control on her own.

Why Regis?

Porter gave a long list of reasons for attending Regis, including that "it had a 125-year tradition," and "an honest-to-goodness campus, with professors (academics as well as industry experts with doctorates) who are dedicated to lifelong learning." She also liked that it was located in Denver, making it physically close enough for her to "attend graduation and maintain a physical tie to the school." In fact, she did graduate from the program and attended commencement ceremonies in May 2004.

Experience as an online learner ...

Porter says that one of the things she liked most about being an online MBA student was that "it gave me the power to manage my education my way. I could manage the pace, within reason. If I wanted to wait and spend the entire weekend studying, I could do that; if I wanted to spread it out and study a bit every day, I could do that. It was fast and furious for eight weeks and then it was on to a new class. I could keep focused and was willing to sacrifice those eight-week increments."

She adds that she spent from 15 to 30 hours per week on her studies and got straight As, usually above 95 percent. "A few classes where I already had lots of experience with the material required only 15 to 20 hours per week." She explains that she "participated more in discussion topics than required. If you needed to spend less time, you could probably get B marks with fewer hours per week, but it still is fairly time-consuming. Don't forget, however, that you get to choose your 15 to 30 hours per week."

Advice ...

Porter had plenty of very sound advice to fill several more pages. Here are three of her nuggets of wisdom:

- **On choosing a program:** "I think as in choosing any personal service, one must evaluate one's own preferences and needs then choose the program that best matches those preferences and meets those needs. What is most important to you—cost, prestige, something else? How do you like to learn—alone, in a group, a little of each?"
- **On faculty:** "Manage faculty the way you manage your own boss/career, by getting clear on the expectations, letting them know if and when you are not able to comply, and negotiating a reasonable compromise when necessary."
- **On interacting with peers:** "Just do it! Approach people; ask their opinions; ask them for clarification; ask them how they came to hold those opinions; ask them to give you an honest opinion on your stance."

Instant Message

"Always be polite, Always acknowledge the other's perspective and offer yours as just another perspective to consider. Always thank others for taking the time to interact with you, and mean it."

—Katherine Porter

Career advancement factor …

Porter explains that she already had a lot of experience and knowledge gained through her career before enrolling in the Regis program but basically lacked the MBA credential. "I probably am slightly more effective in my job, though, because I feel good about having finished that degree. I'm sure it shows in my demeanor and in my decision making. I do have some tools from school that I didn't have before. That additional self-assurance and knowledge will no doubt help if I find myself looking for another job."

Syracuse University (SU)

Students in the Syracuse University iMBA program participate in a week-long residency at the start of each of three terms per year, then work independently for the rest of each term. The residencies are the heart of the learning experience that mixes intense face-to-face interactions with sustained support and interaction throughout the term. The result is strong *esprit de corps* among participants and an uncommon degree of quality and personalized attention.

Christopher Hodges

Age: 45

Employment status: Head of group reporting, finance department, Banco Urquijo S.A., Madrid, Spanish subsidiary of the KBC group of Belgium.

Christopher Hodges earned an undergraduate degree in economics and public administration from Bedford College at the University of London. He has two professional qualifications, an ACIB from the Chartered Institute of Bankers, and an MIL in Spanish from the Institute of Linguists, both earned through distance learning. He is single, and he adds that his "principal responsibilities are juggling my professional, academic, and domestic/private life on my own."

Why SU?

Hodges chose SU because he " was attracted by the residencies and wanted to benefit from a U.S. MBA experience, because the MBA was invented there. Syracuse had been running distance-learning MBAs since the 1970s and their qualification was accredited by the AACSB."

Experience as an online learner ...

Hodges says that the amount of work required was "a shock. I knew it would be demanding but not as demanding as it has proved to be." He adds that the challenge was "getting to grips with the standard of work expected, rearranging my lifestyle to accommodate the academic workload, and learning how to research assignments online. I quickly adjusted and was able to build on assignment preparation experience and that gained from working with fellow students to improve the quality of my work as the program has progressed. I find I'm being introduced to new information sources or techniques all the time."

Advice ...

In regard to choosing an online MBA program, Hodges is a strong proponent of residencies, saying he "is able to meet faculty and students for a week, which builds a sense of commitment and strengthens relationships; residences also provide an effective launch pad for virtual team working." He sums up his overall experience as being "totally positive," commenting that "I enjoyed researching and writing case studies relating to famous companies or people and have got a lot of pleasure from seeing how I've risen to the challenge and have produced, in some instances, what I consider to be some of by best work, academic or professional." He adds that prospective students must "understand the commitment you're taking on; the level of commitment expected is extremely high, and it is not possible simply to get by."

Career advancement factor …

He says that his aim is to use the MBA "as a stepping-stone to a more responsible, better-paying job after graduation." He also notes that the course modules he has taken "have improved my current job performance in terms of analyzing and understanding issues, presenting recommendations, and team management."

Mike Venable

Age: 31

Employment status: vice president of operations, Countrywide Financial.

Mike Venable earned an undergraduate degree in operations management and accounting in 1995 from the University of Texas. His work background includes stints as a credit analyst for a major bank in Dallas and working in operations for a mortgage corporation in Philadelphia. He is married and does not have any children.

He graduated from the Syracuse iMBA program in May 2004. His focus was in finance and entrepreneurship.

Why SU?

Venable says he reviewed and interviewed four schools that had online curriculums when he was searching for an MBA program. "What set Syracuse apart was the three residencies. This element of the program allowed you to meet new friends, colleagues, and, most importantly, your professors. I felt like part of the student body at SU rather than an individual just sending in tuition payments from afar every semester."

Experience as an online learner …

"The Blackboard application is an amazing tool," says Venable. "It makes you feel like you are on campus every day. The most educational piece of the coursework for me was the case studies. I enjoyed reading about company issues and problems and what they did to resolve them. I cannot single out one portion of the coursework I did not enjoy. All of it was a learning experience."

Advice …

Concerning the process of choosing a program, Venable says he did research online and called friends who had completed their MBAs for pointers. Venable also advises students to "be educated on the main Microsoft applications" because "they are used frequently throughout online courses."

Career advancement factor ...

"The iMBA courses were relevant and difficult but, more importantly, they were practical," says Venable. "The lectures, group projects, and tests could be applied to real-life work environment situations. Many times I can remember including things I learned in a class into a meeting agenda, business project, or seminar."

Instant Message

"Once I narrowed down my selection, I began calling around to the schools, and I asked a series of questions that pertained to five criteria: accreditation, flexibility, faculty, administrative and support services, and cost."

—Mike Venable

University of Florida (UF)

The UF program is divided into seven four-month terms. The curriculum has been carefully designed to maximize the MBA educational experience while allowing the student to work almost exclusively from their home or office. Students are required to meet in Gainesville once every term to take finals and participate in case presentations.

Scott Henninger

Age: 38

Employment status: Production manager of a cement plant in Tennessee.

Scott Henninger earned a Bachelor of Science degree in Physics, with a minor in Math, from King College. He also earned a Bachelor of Science degree in Mechanical Engineering from the Georgia Institute of Technology. He is married and does not have any children.

Prior to enrolling in the UF program he considered himself "fairly Internet and computer savvy. There was very little adjustment required other than becoming familiar with the conferencing software, presentation recording software, and acclimating myself to the different types of assignments and tools the school's website offers."

Why UF?

Henninger says he chose UF because he "wanted a well-respected degree. I placed a high emphasis on national rankings. Second, I looked for a school with a structured program that allowed me enough flexibility to maintain my current erratic work schedule without requiring significant periods on campus."

Experience as an online learner ...

"I have been very surprised at the ability of the school and its professors to provide quality learning through this medium," says Henninger. "I was skeptical at first, but I must say that I feel we learn as much as, if not more than, regular on-campus students. The work is challenging, but in some ways the online format allows for greater learning." He adds that "surprisingly, the team method works well in an online environment."

Instant Message

"I have learned a great deal by reading classmates' postings to questions or assignments on these discussion boards. People tend to participate more in this format."

—Scott Henninger

Advice ...

"Use the discussion boards," says Henninger. "There is a great deal of valuable information exchanged here from teammates that may be able to provide many different perspectives."

Career advancement factor ...

Henninger explains that he has not been promoted yet, adding that he is "now much more confident in my work and feel that I am well positioned for future promotions within our company."

Kimberly Levin

Age: 34

Employment status: Pharmaceutical representative, Merck & Co., Inc.

Kimberly Levin earned her Bachelor of Arts degree in Mathematics from the University of Delaware in 1992. She taught high school math for five years before moving to the corporate world. She is married and does not have any children, saying that she and her husband are putting off having children until after she graduates. "We made this decision because work and school creates enough stress," she says.

Although she claimed to have a "decent amount of computer experience," before enrolling in the program, she added that she is "not an IT geek. Because I work out of my house, my work requires constant communication through syncing handheld devices to my laptop and downloading my laptop through the company intranet."

Why UF?

Levin did her homework before applying to UF, saying that she "contacted the school and asked for some references of students that attended their online program. I e-mailed some and spoke live to others. I was satisfied with what I learned." She adds that UF's ranking by the *Wall Street Journal* and *U.S. News and World Report* also helped with her decision making process. "I wanted the school to have some clout," she says.

Experience as an online learner ...

"At first it was an adjustment for all of us," says Levin. "But the professors in the first term are very aware of the learning curve. In fact, the professors are very hands on. Most professors respond to e-mail or discussion questions within several hours." She says that her coursework can take up to 30 hours per week and at other times as low as 5 hours per week. "It depends on the workload." She explains that "team projects can be very intense," referring to a project in which she was on a team that did a study about Vietnam that resulted in a 75-page report. "This country analysis was an eye-opening experience. It is a lot of fun to throw ideas back and forth and fight for what you think is the best way to accomplish a task."

Advice ...

Levin has some straightforward words of advice: "If you don't interact with your peers, you are not going to get as much out of the program. Just because you are not sitting in a classroom together does not mean you cannot benefit from each other's knowledge and experiences."

Career advancement factor ...

Levin has been promoted already at her current job, and she says that she has "found that the knowledge I have gained has helped me assess work situations differently than I previously would have. My graduate school experiences have helped mold me into who I am today."

Instant Message

"The teamwork aspect sheds a lot of light on the real-world aspects of business. Everyone has different personalities, and we must learn to deal with all kinds of people from all walks of life."

—Kim Levin

University of Maryland University College (UMUC)

The fully online UMUC program is designed to be interdisciplinary, integrated, and applied. The program consists of one 1-credit foundation course and seven 6-credit seminars. The objectives of the program are to explore the evolving nature of corporations, blend leadership with change management, better measure an organization's intellectual assets, merge product development with entrepreneurship, and foster new approaches to measuring the economic performance of organizations.

Linda Couch

Age: 43

Employment status: Business unit strategist, IBM Global Services.

Linda Couch is a graduate of the UMUC online MBA program. She completed her degree requirements in December 2002. She has an undergraduate degree in mathematics from Johns Hopkins that she earned in 1990. She has held a number of positions in engineering, marketing, and general management with IBM since 1988.

Couch is a single mother with one adult daughter. During her stint as an online MBA student, she was on a five-year assignment for IBM in Tokyo. She is a veteran computer and Internet user.

Why UMUC?

Couch says that she chose UMUC because it did not have an onsite requirement, was accredited, and she had previous experiences with UMUC that were positive. She adds that she first considered going the traditional MBA route, "but the few English programs based in Tokyo were not convenient given my extensive business-travel schedule. So I decided that an online MBA was appropriate for me."

Experience as an online learner …

Couch says that she found her online experience "very, very rewarding. First of all, it was relevant because it was very much like my work environment—remote, asynchronous, and including participants that I never met in person. I learned a lot and felt that I worked just as hard, if not harder, than any classroom student." She adds that "the faculty was amazing. With the exception of one course, professionals, not full-time, career academicians, taught all my courses." She also mentions that the "courses were very challenging. There was so much reading."

> **Instant Message**
>
> "I learned a lot from the discussion threads. Almost everyone would support their arguments with examples or analogies from their own business experiences. Reading those pieces was extremely informative."
>
> —Linda Couch

Advice …

"Unless you are doing an MBA for the fun of it, do the due diligence you would do for any other MBA," she says. "Ensure the total costs (including books and other materials) are within your budget and ensure that the program is accredited. Make sure you understand how online the program really is. When I researched for my program, most of the schools I found offered combinations of onsite and online work. Decide which type(s) will work for you and ensure that you understand exactly what the school offers."

Career advancement factor ...

Although Couch had a lot of management experience under her belt when she entered the UMUC program and understood much of the material presented, she says that she "found a framework that made it easier for me to apply both old and new knowledge. In addition, I believe the MBA on my resumé will position me more positively than other candidates who may have similar work experience but lack that Master's level of study."

University of Colorado at Colorado Springs (UCCS)

The UCCS MBA program is committed to blending business practice and research into every aspect of its curriculum. The program is offered in two delivery methods, on-campus and fully online, with various specializations. This dual mode of delivery allows students to begin their MBA either on campus or online as well as to finish the program in either format.

Errol Robateau

Age: 33

Employment status: Employed with an affiliate of Exxon Mobil Corporation in Belize.

Errol Robateau earned his Bachelor degree in Accounting from St. Louis University. He has worked for a public accounting firm and has his CPA. He was nearing completion of his online MBA program at UCCS, with a double emphasis in finance and management, at the time of this communication.

He is married with three children. He and his wife are busy people, active in their church. He says that he is "quite fine working alone and meeting deadlines"—two facets of his personality that have helped him complete his MBA studies.

Why UCCS?

Robateau used some of the search methods suggested in this book, starting out with the *Business Week* and *U.S. News and World Report* websites. He says he chose UCCS because it was an AACSB accredited program, had a reasonable cost, and did not require campus visits.

Experience as an online learner …

Robateau explains that the UCCS faculty "were very responsive to our needs and provided great support along the way." He adds that "the ability to use the Internet to deal with real-world issues was great. It was not all textbook learning. The online experience included online financial real-world business data sites, which added to the learning."

Advice …

Robateau has some solid advice for students thinking about earning their MBA online. "Starting is easy," he says. "But completing your online degree requires discipline, perseverance, and an unwavering commitment to completing your degree." Also he strongly suggests that prospective students "start the application process early. I suggest starting everything at least one year before you plan to actually begin classes. This gives you enough time to choose the school, ask questions, obtain recommendations and transcripts, and complete the essays and the GMAT."

Instant Message

"Start slow with maybe one class until you get used to it, and then add more classes later. I find that two classes per semester is adequate if you have a full-time job with a family."
—Errol Robateau

Career advancement factor …

Robateau explains that he seems to be getting additional respect at his job as a result of his MBA experience. "In addition, I have been given more responsibilities that are in line with my MBA coursework. My company values an MBA, and therefore opportunities for advancement in our global company are now endless."

Jennifer Skipton

Age: 38

Employment status: RF performance engineer manager for AT&T Wireless.

Jennifer Skipton earned an undergraduate degree in electrical engineering from the University of Iowa. Her professional work experience has been primarily in the telecom sector. She is single, in a long-term committed relationship, and does not have any children. Skipton is also a volunteer with the Make-a-Wish Foundation.

She is Internet and computer savvy, claiming that "there is not anything I feel can be done to or with a computer that I can't figure out. The online learning format was easy to adjust to as long as you run through the tutorial."

Why UCCS?

Skipton searched the Internet for online MBA programs. "UCCS provided what looked to be a challenging program," she claims. "My biggest concern was to find something challenging. I want to feel as though I am earning my degree and not as though I just paid a high price for something worthless."

Experience as an online learner ...

Skipton explains that she is "gaining real-world experience in being a self-starter, which is important in the business world. Courses have been challenging, particularly the accounting courses, because that is not my background. I find the courses to be very relevant to business, and the interesting part is they also apply to my investment club and provide a great understanding of the stock market and stocks in general."

Advice ...

"Take it serious," says Skipton. "Keep on your studies. You must be motivated because there is no one prodding you to do the homework. Don't waste your time if you aren't serious about it. Read the books, no matter if they are math-based or not. Plan your time wisely and, if possible, plan ahead."

Career advancement factor ...

Skipton moved to a manager's position prior to enrolling in the UCCS program. She says that so far "the program has helped me to understand not only what I have done right to get this position, but also what things I need to improve on to move from being a manager to a true believer.

The Least You Need to Know

- Through as much due diligence as possible, make sure you understand exactly what the curriculum, faculty, and students are like.
- Don't underestimate how much dedication, commitment, and time is really required to earn an MBA online.
- Family and employee support is vitally important to your success and sanity.
- Be open to interacting with and listening carefully to your peers in order to get as much as possible out of the overall learning experience.
- Start the application process well enough in advance to be properly prepared to tackle admission requirements, such as the GMAT.

Chapter 20

A Brief Review and a Bit of Advice

In This Chapter

- An optimistic point of view
- Some suggestions about taking responsibility
- Last-minute tips
- Some personal preferences
- Final good-luck message

This chapter consists of some final words of advice sprinkled with my opinions about online education in general. Also just like in any online or on-campus classroom experience, there's a review of what you may or may not have learned from reading this book.

You should have a keen understanding of how to choose the program that is right for you, how to succeed as an online student, and what you need to do to take your degree to the next level of your career.

But, like anything in life, nuances can alter your ultimate pathway. In the online education world, those nuances deal primarily with how the institution meets its promise to provide you with a meaningful and effective education.

Unfortunately, you won't discover how good a program really is until you're fully enrolled in the thick of it. I can say, however, that through literally hundreds of in-depth interviews I've conducted with educators who work in online learning departments across the country, that I have developed a very strong sense of optimism about this form of teaching and learning. At the same time, I have developed a sense of cynicism about higher education, in general. Much of this diametrically opposed philosophy comes out in an occasional column that I write called "The Digital Optimist."

The Digital Optimist

Let me begin by saying that the people who work in online higher education are some of the hardest-working people I have ever met in my life. I can't tell you how many Saturday-afternoon and Sunday-evening conversations I have had with educators in this field who have no qualms about conducting business on what should be their days off. A colleague of mine, who also works in this field, jokingly says, "Only real men work on Sundays." I'm sure there's some religious opposition to that statement. But, overall, the people in the world of online education are truly dedicated professionals who have a passion about making this kind of teaching and learning work.

At some institutions, however, these passionate online educators are met with some resistance from colleagues who don't see online teaching and learning in the same light. In short, not all of the academic world is jumping on this train. At some institutions, the resistance to online education, especially to fully online degree programs, causes administrations to not adequately support the passionate academics who are creating these new and exciting teaching and learning environments.

Nonetheless, my experience investigating all these online MBA programs and communicating with administrators, faculty, and students has shown that all the regionally accredited schools are doing everything they can to make online education work. These programs are always in a continuous improvement cycle. The administration and faculty listen to students and corporate America and merge changes into their courses to make these programs better.

Of course, a traditional face-to-face MBA program does have its important elements that cannot be replicated online. A traditional program's culture and community, for instance, can never be converted to a virtual space. Live classroom connections obviously have benefits over and above what any online program can offer.

Also, online or on-campus, business and academia often can't seem to get on the same page. Just read some of Peter Drucker's work to get a sense for his views on the growth of our knowledge society and how traditional higher-education institutions are becoming less important.

Get On the Phone

So how do you find out which schools may be contributing to our knowledge society and which schools are not? This will sound overly simplistic, but you have to try to make contact with the faculty, administrators, and students in these programs and make a judgment call based on what information, or lack of information, they divulge to you.

You should have noticed that throughout this book I suggest that you call the people who run and teach online programs and ask a lot of questions. Don't be satisfied with talking to only an enrollment counselor/sales agent. Before you go through any admission process, make sure you speak with a college dean, or program director, or department chairperson, or some faculty members, and, if possible, some students (current or alumni) of the program.

Look through all the chapters of this book and write down those questions I suggest, or devise some of your own, that can help you dig deeper into whether you are the right fit for any particular program. Keep this list next to the telephone as you make these calls. Take notes and compare schools as you sift through all this information. Also keep accurate records of all your online research.

Guide on the Side

Don't rely on only what a school's employment counselor tells you. At some colleges and universities, enrollment counselors are singularly focused on getting you to fill out that application form and obtaining your tuition dollars as soon as possible.

Take Responsibility for Your Path

When all is said and done, your assertiveness and your ability to communicate and interact with faculty and fellow students in a professional manner will make all the difference in your success. If you sit back and wait for the institution to pour knowledge into your brain, and guide you every step of the way, all you'll become is a bucket that can be emptied. If you take an active, somewhat outspoken but professional and humble role in your education, you will reap more learning rewards than you could ever imagine.

In short, you are the master of your educational fate. Use your professors to your advantage. Question them, ask them for help, ask them to clarify things when you are confused or when you disagree with something.

In general, professors want to help you, regardless of their status as part-time adjuncts or full-time tenure-track faculty. In fact, many times that part-time adjunct with only a Master's degree and the practical, on-the-job experience can provide a better learning experience than the seasoned professor with a Ph.D. who is more concerned about his or her research than teaching. Of course, the opposite of that supposition is true as well. There are some poor overly stretched adjuncts out there, too.

Guide on the Side

Don't take a backseat to your education. Be an active learner and don't hesitate to ask for help or question something you do not agree with. Also, if something isn't working right online, let the administration or your professor know immediately.

Having said all this as the basis of your higher-education planning, here's a review, and some more opinions and advice, to bolster those plans.

Choose Wisely

Many prospective students get all caught up in an institution's brand-name recognition. However, my opinion is that you should not make that your primary decision factor. Remember, online MBAs are really still a new and growing phenomenon that has yet to reach a full level of maturity and recognition in the marketplace. In short, you can get an excellent education from many not-so-highly-recognized schools.

The institutions with the big academic reputations may give you a better chance of obtaining the best jobs, but they also come with the highest price tags. It's a tough decision to make. Personally, I would send my application to only those programs that impressed me with details about what I will ultimately learn from the faculty and students (review Chapter 6), how it will affect my lifelong learning goals (review Chapter 10), and how it will advance both my career and personal aspirations (review Chapter 18). All these things are much more important than a program's brand-name recognition and perceived value in the job marketplace.

In the final analysis with regard to choosing an online MBA program, it really all depends on the individual. In Chapter 1, for instance, I ask you two all-important questions that need to be repeated here about where you want to take your career and whether you are looking for a credential or knowledge.

Instant Message

"When you are going for job number three, they don't ask you where you got your degree and what your GPA was. Five, six, or seven years down the road, these things almost mean nothing. If you are looking for a job at a medium-sized business in any particular state you choose, you don't need to spend $100,000 to get an MBA."

—Rick Niswander, East Carolina University dean of Graduate Business Programs

Applying and Paying for Your MBA

The application and financial-aid processes can be a real pain in the you know what (review Chapters 11 and 12). Your best course of action here, again, is to simply get on the phone. Have an enrollment counselor help you with filling out the application and a financial-aid counselor help you with loan forms. In short, taking the phone approach could save you untold hours.

How to Be a Good Online Learner

The most vital skills online students can pick up are how to work in virtual teams and how to communicate effectively through modern electronic means, which I covered in Chapter 17 and alluded to in Chapter 18 as well. Also review Chapter 16 about communicating online.

There's a huge difference between online and face-to-face communication, says Maggie McVay Lynch, manager of distributed education at Portland State University. "Most people are not the best communicators in writing," she says. Often, for example, a simple critique of a fellow student's paper can be misinterpreted when provided through an e-mail or discussion board. "The student reads into it and says 'Oh my God, I'm a total failure.' So, there is this whole psychological piece that students need to work through to figure out what is formal communication and what is informal communication. How do you actually engage in interpersonal relationships when you are not seeing people face-to-face? How do you check back and forth, whether it is with your professor or with your fellow students, as to what the meaning really is when you are confused or upset or wondering how you are progressing?"

The large Fortune 500 corporations, in particular, communicate online and work in virtual teams all the time. At the corporate level, it's always referred to as e-learning. Basically, more and more employees are being trained in the online environment, be it through self-paced CD-ROM-based modules with add-on e-mail interaction and discussion boards to web-conferencing events where employees gather synchronously across borders and different time zones to collaborate on group projects and basically learn from each other. Also, instant messaging is frequently the communication method of choice for many corporate employees today.

Moreover, all the information available through proprietary databases available to you through your program's online library services will give you the opportunity to learn how to conduct competitive research. For example, valuable marketing and distribution data found online can help companies make wise decisions geared toward boosting revenues and production efficiencies. In addition, good online research can help put you in touch with the best vendors and suppliers. So in addition to being a skilled virtual team member and communicator, the modern business manager needs to be information literate (covered in Chapter 16).

Instant Message

"Learn something new; expose yourself to different thoughts and different ideas, and new ways to think about things."

—Andrea Davis, vice president of FlashPoint, (human-resource consulting firm)

To sum up how to be a good online learner, take your team projects seriously, learn how to communicate online, and become a skilled online researcher.

My Preference Criteria

Personally, for earning any kind of online degree, my preference is to go with a school that has a few short residency requirements. Of course, I realize that this is not possible for many prospective online MBA students, who perhaps don't have the time or finances to travel away from their jobs and families for any extended period of time. However, if you have the flexibility of traveling to a residency, I think the benefits of meeting in person with fellow students and faculty are well worth it. These kinds of social/academic experiences can really make a difference in forming valuable business friendships and networking opportunities.

I would also pick an institution that has strong ties to corporate America, perhaps is not overly academic in its instruction of business theories and concepts, and has a strong focus on gaining practical knowledge that you can immediately use in your workplace.

Another factor I would consider is how a program presents itself online. I believe a poor website can be a red flag indicating some problems related to a program not getting adequate institutional support. However, a program without adequate institutional support can have an excellent faculty and a good curriculum. So this is one of those gray areas that requires you to dig deeper into the details of a program's curriculum.

Finally, take a close look at how an institution provides its orientation services and other student services (review Chapters 7 and 15). Sometimes a quick face-to-face orientation at a residency is not nearly enough to prepare you for what you'll encounter in your first class.

Also a relatively short online orientation class might also not be enough. Maggie McVay Lynch, who did her doctoral dissertation research on online orientation methods, says that an online orientation should "put you in the environment that you are going to be working in for the time you are in the curriculum, so you can experience and work through any problems right up front before you actually take a class. It also gives you the opportunity to figure out what kind of resources you will have to assist you when the instructor or help desk is unavailable."

The other vital student service you'll more than likely take advantage of early on is technical support. The world of information technology is certainly less than perfect. When something goes wrong on the technical side, you'll want to immediately talk to a computer geek who can pull you out of what can be a cyberhell.

Finally, review what a school's alumni services are all about. Those institutions with large alumni networks could turn out to be a great way for you to make connections with other working professionals who can help you with your career-advancement strategies.

Instant Message

"If the orientation is fully online, hopefully it will step you through the process of using all the tools you will be using in the program."

—Maggie McVay Lynch, manager of distributed education at Portland State University

Good Luck

Phew! It's good to be at this point in the book. What a journey! To say the least, I wish you all the luck in the world. Online education is really a viable option, and it's definitely becoming more a part of our educational systems, not just at the MBA level, but in all higher-education disciplines. So take a deep breath, and start flying through cyberspace to pursue what the Internet is really all about—that is, to learn and teach and share and grow.

The Least You Need to Know

- The vast majority of regionally accredited online MBA programs are continuously improving based on the input they get from students and corporate America.
- Use the phone to your advantage and call program administrators and faculty with a list of questions you've developed from reading this book.
- Choose a program based on your aspirations and what you will ultimately learn, instead of basing your decision only on an institution's brand-name recognition.
- Learning how to communicate, work in virtual teams, and conduct effective research online are the three most important skills you'll pick up as an online student.
- Take a closer look at a school's ties to corporate America, how it presents itself online, and what kind of student services it really offers, especially its orientation, technical support, and alumni services.

Appendix A

Glossary

802.11 WiFi networking connectivity service This is a specification that allows your computer to connect to the World Wide Web via high-frequency radio waves. If you and your laptop, for instance, are in an area where a wireless hub device is installed, and you have an 802.11 WiFi networking connectivity service plan and a wireless network card installed in your laptop, you can go online without having to plug into a modem.

academic advisor This is a professional staff member of an institution (usually a professor) who has been assigned to assist a certain number of students with the course-selection process and other decision-making processes concerning one's academic and professional objectives.

accreditation This is a process in which educational institutions are recognized as viable places to learn. Standards are established by various accrediting agencies that are composed of educational experts. If an institution meets the standards set by the agency, which is accomplished through a peer-review process, it is acknowledged with accreditation status.

adjuncts These faculty members are part-time teaching employees. In online MBA programs, an adjunct will typically hold a full-time teaching position at another institution, or they may hold a full-time management-level position with a corporation. Some adjuncts teach part-time for multiple institutions.

adware This is software that generates advertising messages that pop up all over your computer screen while you are surfing the web, or, in some cases, when you are not surfing the web. Often secretly installed on people's computers when they download freeware or when they click on a button at an unethical website that installs adware on unsuspecting visitors.

asynchronous communication This does not occur in real time. A discussion board, where students post topics and responses whenever they desire, is a form of asynchronous communication.

Bloom's Taxonomy This is named after Benjamin Bloom, an education professor and researcher from the University of Chicago who, in 1956, identified six levels of learning: knowledge, comprehension, application, analysis, synthesis, and evaluation.

broadband This allows for more types of data to be transmitted over channels simultaneously, such as coaxial and fiber-optic cable channels that have a wider bandwidth than traditional copper telephone line channels (and hence data travels faster). Internet users with broadband access can view web pages more quickly than Internet users with dial-up Internet access.

Carnegie classification As noted at www.carnegiefoundation.org, this "is a taxonomy of colleges and universities. It is *not* a ranking of institutions, nor do its categories imply quality differences. Each institution is assigned to one of several categories based on descriptive data about that institution. The categories are intended to be relatively homogeneous with respect to the institutions' functions as well as student and faculty characteristics."

competency-based learning This is an education practice that measures and demonstrates what a student is capable of executing as a result of what he or she has learned. Related to competency-based learning are learning outcomes, which are the clearly stated capabilities or desired results of a learning experience.

course management system This is software that provides most of the tools and interface to present an online course on both the student's and faculty member's computer. It is the shell that holds all of an online course's functions, including the course syllabus, discussion board, live chat room, reading materials, lectures, assignments, a grade book, electronic file exchange functions, and access to outside resources such as the campus library.

curriculum This is a set of required courses that a student must pass to earn a degree.

curriculum vita This is similar to a resumé in that it lists a person's employment history and education. In higher education, it is usually a much longer document that also includes a faculty member's full publishing history, professional memberships, special recognition and awards, and other biographical information.

deductive reasoning This is the process of using generalizations to draw a specific conclusion.

distance education This refers to teachers and students in any given course that are not located in the same physical space.

educational technologies These are the electronic and/or web-based functions, features, and tools of a course of study or program used by both students and faculty. Educational technologies can include CD-ROMs and DVDs, all education-related software, video- and audiotapes, Internet-based communications, telecommunications, and streaming multimedia.

for-profit higher-education institution This institution operates under the notion of accruing earnings that can be utilized for the institution's improvement but also for the benefit of the private shareholders and/or individuals who own the corporation that runs it.

Free Application for Federal Student Aid (FAFSA) This is a form in which students provide their income, asset, and tax information to be considered for federally funded financial aid, including government-backed subsidized and unsubsidized Stafford Loans for graduate-level students.

fully online MBA program This means that every course required to graduate can be completed through an Internet connection without ever setting foot on campus.

graduate-level certificate program This is a non-degree-granting curriculum of graduate courses. Upon successful completion, students are awarded a certificate. The number of courses in any certificate program varies by institution. Most award credit that can be applied toward earning a Master's degree.

higher-education web portals These are relatively large websites that offer a comprehensive gateway to a wide variety of information related to higher education. These web portals typically have links to other education-related websites; access to online communities with discussion forums; and possibly live chat rooms, specialized content about specific topics of interest, a search engine and directory function for finding degree programs, and a variety of online shopping services.

hybrid learning Also known as "blended learning," this is a form of education that replaces a portion of the traditional face-to-face classroom with an online learning format.

independent self-study This is a teaching and learning format where individuals enroll in a class of one (their self) and are typically guided by a faculty/mentor/coach with whom they can communicate for assistance with achieving their course objectives within a specified time frame.

inductive reasoning This is the process of using specific observations, situations, cases, etc. to draw a general conclusion.

information literacy The Association of College and Research Libraries (ACRL) defines information literacy as a "set of skills needed to find, retrieve, analyze, and use information. It includes the technological skills needed to use the modern library as a gateway to information. It enables us to analyze and evaluate the information we find, thus giving us confidence in using that information to make a decision or create a product."

instructional designers These professionals help with the organizational structure and methods used for presenting online courses. They will introduce faculty to online teaching strategies, course content resources, student activities, testing methods, and what kind of technologies may best fit their desired teaching goals.

lock-step cohort online MBA program This is a program in which a group of students are enrolled and all take the same predefined courses together and in the same sequence as strictly outlined by the school.

netiquette This is a term that came of age with our adoption of the Internet. It refers to the practice of being civilized in both asynchronous and synchronous online communications. The short definition is practicing etiquette on the Internet.

non-AACSB-accredited school This can either mean that a school has not sought out AACSB Accreditation or would most likely not achieve it if they did seek it out, perhaps because they don't meet AACSB's criteria for a variety of reasons.

nonprofit higher-education institution This institution operates under the notion of serving the public good, with all earnings being utilized only for the institution's improvement.

online discussion board This is also referred to as a discussion forum or group, or message board, and is where faculty and students in an online class post questions, responses to questions, opinions, and basically enter into dialogues with each other asynchronously.

online learning A type of distance education that entails students learning and interacting with their instructors, and with other students, over the Internet. It can include electronic communications, distributions and displays via e-mail, electronic discussion forums, chat rooms, streaming audio and video, electronic simulations, and other education technologies.

pay-per-click (PPC) marketing This is where an advertiser pays a predetermined amount of money to a web publisher for every time a visitor clicks on an advertisement or link that is listed on a hosting website.

pay-per-lead (PPL) marketing This marketing is where an advertiser pays a web publisher to help generate information about as many prospective customers as possible, typically through an online form that the prospective customers fill out and submit online.

pedagogy This is a term that is used to describe how teaching and learning occurs in a course. It is often referred to as the art and science of teaching and learning, or the study of the manner and function of educational concepts and theories and how knowledge and learning is applied and accomplished.

plug-in This is an application that complements the capabilities of a web browser. Once installed on your computer, plug-ins are activated to display multimedia files.

residency requirement This means that, as part of the online MBA program you are enrolled in, you'll be required to pay a visit to the institution's main campus or an institution's satellite or off-campus office for a predetermined amount of face-to-face instruction.

simulations These are electronic replicas of business challenges users interact with online and make decisions about. The simulations then assess the user's behavior and choices and provide feedback. To see a demonstration of how electronic simulations work in graduate-level business courses at the University of Phoenix, visit www.phoenix.edu/simulations.

spyware This is software that watches where you travel in cyberspace. Unbeknownst to the user, it tracks your clicks and typically uses that information to send you unsolicited e-mails. Often secretly installed on people's computers when they download freeware or when they click a button at an unethical website that installs spyware on unsuspecting visitors.

Stafford Loan See *subsidized federal Stafford Loan* or *unsubsidized federal Stafford Loan*.

subsidized federal Stafford Loan This is awarded to a student based on financial need, and it includes the provision of not being charged any interest while you are attending school and you continue to meet the basic eligibility requirements of the loan.

synchronous communication This is live, occurring in real time. A live chat session is a form of synchronous communication.

teaching, learning, and technology center (TLT) This is composed of a group of information technology professionals who build and maintain the electronic and web-based infrastructure, software functions, and content used in online courses.

tenure This is a system whereby faculty can obtain lifetime job security by passing a long-term evaluation period in which they must demonstrate academic achievement, typically through publishing research and contributing substantially to a body of knowledge.

theory of constraints This was created by Eliyahu Goldratt, a physicist and business consultant, who developed a management practice and philosophy that identifies and measures multifaceted systems and facilitates continuous improvement by limiting or eliminating constraints that prevent businesses from reaching goals.

unsubsidized federal Stafford Loan This is a loan that is not awarded to a student on the basis of financial need, and it includes being charged interest from the time the loan is granted.

virtual universities These are higher-education institutions that do not have a traditional physical campus but instead operate out of a central office that is the management hub of its distance-education-only degree programs and courses.

web conferences These are when two or more people in separate locations communicate, with audio, video, and other presentation software, in real time over an Internet connection. Web conferencing software allows participants to talk with each other if they have a microphone hooked up to their computers with a sound card and speakers. Functions for conducting live polls are also used in web conference.

webinar This is a live, synchronous seminar viewed through a Web browser with audio communication through a teleconferencing connection or voice over Internet connection. They are typically recorded for viewing asynchronously.

whiteboard tool This allows users to draw, erase, and point to elements on a computer screen in real time. They are very typically used in web conferences.

Appendix B

Resources

Here is where you will find a complete list of all the online MBA programs available today. The details of each program are provided as follows:

- Name of institution
- City and state where institution's main campus or headquarters is located
- The web address of the program's main page
- The institution's accreditation status, noted as follows:

  Regional—Regionally accredited

  DETC—Nationally accredited by the Distance Education and Training Council

  AACSB—Professionally accredited by the Association to Advance Collegiate Schools of Business

  ACBSP—Professionally accredited by the Association of Collegiate Business Schools and Programs

  IACBE—Professionally accredited by the International Assembly for Collegiate Business Education
- Types of degree programs the institution offers. The key for identifying program types is:

  * Offers a general MBA program

** Offers a general MBA and MBAs with concentrations

*** Offers a general MBA and/or MBAs with concentrations as well as Master of Science programs with concentrations in business-related fields

**** Offers Master of Science programs in business-related fields

Offers an Executive MBA program

- Whether a program has a residency requirement, signified as "None" for no residency requirements and "Yes" for some residency requirement

Finally, please be aware that web addresses frequently change. If the web address provided in this list does not take you to the program's website, your next best option is to key in the institution's name into your favorite search engine to find its primary website and then do a search to find its online MBA program website.

Online MBA Programs in the United States

Alabama

American College of Computer & Information Sciences
Birmingham, AL
www.accis.edu/prospective/degreeprograms/managementandbusiness/mba/index.asp
DETC
*
None

Andrew Jackson University
Birmingham, AL
www.aju.edu/mba.htm
DETC
*
None

Auburn University
Auburn University, AL
www.auburn.edu/distance_learning/auonline/auol_credit_courses.php
Regional, AACSB
*, #
Yes

Columbia Southern University
Orange Beach, AL
www.colsouth.edu/distance_learning/College_degree/mba.html#
DETC
**

None

University of North Alabama—College of Business
Florence, AL
www2.una.edu/business/mba/index.html
Regional, AACSB
**, #
Yes

Arizona

Arizona State University—Main
Tempe, AZ
http://wpcarey.asu.edu/MBA/online/about.cfm
Regional, AACSB
*

Yes

Northcentral University
Prescott, AZ
www.ncu.edu/
Regional
**

None

University of Phoenix
Phoenix, AZ
www.uopxonline.com/programs.asp
Regional
**

None

California

California College for Health Sciences
National City, CA
www.cchs.edu/Programs/Business.php
DETC
**
None

California National University for Advanced Studies
Northridge, CA
www.cnuas.edu/pages/AcademicPrograms/AcademicPrograms.shtm
DETC
*
None

California State University Dominguez Hills
Carson, CA
http://mbaonline.csudh.edu/
Regional
**
None

National University
La Jolla, CA
www.nu.edu/Academics/OnlineEducation/OnlineDegreesandProg.html
Regional, IACBE
***, #
None

Touro University International
Cypress, CA
www.tourou.edu/cba/mba.htm
Regional, IACBE
**
None

William Howard Taft University
Santa Ana, CA
www.taftu.edu/ba1.htm
DETC
**
None

Colorado

American Graduate School of Management
Englewood, CO
www.agsm.edu
DETC
#
None

Aspen University
Denver, CO
www.aspen.edu/programs/graduate_programs.htm
DETC
**
None

Colorado Christian University
Lakewood, CO
www.ccu.edu/mba/
Regional
*
None

Colorado State University
Fort Collins, CO
www.learn.colostate.edu/degrees/mba.asp
Regional, AACSB
*
None

Jones International University
Englewood, CO
www.jonesinternational.edu/ourPrograms/program.php?prg=1
Regional
*
None

Regis University
Denver, CO
www.mbaregis.com/
Regional
**
None

University of Colorado at Colorado Springs
Colorado Springs, CO
http://business.uccs.edu/mba/index.php?page=11
Regional, AACSB
*
None

District of Columbia

Howard University
Washington, DC
www.howarduniversityonline.com/index.learn?action=Programs
Regional, AACSB
**
None

Florida

Embry-Riddle Aeronautical University
Daytona Beach, FL
www.erau.edu/db/degrees/ma-mbaaonline.html
Regional
**
None

Florida Atlantic University
Boca Raton, FL
www.itss.fau.edu/vmba.htm
Regional
**
None

Florida Metropolitan University
(Member of Corinthian Colleges, Inc., based in Santa Ana, CA)
http://www.fmuonline.com/degree_business_masters.html
Accredited by the Accrediting Council for Independent Colleges and Schools (ACICS)
**
None

Florida State University
Tallahassee, FL
www.cob.fsu.edu/grad/pmba/
Regional, AACSB
**
None

Nova Southeastern
Fort Lauderdale, FL
www.huizenga.nova.edu/programs/flexible_formats.cfm
Regional
**
Yes

University of Florida
Gainesville, FL
www.floridamba.ufl.edu/futurestudents/internet.asp
Regional, AACSB
*
Yes

Georgia

Brenau University
Gainesville, GA
http://online.brenau.edu/programs.htm
Regional
**
None

Georgia WebMBA
(courses offered through a consortium of five institutions)
Georgia College & State University, Georgia Southern University, Kennesaw State University, State University of West Georgia, and Valdosta State University
www.webmbaonline.org/
Regional, AACSB
*
Yes

Iowa

Upper Iowa University
Fayette, IA
www.uiu.edu/distance/online/on_graduate/mba1.html
Regional
**
None

Illinois

American Intercontinental University
Hoffman Estates, IL
http://business-administration.aiuonline.edu/mba.asp
Regional
**
None

Auburn University
Auburn, IL
www.auburn.edu/distance_learning/auonline/auol_credit_courses.php
Regional, AACSB
**
None

Cardean University
Deerfield, IL
www.cardean.edu/mba_cardeanMBA.htm
DETC
**
None

Keller Graduate School of Management of DeVry University
Oakbrook Terrace, IL
www.keller.edu/programs/mba.html
Regional
**
None

National-Louis University
Chicago, IL
www3.nl.edu/academics/cmb/onlinemba/index.cfm
Regional, IACBE
*
Yes

University of St. Francis
Joliet, IL
www3.nl.edu/academics/cmb/onlinemba/index.cfm
Regional
*
None

Indiana

Indiana University Kelley Direct
Indianapolis, IN
http://kd.iu.edu/prospective/default.aspx
Regional, AACSB
***
Yes

Indiana Wesleyan University
Marion, IN
www.iwuonline.com/ws_masters.html
Regional
***
None

Kansas

Ottawa University
Overland Park, KS
www.ottawa.edu/gradbusinessadmin.htm
Regional
*
Yes

Kentucky

Morehead State University
Morehead, KY
www.morehead-st.edu/colleges/business/mba/
Regional, AACSB
*
None

Sullivan University
Louisville, KY
www.sullivan.edu/programs/GradProg.htm
Regional
**,#
None

Maryland

Capitol College
Laurel, MD 20708
www.capitol-college.edu/academicprograms/graduateprograms/mba/
Regional, IACBE
***
None

University of Baltimore
Baltimore, MD
www.ubonline.edu/home.nsf
Regional, AACSB
**
None

University of Maryland University College
Adelphi, MD
www.umuc.edu/grad/degrees/degrees_home.shtml
Regional
***
None

Massachusetts

University of Massachusetts—Amherst
Amherst, MA
www.isenberg.umass.edu/MBA/PartTime_MBA/Online/
Regional, AACSB
*
None

Western New England College
Springfield, MA
www1.wnec.edu/business/index.cfm?selection=doc.1279#online
Regional, AACSB
*
None

Nichols College
Dudley, MA
www1.wnec.edu/business/index.cfm?selection=doc.1279#online
Regional
**
None

Suffolk University
Boston, MA
http://209.240.148.229/online/index.html
Regional, AACSB
**
None

Worcester Polytechnic Institute-Advanced Distance Learning Network
Worcester, MA
www.wpi.edu/Academics/ADLN/Programs/Management/mba.html
Regional, AACSB
**
None

Michigan

Baker College Online
Flint, MI
www.bakercollegeonline.com/
Regional
**
None

Davenport University
Grand Rapids, MI
www.davenport.edu/du/currentstudents/newprograms/programsregistration/programs/mba/default.htm
Regional, IACBE
**
None

University of Michigan—Dearborn
Dearborn, MI
www.webmba.edu/
Regional, AACSB
*
None

University of Michigan Flint—NetPlus MBA
Flint, MI
www.umflint.edu/departments/som/mba/
Regional, AACSB
*
Yes

Minnesota

Capella University
Minneapolis, MN
www.capella.edu/reborn/html/schools/business/index.aspx
Regional
***
None

Missouri

Park University
Parkville, MO
http://parkonline.org/
Regional
**
None

Stephens College
Columbia, MO
www.stephens.edu/academics/graduate/mbaprogram/
Regional
**
Yes

Webster University
St. Louis, MO
www.webster.edu/worldclassroom/
Regional
***
None

Nebraska

Bellevue University
Bellevue, NE
www.bellevue.edu/Online/programs/mba.html
Regional, IACBE
**
None

University of Nebraska Lincoln
http://mba.unl.edu/distance.html
Lincoln, NE
Regional, AACSB
*
None

New Hampshire

Southern New Hampshire University
Manchester, NH
www.snhu.edu/Southern_New_Hampshire_University/Distance_Ed/DE_Course_Information/DE_Grad_Programs.html
Regional
***
None

New Jersey

Seton Hall University
South Orange, NY
www.setonworldwide.net/page/PFPD+MASCL+Program+Overview!OpenDocument
Regional
Master of Arts in Strategic Communication and Leadership
Yes

New York

Empire State College—State University of NY
Saratoga Springs, NY
www.esc.edu/ESConline/Across_ESC/grad.nsf/wholeshortlinks2/MBA?opendocument
Regional
*
Yes

Marist College
Poughkeepsie, NY
www.marist.edu/gce/elearning/
Regional, AACSB
*
None

Mercy College
Dobbs Ferry, NY
http://grad.mercy.edu/mba/learning.htm
Regional
*
None

New York University School of Continuing and Professional Studies
New York, NY
www.scps.nyu.edu/departments/degree.jsp?degId=31
Regional, AACSB
****

None

SUNY Institute of Technology at Utica/Rome
Utica, NY
www.sunyit.edu/academics/programs/mba/
Regional, AACSB
***

None

Syracuse University
Syracuse, NY
http://whitman.syr.edu/prospective/imba/index.asp
Regional, AACSB
*

Yes

North Carolina

East Carolina University
Greenville, NC
www.ecu.edu/cs-bus/grad/Internet-Option.cfm
Regional
**

None

Pfeiffer University
Charlotte, NC
www.business.ecu.edu/grad/internetlearning.htm
Regional
*

None

Ohio

Franklin University
Columbus, OH
www.franklin.edu/prospective/online/mba.html
Regional, IACEB
*
Yes

Tiffin University
Tiffin, OH
www.tiffin-global.org/index.learn?action=Graduate&subaction=business
Regional, ACBS
*
Yes

Oklahoma

Cameron University
Lawton, OK
www.cameron.edu/online/mba.html
Regional, AACSB
*
Yes

University of Tulsa
Tulsa, OK
www.imba.utulsa.edu/
Regional, AACSB
*
Yes

Oregon

Marylhurst University
Marylhurst, OR
www.marylhurst.edu/online/programs/mbaonline.html
Regional, IACBE
**
No

Portland State University
Portland, OR
www.emba.pdx.edu/about/about.html
Regional, AACSB
*

Yes

Pennsylvania

The American College
Bryn Mawr, PA
www.amercoll.edu/current_students/graduate_school/msfs.asp
Regional
****

Yes

DeSales University
Central Valley, PA
www4.desales.edu/~drs2/onlinecourses/courses.htm
Regional
**

None

Drexel University
Philadelphia, PA
www.drexel.com/Fields_of_Study/Business.shtml
Regional, AACSB
**

None

Pennsylvania State University
University Park, PA
www.worldcampus.psu.edu/pub/imba/afs_prog_desc.shtml
Regional
*

Yes

Rhode Island

Salve Regina University
Newport, RI
www.salve.edu/catalogs/graduate/esalve.cfm
Regional, IACBE
***
Yes

South Dakota

National American University
Rapid City, SD
www.national.edu/distance/mba/index.html
Regional
*
None

Tennessee

Tennessee Tech University
Cookeville, TN
www.tntech.edu/mba/
Regional, AACSB
*
None

Texas

Amberton University
Garland, TX
www.amberton.edu/DistMBA1.htm
Regional
***
None

Dallas Baptist University
Dallas, TX
www.dbu.edu/online/degrees_offered.asp
Regional, ACSB
**
None

University of the Incarnate Word
San Antonio, TX
http://online.uiw.edu/
Regional
**
None

University of Texas at Dallas
Dallas, TX
http://som.utdallas.edu/globalmba/index.html
Regional, AACSB
*
None

University of Texas System—UT TeleCampus
Austin, TX
www.telecampus.utsystem.edu/index.cfm/4,627,82,56,html
Regional, AACSB
*
None

West Texas A&M University
Canyon, TX
http://wtcis-3.wtamu.edu/college/opening1.htm
Regional
**
Yes

Utah

Western Governors University
Salt Lake City, UT
www.wgu.edu/business/programs.asp
Regional
**
None

Virginia

American Military University
C/O American Public University System
Charles Town, VA
www.apus.edu/AMU/Academics/SubPrograms.aspx?paid=1895
DETC
**
None

Liberty University
Lynchburg, VA
www.liberty.edu/Academics/Graduate/index.cfm?PID=5638
Regional
*
Yes

Regent University
Virginia Beach, VA
www.regent.edu/acad/schbus/academics/online_programs.htm
Regional
*, #
Yes

Vermont

Norwich University
Northfield, VT
http://www3.norwich.edu/mba
Regional
*
Yes

Washington

City University
Bellevue, WA
www.cityu.edu/student/dl/cuol.aspx
Regional
*
None

Wisconsin

University of Wisconsin Whitewater
Whitewater, WI
http://academics.uww.edu/business/onlinemba/?ad=gec01
Regional, AACSB
**
None

University of Wisconsin Eau Claire
Eau Claire, WI
http://academics.uww.edu/business/onlinemba/?ad=gec01
Regional, AACSB
*
None

Online MBA Programs in Canada and Great Britain

Canada

Athabasca University
www.mba.athabascau.ca
Athabasca, Alberta, Canada
**, #
Candidate for U.S. regional accreditation
None

Lansbridge University
Fredericton, New Brunswick, Canada
www.lansbridge.com/emba/overview.php?CCODE=emba
*, #
None

Great Britain

Edinburgh Business School MBA
Heriot-Watt University
Edinburgh, UK
www.ebsmba.com/
*
None

Imperial College London-Tanaka Business College
South Kensington Campus, London, UK
https://www3.imperial.ac.uk/portal/page?_pageid=58,81111&_dad=portallive&_schema=PORTALLIVE
**

None

University of Liverpool
Liverpool, UK
www.kitcampus.com/programmes/mba.phtml
*

None

University of Manchester
Bangor, North Wales, UK
www.mbs-worldwide.ac.uk
**

Yes

Index

Numbers

A

D

E

F

G

H

I

J–K

L

M

N

O

S

T

U

V

W-X-Y-Z